THE STRANGER NEXT DOOR

The Stranger Next Door

An Anthology from the Other Europe

Edited by

RICHARD SWARTZ

Northwestern University
Evanston, Illinois

Northwestern University Press
www.nupress.northwestern.edu

Published on behalf of the Robert Bosch Stiftung and the S. Fischer Stiftung, and
supported by the Kulturkreis der Deutschen Wirtschaft im BDI e.V.

This anthology appeared simultaneously in Albania, Bosnia and Herzegovina, Bulgaria,
Croatia, Macedonia, Montenegro, Serbia, and Slovenia.

Printed in the United States of America

10 9 8 7 6 5 4 3 2 1

Library of Congress Cataloging-in-Publication Data

Andere nebenan. English.
    The stranger next door : an anthology from the other Europe / edited by Richard
Swartz.
        p. cm.
    "Published on behalf of the Robert Bosch Stiftung and the S. Fischer Stiftung, and
supported by the Kulturkreis der Deutschen Wirtschaft im BDI e.V."
    "Originally published in German in 2007 under the title Der andere nebenan.
Copyright © 2007 by S. Fischer Verlag GmbH, Frankfurt am Main."
    ISBN 978-0-8101-2630-5 (pbk. : alk. paper)
    1. Short stories—21st century—Translations into English. 2. Essays—21st century—
Translations into English. 3. Slavic literature, Southern—Translations into English.
4. Balkan Peninsula—Fiction. I. Swartz, Richard, 1945– II. Title.
PG523.E1 2013
808.8032496—dc23

                                                                        2013008758

♾ The paper used in this publication meets the minimum requirements of the American
National Standard for Information Sciences—Permanence of Paper for Printed Library
Materials, ANSI Z39.48-1992.

Kad slušam tako nekog kako daje opšte i uopštene sudove
(crno ili belo) o zemljama ili narodima, ja nijednog trenutka ne mislim
o tačnosti ili netačnosti tih sudova, jer to zaista ne vredi, nego se pitam
kako je stalo sa razumom i moralom toga koji te sudove daje.

—*Ivo Andrič, Znakovi pored puta*

When I hear someone judge countries or people in broad strokes
(black or white), I don't think for a moment whether these judgments
are right or wrong, because it's really not worthwhile. Instead, I wonder
about the mind set and morals of a person who utters such judgments.

—*Ivo Andrič, Signs Along the Road*

Contents

Preface to the U.S. Edition

The essays and fiction in this volume were commissioned for the German edition, which appeared in 2007, with simultaneous publication in Albania, Bosnia and Herzegovina, Bulgaria, Croatia, Macedonia, Montenegro, Serbia, and Slovenia. These are the countries suggested by its German title, *Der andere nebenan: Eine Anthologie aus dem Südosten Europas.* Since then, there have been translations into Hungarian, Italian, and Turkish as well. For an American reader, "the Other Europe" needs a word of explanation.

The Balkans have been so troubled by violence and misunderstanding that we have the verb "balkanize," meaning to break up into smaller, warring components. While some of the region's artists and thinkers have invariably fallen into nationalistic tendencies, the twenty-one prominent, multiethnic authors represented here, from the erstwhile Yugoslavia and its neighbors Albania and Bulgaria, have chosen to attempt to bridge these divides. As Richard Swartz notes in his introduction, many of these authors now live elsewhere. There are many ways in which they embody the concept of the Other, being strangers themselves and frequently writing in languages that were not their native tongue. Even if they remained in the cities where they were born, the name of their country has likely changed. Here they reflect on their identities and convey with graphic intensity the trauma of the various Balkan wars in the 1990s and their aftermath. The material they relate is dark, but bringing their voices together is a project of understanding. Ethnic conflict of this intensity is an experience that many Americans have not processed or fully considered. As we move into the twenty-first century, perhaps a new generation of writers will tell another story about this region.

INTRODUCTION

Richard Swartz

IN THE NIGHT LEADING UP TO NOVEMBER 11, 1714, KING CHARLES XII OF
Sweden, in disguise and wearing a recently grown beard, reaches Stralsund
after fourteen days on horseback. Flight or homecoming? The Swedish king
finds himself on Swedish soil once more after many years in Turkey, most
recently as a guest of the Turkish sultan near Adrianople. As guest or pris-
oner? In truth it is probably the case that this friendship would not have
existed if the two of them had not shared a common enemy: Tsar Peter the
Great of Russia.

And so this friendship left no lasting traces in either Turkish or Swedish
history, with the exception of a dish that the Swedish king came to enjoy
while living among the Turks. He brought the recipe home to Sweden, and
his subjects enjoyed it as well. What finds its way into the mouth has, as
everyone knows, much better chances of survival than something that has to
be content to stand on a pillar in bronze or marble; and in this case that per-
sistent comestible came to us, curiously enough, by way of a crowned head.

Cabbage rolls—in Swedish, *kåldomar* (from the Hungarian *dolmány,*
actually the term for a short, richly decorated uniform coat like the one
worn by Hussars, which means that the Hungarian in fact must be a loan
word originating from the Turkish *dolama*)—have ever since been a feature of Swedish home cooking: a hot dish made from a seasoned mixture
of ground meat and rice in a casing of blanched white cabbage leaves. As
a child—and I was no exception among Swedish children—I did not care
for them. Cabbage rolls are favored by older, single men and are, like their
Viennese cousin, the *Krautwickerl,* actually much too sweet.

I might never have discovered this connection if I had not made the
acquaintance of the same (in principle) dish in Hungary. There its Turkish origins were denied with a hardheadedness that I found suspicious,
but nevertheless, these Hungarian cabbage rolls tasted better because
they were not as sweet as my Swedish ones. Did the addition of paprika
make the difference? Or the kind of cabbage? Someone had told me that
it was a matter of the proper level of acidity. Friends from the Balkans or
Central Europe—nota bene, the part of Central Europe that once had to
defend itself against the Turks—have often complained to me that one cannot get precisely the kind of cabbage this dish demands either in Berlin or

Stockholm. That might be so. I had by that time long become accustomed to calling it *sarma,* that is, the name commonly used in the greater extent of the Balkans. I became more and more convinced that my friends' point about the importance of the cabbage was correct, but at the same time kept to myself something just as obvious, namely that it was originally none other than the Turks who first prepared this dish.

But soon thereafter, in Bosnia, the significance switched from the cabbage to sour cream, a sour cream so thick that it sticks to the spoon. Without that cream, I was assured, it was completely impossible to prepare an edible *sarma.* So sour cream was the secret. For quite a while I adhered to the sour cream camp, only to later find—in Serbia or Albania, I can no longer remember which—that the sour cream theory had to give way to the meat-filling theory: two parts ground pork to one part ground beef was apparently the only correct ratio, though even this was determined more by cultural than culinary demands, according to where our cabbage rolls were being prepared. Pork was out of the question in large parts of Bosnia, would hardly appear among the Pomaks and Turks in Bulgaria, and is just as unlikely to be used by Albanian Muslims. I soon gave up any discussion of the constitution of the meat and stuck to the quality of the cabbage. I had little or no objection to the sour cream. On the other hand, my Croatian mother-in-law, strictly Catholic and raised on the island of Krk, refused to let any sour cream even come in the vicinity of her *sarma;* whether to achieve some distance from the inferior Muslim and Orthodox recipes, or because of the thriftiness verging on parsimony that characterizes so many of the islanders, is hard to say. And I have no intention of asking.

And so for years and throughout this part of Europe I have enjoyed variations, in total contradiction with one another and yet quite excellent, of what is in essence one and the same dish, though no one wants to admit it. And the only thing that connects the cooks to one another is the deep, occasionally aggressive conviction that, apart from their own version, all other forms of preparation of *sarma* are in fact incorrect and therefore contemptible.

Something shared—an almost identical thing—becomes, when circumstances allow it, all too easily the thing that divides us. That is nothing new, but beyond the world of the kitchen and recipes it can have devastating consequences. This insight lies at the heart of my analogy. And furthermore it seems to be supported by the image of southeastern Europe created by its neighbors, an image that has proved to be remarkably immutable down through the ages, since it stubbornly insists on its supposed truth: southeastern Europe is the most backward region of Europe, full of hate and violence, the powder keg of our continent. According to Otto von Bismarck it was not worth the bones of a single Pomeranian grenadier: an ethnic, religious, and linguistic hodgepodge, no melting pot. For a German or a Swede this world can seem alien, even uncanny. Why this distrust of neighbors? Why this inclination to see them as enemies instead of friends? Why ethnic cleansing as pipe-dream and program?

For this anthology these questions were handed over to those directly involved, in this case twenty-one writers of prose. And that was done despite the fact that, after spending decades in this part of Europe, I have understood that these kinds of questions are to no small degree based on misunderstandings, exaggerations, or prejudices that arise out of ignorance or, worse, indifference. So some of those who were asked might have seen the questions as a provocation.

But the very best questions are often quite simple, questions that seem so obvious and naive that we almost hesitate to ask them. No one likes to appear stupid or naive. Nevertheless I have exposed myself to this danger, and in retrospect I do not regret it, nor do I think I need to apologize.

It is another matter as to whether there are any good or even any answers at all to these questions, as important as they might be. Good authors would rather ask their own questions than give answers. So I had not imagined that the writers whom I approached would sit down like good schoolchildren and answer my questions, since it is generally not worthwhile to tell writers what they should write about. They will in any case write what they want, at least those with talent will (and here we are dealing with talented writers).

And all of them responded as true writers, by relating something of their own: that is, a story. In that way they rewrote the original questions, improved them, or cast them aside, and in their revisions the outlines of something like an answer occasionally can be glimpsed.

With only a few exceptions we find ourselves in the company of the authors whom I wanted to have in the anthology from the beginning. Someone might ask: why no one from Romania? Or Greece? As far as I am concerned, a dozen more might have taken part, but a book requires not only a beginning but also an end. And for that reason a line has to be drawn somewhere, and the former Yugoslavia, Bulgaria, and Albania (often underrepresented) seemed to me in numerous ways to be a reasonable and meaningful limit, even if I would like to avoid the word "border"; if I had taken on the task from the perspective of a customs official or a surveyor, the anthology would have looked quite different. But here we are dealing solely with literature and nothing else.

And for that reason it was not difficult to resist the temptation to do political proselytizing. The purpose of the anthology is, in my view, purely literary. Here is a book of contemporary prose from southeastern Europe, nothing more or less, and that is a good thing. Of course literature has influence on society, but for the most part that influence occurs in a roundabout way or through back doors that remain obscure to us; literature seldom allows itself to be instrumentalized for purely political goals. And its significance should not be overestimated: I am not one of those who believe that literature can change the world. Anyone who would like to work toward such a change, even peripherally, would be wise to become a banker, boxer, or journalist instead of an author. Émile Zola probably accomplished more change in the world through his article *J'accuse* than with all of his novels put together.

Stronger than literature's influence on the world, to be sure, is the influence of the world on literature, or at least on its prerequisites. Once I had put this anthology together, it struck me that something was not right. Again and again I read through the list of authors, without understanding what it was. Were they too old? Too young? Were there too few women? Too few or too many writing in one or another of the languages? Actually this kind of political correctness did not interest me in the slightest; the only thing that counted was literary quality. But suddenly I saw what it was: many of the authors who contributed to this anthology no longer live in their own country. Some of them left to live in what we have to call exile. Some of them have even changed their language, and this is no coincidence. And it ought not to surprise anyone. A person putting together an anthology of German literature in the 1930s would have been forced to look for his or her authors in exile, with the exception of Gerhart Hauptmann, Erich Kästner, Gottfried Benn, and a few others. And so the fact that a majority of the contributions for this anthology of southeastern European literature were composed outside the region already says something about the conflicts and tragedies of today's Balkans. And that accounts as well, I think, for the sorrow and pain that the reader will encounter in this book.

Translated by Linda Rugg

THE STRANGER NEXT DOOR

Why?

David Albahari

WHEN IT GETS GOOD AND DARK, I PUT ON MY SNEAKERS AND GO OUT. THIS is a small place and by nine o'clock at night the streets are deserted. I can walk for hours, from south to north and back again: I won't run into a soul.

One time the priest was there, waiting for me in front of the church. He asked me what I was doing out so late, all on my own. "Taking a walk," I answered. Wasn't I scared? "No, I'm not scared." The priest shook his head and fell silent. I thought he had said his piece. You should be careful at night, he eventually said. I shrugged my shoulders, waited some more, and when I realized that that was all he had to say to me, I turned around and went on my way.

I walked on until I left the town behind me. I crossed the bridge and, when I looked back, the town had vanished. It was shrouded in the dawn mist rising up from the river. I turned to look at the direction I had taken: no mist there and the road, only brushed with dampness, clearly led to a turning into the woods. There it disappeared into the shadows. I took another couple of steps and then stopped. "One day I'll walk on," I thought, "but not this time." I could feel the threads connecting me to the bridge and houses tighten, pulling me slowly but surely back to town. "This isn't a city," my friend Muharem once said, "it's a town." "It doesn't matter," I said. "It can be whatever it wants, but one day I'm going to get out of here." I peered at the bend in the road and tried to imagine what lay behind it. I failed.

It doesn't matter what road I take: sooner or later the priest appears. Does he ever sleep or is he always awake, like me? He says nothing, looks at me, and strokes the beard he doesn't have. Maybe he expects me to ask him something? I put my mind to it, but can't think of a single question. "I'm sorry," I say. The priest does not respond.

First the bakery opens, then the newsstand, then the butcher's, and finally the grocery store. But they all close at the same time, except for the newsstand where the light is sometimes on until midnight.

I return to the bridge and gaze at the bend in the road. Even if I could muster up the courage to walk over to that bend, I wouldn't be surprised if I found the priest standing there. I'll see him now when I turn around, I think, but when I do, there's nobody.

My walks are turning into intricate routes, all of which have only one purpose: to avoid the priest. So I often squeeze through bushes or hedges, jump down into roadside ditches, climb trees, slip into dark doorways, stand in the shadows, and crouch behind parked cars. I have managed to avoid the priest, but now I am coming up against other annoyances. For instance, I chanced upon Mladen and Velimir who, huffing, puffing, and softly swearing, were removing wooden boxes from a hole in the ground behind the culture center, and carrying them approximately a hundred meters away, to another hole on the edge of the little town park. When they caught sight of me they almost dropped the box they were holding, but they quickly recovered and told me that they were playing a joke on Tomislav, the head of the veterinary pharmacy, from whom they had taken a bunch of medicines and chemicals, that was at least two weeks ago, and were now burying them every two to three days in a different place, but he still hadn't noticed a thing. They invited me to help them with the boxes, which I gladly accepted, since the priest was nowhere in sight, and, anyway, I had nothing better to do. "These medicines of yours are heavy," I said, my fingers going numb, and they laughed. It was a somewhat nervous laugh, but that late at night any laugh is somewhat nervous, I thought, making my way home. A rooster started crowing somewhere and the first ray of daybreak soon streaked across the sky.

Yesterday I decided to follow a girl. I hadn't seen her before and presumed she wasn't local but from one of the neighboring villages or hamlets and was attending nursing school here. I glimpsed her through the window of the grocery store and the way she wet her lips stopped me dead in my tracks. She was waiting in line at the cashier's, checking the shiny coins splayed out on the palm of her hand. I turned away, leaned against the lamppost so that I could see the front door from the corner of my eye, waited for her to come out, and then slowly started following her. Sometimes I would let her get a dozen steps ahead of me, other times I was right behind her, once, that was at a pedestrian crossing, I walked in front of her, but even then, though I can't explain how, I had her in my field of vision, and so we continued until she reached the house where, I supposed, she lived. It was one of those matchbox buildings in a new housing development that the military had built several years earlier for officers and personnel from the barracks at the end of town, the opposite end of where the bridge and bend in the road were. I waited for a while, but the girl did not come out and that put an end to my shadowing. I went back to the store the same way I had come. Meanwhile, darkness had fallen and the store, you could see even from across the street, was closed. But a light was still on at the newsstand.

I looked for Muharem to see if maybe he knew the girl from the building, but I didn't manage to find him either. "As if he's vanished into thin air," I said in front of the grocery store, where I was having a beer with Lazar and Nemanja. Lazar belched and farted, Nemanja snickered and said: "Muharem's calling you." And they kept on laughing until I hurled the bottle into the street, where it shattered into smithereens.

I do not read the papers, I do not watch television, I learn about the world from my own experience and from eavesdropping. For instance, at the market, I'll stop between two stalls, pretending to look at something, raisins or walnuts, or chocolate from Germany which reaches our markets in what is to me some unfathomable way, and while I'm standing there I'll pick up snatches of conversation, fragments that slowly open up, though there are those that fall flat, and various sentences, the most important being those sometimes said in a hushed voice. They are the best. That, for instance, is how I learned that the butcher's assistant has a bastard child, though they didn't know where, and that the newsstand owner has some sort of illness that makes his hands shake. At one point I noticed that more and more people at the market were talking in whispers, that gestures and winks were taking the place of words, as if language had suddenly become superfluous or undependable or, perhaps, both, as is often the case. Some of them whispered so softly that I couldn't hear them; others whispered aloud about things and people regarding which I had no clue. The world was undoubtedly changing, although I did not understand why, and for the first time I thought that must be the reason that the priest kept following me around so self-confidently: the world was going through a change, and he probably wanted to explain it to me or to give me words of encouragement or whatever it is that priests do when one world is falling apart and another is just beginning.

"Oh, fuck your priest, of all the people in the world, why ask me about him?" That's what my cousin said. My aunt was married to a Croat, an army major, and they lived in one of those army buildings. The major, they said, was the terror of the military, but at home he was as meek as a mouse. And my cousin behaved accordingly: as if the major, his father, didn't exist. We were standing in front of the open apartment door and could hear the loud blare of the TV inside. My cousin poked his head back in and shouted at his father to turn that shit down right now. "Otherwise," he screamed, "somebody's going to come and take it away from you." I couldn't believe my ears. Mind you, since the whispering had died down at the market, I'd stopped believing my ears anyway, because even when I did hear it, I couldn't understand what they were talking about. Names dropped off of lips like autumn leaves and, like leaves, they were all similar, making them hard to remember. In the end, my cousin asked me if I wanted him to beat up the priest. "Why?" I asked. "He hasn't done anything to me," "That's why he should be given a licking now," my cousin said, "because later, if he does do something to you, there'll be no point." He stepped back into the apartment and started to close the door. "Get it?" he asked. "Yes," I said, but when he had shut the door, I closed my eyes and whispered: "No, I don't."

I imagined myself walking beside her, talking to her about the meaning of life. My sentences pour out like honey and every so often she, not hiding her admiration, looks at me sideways, lifting the bangs off her brow. In my mind's eye, we stroll down to the bridge, cross it, and I take her by the hand as we walk to the bend in the road. She hesitates, but I draw her to me protectively, I put my arm around her and take first one step, then another, and another, until slowly, step by step, we enter the darkness.

One night, while I was hanging around, leaning against the tree opposite the entrance to her building, I dozed off. I don't know how sleep got the better of me, but at some point I woke up and didn't know where I was. Clouds blanketed the sky, the nocturnal darkness was dense, and an unpleasantly warm wind was blowing. Then I heard muffled noises, a mixture of grinding, grating, and metal, and slowly, crouching low, I started inching my way toward the sound. About midway I had to stop because I noticed the beam of a flashlight. I saw a pair of heads peering at the tenants' names next to the door buzzers. Actually, they were peering at the back of the metal directory and at the colored wires leading to a hole in the wall by the front door. I crouched behind a bush. I couldn't see their faces. One of them had a square head, just like Tomislav's, who ran the veterinary pharmacy, but he was not as tall, and as for the other, I was sure I had never seen him before. The flashlight kept going on and off, their hushed voices intermingling with the other sounds, and suddenly I felt sleepy again and had to sit down and rest my head on my knees. When I opened my eyes, it was dawn. The two of them had disappeared and the metal directory was gleaming in its usual place. I walked over to study it. There was nothing to show that somebody had been fiddling with it during the night. I tried to picture a screwdriver and after a while it appeared in the far recess of my mind: I could clearly see it lying on a shelf, it had a yellow, transparent handle, with the manufacturer's logo on it, and was leaning against a hammer.

"Now I just have to figure out where it is," I told the officer coming out of the building, "and then go and get it." "What are you looking for," asked the officer, "and why?" I waved in a vague direction. "I need a screwdriver to check something," I said. "The light in the stairwell isn't working," said the officer. "Exactly," I said, "the light in the stairwell isn't working." So I didn't have to go all the way home for my tool kit, the officer said, I was free to go to his apartment, number twelve on the third floor, and tell his daughter that he had sent me for the screwdriver. "Yes sir," I said, stiffening. "At ease," replied the officer and departed.

I didn't go for the screwdriver right away. I was sleepy again, so I sat down in a corner, rolled myself up into as small a ball as possible, and dozed off. I dreamed about the postman. He was carrying a bag but there was no mail in it. "I delivered everything already," he said as if justifying himself, "there was nothing for you." "Not even a paltry postcard," I asked, "or a reply card?" The postman lifted up his bag and turned it upside down. True enough, nothing fell out, not even a scrap of paper. "So what are you going to do," asked the postman, "now that nobody's writing to you?" "I'll figure something out," I said. I kept telling myself: "It's time to wake up, time to wake up," and wake up I did. The postman was gone and instead I saw clusters of people, big and small, passing by the building, all moving in the same direction. I stretched, got to my feet, and headed for the third floor.

An unbearable silence filled the corridor of the building. Most of the apartments had pairs of slippers or clogs on their doormats, some placed neatly, others knocked over and lying helter-skelter, as if their owners had been in a hurry to go in and shut the door behind them. The door of apartment number twelve bore a copper plate, which said: S. Kulenović, Officer of the JNA.* I ran the tip of my index finger over the letters. Then, without breaking the fluidness of the movement, I ran my finger across the surface of the door until it touched the doorbell. I pressed and heard a fluttery tone, like a bird chirping. I liked it, so I pressed the bell again, and continued pressing it, listening to the chirping. I heard a voice inside and then the door was yanked open. "For God's sake," said the girl, "what's going on. Where's the fire?" I pressed the bell one more time and let my hand drop. "What's going on?" the girl said again. "Why are you leaning on the doorbell?" If I had had any doubts to start with, now I was certain: standing in front of me was the girl from the grocery store. I said I had come for a screwdriver, her father had sent me, I had to check something in the fuse

---

* Yugoslav People's Army. —Trans.

box downstairs. "And where is he?" asked the girl. "Why didn't he come with you?" I shrugged and said: "I guess he had to go to work." The girl cocked her head to get a better look at me: "To work?" she asked. "What world do you live in?" These were already hard questions, I didn't like them, so I turned around and headed back downstairs. "Hey," shouted the girl, "what about the screwdriver?" "I'll come back tomorrow," I said, and started running down the stairs, two, three steps at a time. The postman had woken mc up too early, after all: I had a headache.

Speaking at one end of town was a bald man, with a mustache and a frown. Speaking at the other was a dark-haired man, with a beard and big glasses. I couldn't listen to both of them at the same time, so I had to keep running back and forth, but by the time I reached one end, I had forgotten everything that had been said at the other, and so, except for sore feet and legs, I got nothing out of it at all. True, there were some young guys at either end who laughed whenever I came running up, all hot and sweaty, though there were others who threw me dirty looks, and once one of them said loudly that everybody would have to make up their minds where they belonged, and that nobody, not even that dimwit over there, would be able to straddle two stools. I wanted to go over and tell him what I thought about his stools, but then I saw his eyes and, no, you don't go near eyes like that, and I didn't.

The following evening, when it was good and dark, I headed for the new housing development, armed with my screwdriver. Flitting from shadow to shadow, I would occasionally see people's silhouettes. The night used to be mine alone, and I did not like having to share it. Had I not been carrying the screwdriver, I would have certainly walked up to some of those silhouettes and asked them what they were doing out so late at night. "Just in case," I said to the screwdriver, "I'll steer clear of the silhouettes the way I do of the priest. The time is coming," I said to the screwdriver, "when we won't be able to believe anybody." The screwdriver looked at me. "Don't ask me how I know," I said. "Some things you just know," I told it, "that's all."

There was nobody in the new housing development, not even a light in any of the windows, but I could feel lots of eyes watching me, and I didn't like it. Holding the screwdriver, I walked through the development into the dark. Then, following my own private pathways, I came back, hid in a dark shadow, and stayed put. The silence grew louder and louder, but I was patient, I waited for it to become unbearably loud, then I stood up and, darting like a cat from shadow to shadow, made my way to the front door of the building. I had stuffed the screwdriver inside my shirt; I couldn't stand its gleam anymore; now I took it out again and went over to the directory. I turned three screws, the fourth was missing, and removed the metal plate. I peered into the hole in the wall, but except for wires and the odd clump of plaster, there was nothing there. Then I looked at the back of the directory and saw that there were black dots next to some of the names. I read them out softly: Begić, Mehmedinović, Džindo, Kulenović. Others had little circles next to them: Popović, Mikić, Pavlović, Bratić, Jovanović; and still others had little crosses: Krešić, Marinković, Bagić. What did it all mean? I looked at the screwdriver, but it was silent. I thought of going to the Kulenović apartment, maybe the girl could tell me; instead, though, I gazed at the dot next to their name, wet my index finger with saliva, and wiped it off.

Over the next few nights I checked out the other buildings in the development, and everywhere it was the same story: I would unscrew the directory and when I turned it around to look at the back, I found the same symbols. In some places there were more black dots, in others more crosses, and in still others more empty circles, but all three symbols were everywhere and there was not a building where the tenants were all marked with just one symbol. They must have meant something to somebody, I don't believe that those two guys were doing this just for fun, just as I didn't believe that they had put those markings there themselves. Who knows how many young guys, equipped with flashlights, screwdrivers, and magic markers, had taken part in all this, not to mention the people who had thought the whole thing up, because nothing happens by itself, everything needs some sort of impetus, just as I can't go to the cemetery unless it's for a funeral, for me that is a kind of impetus, because in any other situation I see no point in going somewhere to be with the dead. The dead are dead and there is nothing to be added. Or taken away. There is no light, no glow, just darkness.

"I should have slept through it all," I told my face in the mirror. I didn't like what I had seen, but there was nothing I could do about it. "I constantly have the feeling," I told my face in the mirror, "that my hands and feet are tied and that I can't walk, I can only hop. Do you know," I asked my image, "how exhausting that is? Do you know," I asked it, "that at night I'm so tired, so bushed, that I can't even shut my eyes, I sleep with them open? Do you know," I asked, but then I waved my hand dismissively and turned away. Anyway, mirrors lie.

The days became longer, but at the same time shorter. The mornings dragged on, afternoon never seemed to come, then it would be evening and, in a hand clap, the night would be gone. Occasionally you could hear an explosion in the distance, or a burst of rifle fire, and then everything would stop: people, the day, time, even the sun in the sky would stop and peep from behind a cloud. Somebody tried to tell me that it was hunters and fishermen, that fishermen were using dynamite to catch fish and hunters were out shooting foxes. "That explains the explosions and the gunshots," they said, "no need to attach any importance to it." "Fine," I said, "I won't attach any importance to it, a gunshot is just a gunshot, that's all, anyway all this is making me terribly sleepy." So I went into the courtyard, sat down under a pear tree, and fell asleep. When I woke up, it was so quiet that I thought I was still asleep. Then I saw a cat at the other end of the yard. It was eyeing a bird perched on the gate and gradually crept closer, its movements slow but utterly deliberate, its muscles taut, ready at any moment to pounce and nab its prey. Then from a distance came a clap of thunder, the bird took flight, the cat lunged in vain, and I scanned the blue sky, amazed that there was not a single cloud, the thunder had turned into a rumble, and a tank pulled up in front of the house. As I got to my feet and headed for the fence, the turret of the tank started turning until its cannon was aiming straight at me. I peered into the opening and wondered what really passed through it. The turret started turning again, resuming its earlier position, its caterpillar tracks creaked, the tank moved on, and out of one of the openings appeared an unreal white hand holding a sheaf of papers, which it tossed into the air. The papers swirled in the air like doves, and I ran after them shouting something, but I don't know what.

After the tanks came people with suitcases. They were heading for the bus station, mostly in columns: first the father, followed by the mother, then the children, in order of height or age. The smallest child usually cuddled a toy, a teddy bear or plush giraffe; the eldest child, walking behind the mother, carried a cat or a birdcage or a plastic bag of water with goldfish inside. The mother lugged a suitcase and bundled bed linen, the father carried two suitcases and a backpack. As the crowds pressed in around the buses at the station, the goldfish would spill out of the bag of water or the cat would cut loose, and the sound of swearing and grunting would be augmented by that of the children crying, but still, nobody spoke, nobody waved, not those who were leaving, not those who were staying.

In the evening, when it gets good and dark, I don't know what to do anymore. I put on my sneakers and stand by the window. I count the silhouettes moving in all directions; I count as high as I can, and then start all over again. Maybe it would be better for me to take off my sneakers so that my feet don't sweat unnecessarily, who knows how long this can last? Every so often, a fire flares up somewhere, reddening the sky, but nobody seems to put it out. And who is there to do it? Soon, nothing but silhouettes will be left in town. I think of my friend Muharem, of how he said that we live in a town, not a city, and I try to work out how long it's been since we last saw each other. Yesterday I wanted to go to his house, but I came up against a barricade and a man I had never seen before, dressed in a green camouflage uniform, told me to turn back. "I'm looking for a friend," I shouted in an attempt to persuade him to let me through. "There are no friends over there, you fool," the man said to me. "So shove off," he added, tapping the handle of his pistol. "All right," I said, shaking my head. "Hey," said the man in a sinister voice, "that's not you being mad at me now, is it?" I had never heard a voice like that before, but I knew not to argue with it, let alone look at him, so I stared at the ground and merely said: "Of course not," and then added: "I'm sorry." I could feel his eyes boring into my back as I walked away, and the whole time I kept thinking what I would do if I heard a gunshot and wondered if by the time you heard the shot it wasn't too late to do anything anyway.

They were taking my space away from me, like toys from a child at play. Whatever direction I took, toward the bridge or toward the barracks, there was somebody advising me to turn back. On the third side was a forest, which I had always been told was enchanted, and on the fourth were cornfields. I would never dare to go into the forest, and the sheaves of the corn leave ugly stains on my skin. All in all, I don't have much choice: I go out in front of the house, sit on the bench, watch the people leaving, the women crying, the children looking around and still trying to smile and blow kisses, but when I feel the pressure build in my head I go home, pull the thick curtains closed, and try to forget everything I've seen, but the more I tell myself that I haven't seen or heard something the more clearly I can see and hear it. In the end, I go into the bathroom and douse my head with cold water. I feel better for a moment, but then it starts all over again. I see my aunt and her son lugging their suitcases, discarding the bundle of linen that somebody quickly picks up and carries off. I'm tired and I want to lie down, I say to the empty room. The words bounce off the walls, flutter around the room, and then collapse onto the floor. There is a soft sough when they fall, like a plum blossom dropping to the ground.

"The sun is nowhere to be seen," somebody said yesterday, and it really was an awful day, cloudy and listless, full of smoke from the heaps of ash, with a stench that I simply couldn't place. By noon I thought I would go berserk if I stayed in the room, so I went out. Standing in front of the house was a corpulent man with long hair and a beard. "Are you one of us," he asked me, "or one of them?" "Of course I'm one of us," I said. The man looked me up and down. "Fuck it," he said. "It takes all kinds, but never

mind," he went on. "What's important is that they've gone." "All of them,"
I asked, "everybody?" "The ones and the others," the man confirmed. I
opened the gate and stepped onto the sidewalk. "Where are you going with
that flower in your hair?" the man asked. I touched my hair: there was no
flower. He roared with laughter; even his stomach was shaking. He waved
me past. "But watch it," he added. "There are still some ugly customers
around. Avoid the dark." I headed for the new housing development, and
it was only then that I noticed the dead people lying in the street: the wind
had hiked up a woman's skirt and for an instant I saw her bloodstained
underwear; two pigs were grunting around the bodies of two men who
were holding hands; another woman was leaning against a tree, and, if it
hadn't been for the big red blotch on her breast, I would have thought she
was asleep. I felt nauseous, but I didn't want to vomit, at least not as long as
that fat man's eyes were on me. I went behind the corner, leaned against the
wall, and threw up yellow mucus. I didn't feel any better, though; in fact I
didn't feel anything. If I hadn't been so scared I would have plonked myself
down right there and then and gone to sleep. Nothing is as comforting as
sleep. Then I heard footsteps and, when I looked up, I saw Slobodan and
Jovan. They came over and patted me on the shoulder. "It's a good thing
it's you," Jovan smiled, "because Fatso over there thought you weren't one
of us, so he sent us after you to see what you were up to." We stared at my
yellow puke. "You know what," said Slobodan, "you should get yourself a
weapon; it isn't right that everybody else is armed and only you go around
with your pants down. Fatso's got two guns anyway," he went on, "I'll tell
him to give you one." He went to the corner and shouted: "Bring over one
of those submachine guns." We could hear Fatso shout something back.
"C'mon," Slobodan roared, "bring that gun over." "Fuck it! I don't know how
to fire a gun," I said when they put the submachine gun in my hand. Jovan
shrugged. "You'll learn," he said, "once you've got a target. And remember,
if you don't fire first, you won't have time to be second."

With the submachine gun in my hand, I continued on my way to the
new housing development. Even if I had wanted to look for a target, I
wouldn't have found one, because the streets were deserted, with only the
odd dog trotting by or cat stretching on a doorstep. One cat even came up
to me, arched its back, and brushed between my legs. I pointed the gun at
its head and said: Bang! The cat rose on its hind legs, trying to smell the
barrel. It must have really reeked, because the cat suddenly pulled back and
shook its head. I raised the tip of the barrel to my nose. That's what death
smells like, I thought, feeling my finger stiffen around the trigger. I lifted
my head and saw a big milky cloud in the sky. The cat had gone by then.

"Are you my target?" I asked the cloud. The cloud was silent, and so, a bit later, was the submachine gun.

By the time I spotted the priest, it was too late. I had nowhere to hide. "I've been looking for you," said the priest. "When?" I asked. "Where?" The priest slowly spread open his arms. "Everywhere," he said, "but I see you've managed without me." He pointed at my gun. "Where did you get that from?" he asked. I indicated somewhere behind me. "From there," I said. "Just be careful with that," said the priest, "because it can be God's implement but also the devil's." I had never thought of a submachine gun as an implement, but there's always time to learn something new. The priest asked me where I was going and I said I was going to the new housing development. He again advised me to be careful about what I got up to. He raised his hand and drew the sign of the cross above my head. "That's all I need," I thought, as I felt the cross touch my hair.

When I got to the building, officer Kulenović was lying on the concrete path, blood trickling from the wound in the back of his head. Dragan, known as Tomcat, was crouching beside him, smoking. "Imagine," he said when I managed to stop, "the lunatic wiped off the symbol on the directory. He probably hoped we wouldn't know he's a Muslim, as if we're idiots and don't know who's who in the army." I looked at the front door and saw the directory swaying, though there was no wind. "And the daughter," I asked, "what about her?" "They're questioning her in the apartment," Dragan said, "because she's clearly a spy, too, the fucking whore. Tell them to hurry up," he said when he saw me heading for the building. "I don't want to be here all night." Slowly I climbed up the stairs, thinking that I'd never make it to apartment number 12. The door was open, the front hall empty, like the dining room. Then I heard voices in the bedroom, so I walked over and looked in. One of them was pinning down her arms, the other pressing her thighs, thrusting himself between her legs. I raised my gun, took aim at the man standing over her, fired, and, without taking my finger off the trigger, aimed the barrel at the other one. When I removed my finger, the silence was so loud I thought I would go deaf. The girl covered her face with her hands, but her thighs and stomach were still naked. I stepped toward her, the parquet creaked, and she peeked at me through her fingers. I jumped over the man who had been standing between her legs and gazed at her nakedness. "I did not like what I saw," I said later while I was tying her hands and legs to the bed frame. Before that I had dragged the two men into the bathroom, first one and then the other, and dumped them in the bathtub. When the doorbell rang, she began to strain against the ropes. "Don't worry," I reassured her, "I locked the door." And sure enough, a bit later the doorbell stopped ringing and a deafening silence once again filled the apartment. I was feeling tired and went into the dining room, turned on the television, and lay down on the couch. The screen was showing a green soccer pitch and players bravely chasing the ball. I heaved a sigh and fell asleep.

When I woke up, the players were still running, the pitch was still green, the referee was blowing his whistle, the spectators were shouting, a player was running back and forth near the corner flag. I could hear her sobbing in the other room. I got up and went into the kitchen to look for the right tools. The major must have liked roasts, because I found a number of sharp, big knives in the drawer, one of which had a greasy handle. I took it out and tested it on the cutting board. It went through the wood like margarine, and as I wiped it clean with a dishcloth, I felt this tranquillity take hold of me. I am as peaceful as a tomb, I thought to myself, but when I went up to the girl and confronted that space between her legs, I could feel my hands begin to shake. She lifted her head just as I was touching the inside of her left thigh with the tip of my knife, and that movement of hers—like the words that quickly followed: "What are you doing?"—made my hand wobble, and the blade slipped down her thigh. A jagged rivulet of blood appeared, but when I righted the tip of the knife and drew it straight down toward her knee, new rivulets began streaming down in straight, almost parallel lines. The girl moaned and every so often her thighs went taut, but when I cut deeper into the skin near the groin and separated it from the flesh with the tip of the knife, she screamed and her body arched into the air. I grabbed the skin and yanked it toward me with all my strength, but instead of the whole strip of skin, only a small part of it was left in my hand. The girl stopped screaming and looked up at me. Her eyes were brimming with tears, which I also didn't like, because I get a headache when somebody cries. I need another rest, I told her, and went into the dining room. The television was still on, except now it wasn't soccer on the screen, it was a children's program. I lay down on the couch, but the pain in my head was piercing. All this time, adult actors were pretending to be children, grimacing the way no child ever does. If I had had the submachine gun at hand, I probably would have fired it at the screen, but I had put it down somewhere and couldn't remember where. I went and asked the girl if she knew where I had left the gun. She didn't say anything, she just shook her head. I looked for the knife, wiped it, and leaned over her. The incisions had to be deeper, I realized that, so I pressed the knife harder into the girl's right thigh. She made not a sound now, she just gritted her teeth and bit her lip, but when at last I pulled the strip of skin, she screamed so loudly that I jumped. Her whole body shook, blood streaming down both thighs, and I stood immobile between her legs until there was the sound of her voice. She asked: "Why are you doing this to me?" And I said: "I don't know."

Because I honestly did not know.

Translated by Christina P. Zorić

Rootlessness

Vladimir Arsenijević

HE'S STANDING AT THE DOOR OF THE *MODTAGE REGISTERING CENTRUM** in Avnstrup, legal at last, free at last, only yesterday he had been knocking back hectoliters of beer with the others, day in and day out, in the kitchen upstairs, rehashing all those stupid asylum-seeker and refugee stories, and now here he is, leaving, in his frayed white T-shirt, a Geneva Convention travel document in his pocket, that dark object of desire of every Asylansøger in the Kingdom of Denmark, and they are still back there, tongue-tied and passive, until they are all packed off, kicked out of the Reception Center, and dispatched from the comforts of Denmark straight back to where they came from, each to his own shithole, but not him, he is legal at last, legal at last, free at last. Lars, one of their "carers," brushes past and flashes him a look with his narrow, Eskimo eyes, points to the bus station, raises his eyebrows in surprise (why is he standing there? why is he just standing there instead of getting a move on?). He wonders that himself, and yet—he does not leave, the dreaded moment has arrived (dreaded, Dren, why dreaded?), though the whole thing took only six months, and it all went faster than he expected. Certainly the awful situation back home had helped. The awful situation back home *always* helps, and now here he is, hesitating in front of the glass doors of the reception center, not moving, even though he feels that there are some things that Fate has got right, because there are shimmering opportunities in the offing, because anything is better than Prizren, and because anything is better than Avnstrup. So, destination: Copenhagen, he thinks to himself, filling his lungs with the crisp morning air; destination: a normal life, and he smiles at Lars who smiles back and raises his hand to his forehead like a salute, and Dren— Dren Kastrat, the twenty-one-year-old refugee from Kosovo—finally pulls himself free after six months of vegetating in the asylum world of red and brown bricks, and now bold and full of sudden enthusiasm, in possession of

* Reception and Registration Center. —Trans.

a new travel document, in possession of freedom, in possession of all these shimmering possibilities, his step light, he heads for the bus station . . .

Sitting in the taxi—a brand new cream-white Mercedes—they entered town from the east and Ulrike from the Berlin Center for Intercultural Dialogue kept leaning across Marija, poking her elbow in Marija's stomach, wanting to show her the various sites they were passing that she thought were especially interesting.

The taxi was driving through the rather grim outskirts of onetime East Berlin and Marija found nothing particularly interesting there. She was simply too tired and overwrought. She had arrived tired from Budapest. All she had on the plane was coffee. They did not serve alcohol. Her whole body was tingling unbearably, and her claustrophia was getting worse by the minute. Plus there was that uncontrollable fatigue, that throbbing headache, the stomach gases—she simply didn't know which to deal with first. And so now, in the taxi, she kept furtively licking her swollen lips and gulping, hoping to get a grip on herself.

But Ulrike Kruger, the blessed intercultural Ulrike Kruger, seemed not to notice a thing. She kept getting into her face, digging her sharp elbow straight into her kidney, and talking, talking, talking, thrilled that Marija was really here, that she was alive, that all of her own tireless humanitarian work had paid off and was producing visible results. Clutched to her flat, sunken chest was the German edition of Marija's novel *Rootlessness* (her only translation into German; the Fischer Verlag edition had bombed commercially—never mind, Ulrike had repeatedly said in her emails that it was one of her favorite books), and she was grinning so broadly that Marija Pavlović had a full view of the woman's galloping periodontitis. However, she was too dispirited to smile back. She had accepted the invitation to spend a year in Berlin and now here she was.

And that was that.

What was so special about it and why all these knowing smiles? She had been invited to come in '97, at the time of those marathon anti-Milošević winter demonstrations, but she had been in no state then to accept. They renewed the invitation in the fall of '98, during those first threats of bombing that never materialized, but still she wavered, and the whole thing sort of kept rolling along, until the bombing of Serbia and Montenegro, which started in March of '99, accelerating matters dramatically. Suddenly it was as if she was the only person who had to be pulled out of that hell. It was a mission of pressing importance, but she really did not need such help—she had been living in Budapest at her best friend Nives's since the beginning of the year. But, Ulrike Kruger, Hans Dietrich Olaf, and others from the center with whom she had been in constant touch could not have known that because they only communicated with her through email. And when, slightly embarrassed by their concern for her well-being and life, she informed them of where she was now living, it briefly raised some doubts about what to do next, which annoyed her, so that, even before having taken stock of Ulrike's periodontitis, and even before she had felt the sharp edge of the woman's elbow and listened to her quivering sighs, she had not been in the best of moods.

And so she did not return Ulrike's smile, she just silently kept looking out of the taxi window. Her fellow passenger coughed. "OK, Marija," she said, "just take a gooood look at this," and, leaning over, planted her elbow in her kidney again. A blinding pain shot through her head. She thought she would jump out of her skin. "If you would be so kind," she managed to say through clenched teeth, when she could not stand it for a second longer, and finally pushed Ulrike's elbow away.

Thin and long-limbed, in a stained blouse and a wrinkled skirt that was too short, Ulrike Kruger abruptly withdrew to her side of the cab and regarded her with the uncommunicative, surprised look of a marsh bird. "You must be tired," she observed.

"Indeed I am," Marija agreed tersely, her eyes fixed on the streets that kept fanning out, multiplying, branching off and, as they drove deeper into the city, getting denser on the other side of the immaculately clean window.

Then everything happened so fast it surprised Dren himself, life with Lola in the anarcho-antifascist squat of *Subversiv* in Nørrebro: he met Lola by accident, in the street, and immediately fell madly in love with her. True, she was chubby, was Lola, but she had white hair and those unusual gray-green eyes, and she fell for him right away too, his lanky limbs and thin chest, his ruddy cheeks and warm dark eyes. She didn't believe he was from Kosovo. People from Kosovo surely did not look like him. "Wait, are you really from Kosovo?" she asked in disbelief. "What did you say your name is? Dren," she repeated after him, so she would not forget, "Dren Kastrat," and Lola laughed, did Lola. She laughed, as they shared a tea. Then she brought him over to her place, to *Subversiv*, and now here he is, Dren, lying on the mattress in her room, waking up every morning happy, his hair a bit longer than it was in Avnstrup, and shaggy, dyed jet black. Usually he wears a black shirt and short leather jacket, tight jeans and high-top sneakers, two earrings on his left ear and one in his right nostril. Back home in Prizren he kept getting beaten up because of the way he looked, but here in

Nørrebro, in the *Subversiv* squat, nobody bothers him, nobody throws him dirty looks, and he simply can't get used to it . . .

Winter is slowly approaching and the news from Kosovo is getting worse and worse. Dren talks to his father at least twice a week. Though it isn't anywhere near as bad in Prizren as it is in Prishtina or Rahovec, or Gjakova or Deçan, or many other places, he is still worried, his father is old and ever since the bombing started even the tense, relative peace that had reigned in town has gone. People are dying and disappearing, the Serbian army and police are rampaging through town, civilians are leaving in the hundreds, in the thousands, and his father won't even discuss it—he just hems and haws on the phone, as if he doesn't know what to say anymore, but Dren tries to phone regularly, though it is harder and harder for him to get through, and since late March, since NATO bombed Prizren, and since almost half the city fled for Albania in fear of Serbian reprisals, he has been unable to get through at all. Still, every day he keeps trying, becoming more and more morose. And Lola, well let's say that Lola tries, but in honesty, it is all too complicated for her. "He must have fled to Albania," Dren mutters to himself, and that in Danish, impatiently rolling a cigarette, and Lola says absently: "Well, that's great, isn't it?" streaking her naturally white hair red. She yawns briefly. She is not particularly interested in all this. That night, Lola is especially gentle and passionate in bed, and, for the first time, he cannot get an erection, but Lola doesn't mind, she hugs him and nestles in the crook of his arm, smiling, kissing Dren's nipples, but he feels nothing. He is thinking about his father, he is thinking about home, about Prizren, he is thinking about Kosovo, and again about his father, and so in a circle, all the while staring dully at the top of Lola's head, her hair red, red . . .

Marija lives in a small street in Berlin's Prenzlauer Berg. Her balcony overlooks the street and is opposite an unusual-looking building that keeps drawing her attention. Unlike the well-tended building she lives in, the facade of this other building is peeling and cracked. It is covered in graffiti, and a big toy rabbit, hanging out of the window on old, stretched suspenders, sways there day and night. Coiled around its right leg is the cord of an antiquated telephone. The rabbit is missing an eye and written on its stomach in black spray paint is the circled letter A. "Ja, Marija, that is an anarchist squat," Ulrike explained to her once, "there were dozens of them all around here, but their number has been dwindling of late," as if she herself was not sure whether this was a pity or not.

With the advance of spring, Marija spends more and more time on her balcony, reading for hours or keeping an eye on the squat across the road.

She read on the Internet that it is called *Subversiv,* that it is connected to several squats of the same name across Europe, that the people who live there are members of an organization called *Autonome,* that on several occasions the German police tried, unsuccessfully, to evict them, and that violence could erupt there during Berlin's traditional May Day demonstrations. Marija is aware of all this, but it does not worry her too much; on the contrary. She likes colorful neighborhoods.

Living in the apartment below is Fatmir Berishaj. Like Marija, he is in Berlin at the invitation of the Center for Intercultural Dialogue and came not from Kosovo but from the moderate comfort of Klagenfurt, where for years now, as the city's town clerk, its *Stadtschreiber,* he has been enjoying all the amenities of a relaxed, well-heeled Austrian life. He came to Berlin somewhat earlier than Marija, and when she arrived he welcomed her warmly, but since then he has kept a polite distance.

To be honest, that suits Marija perfectly. They know each other well enough from before, and she finds the pomp and ceremony that Fatmir surrounds himself with as Kosovo's most prominent, widely translated poet, pretty silly.

Truth be told, Marija avoids company as such.

In the morning she writes. In the afternoon she cooks. At night she drinks.

She doesn't need anybody for any of that.

As for her social life, she sees no one; Ulrike comes by two or three times a week, but that's all. On her way, Ulrike always picks up Fatmir, and they sit in Marija's dining room, and sometimes even enjoy themselves, like now, here they are in the dining room. Ulrike is smiling, Fatmir is friendly, Marija is friendly as well. The two of them smile like old acquaintances. They chat easily, but as soon as Ulrike steps out for a second, as soon as she goes to the toilet, the atmosphere at the table flags. A few seconds of silence ensue. Fatmir's head sinks into his shoulders, his brow furrows, his face is grayer than it was just a minute ago. He drums his fingers on the table and says, in perfect Serbian: "Eh, Marija, good old Marija," smiling enigmatically, and when Marija raises a questioning eyebrow, he just shrugs noncommittally, and even more noncommitally smiles, and the two of them, as if by agreement, withdraw each into their own cocoon, saying nothing, not moving until Ulrike's return.

But it is all fine—Ulrike is not particularly sensitive to such things. Considering all the hatred that exists between Albanians and Serbs, a hatred unequaled elsewhere in Europe, Marija and Fatmir are communicating exceptionally well, in her opinion. There is a spark of friendship between them, and an atmosphere of mutual respect and understanding that runs deeper than that vapid politeness that is invariably assumed by people from warring sides whenever you put them together on neutral turf. In the final analysis, both are prominent critics of negative, retrograde tendencies in their respective societies, and have been invited here as such. Admittedly, the center's board had not been overjoyed by the choice of two somewhat older writers in exile, but there is nothing to be done about that. Such are the times. The competition is tough. There are lots of players in the penalty box of the nongovernmental sector. They are all angling for a goal. The results are not always spectacular, and Ulrike, sitting there on Marija's toilet, knows it only too well. That is why she feels a special tenderness and friendship for both guests this afternoon. Soon she will head for home— she mustn't forget to kiss them both before leaving, Fatmir twice and Marija three times. Marija is a Serb and the Serbs, like the Poles, kiss each other three times. She likes that, does Ulrike, and anyway, cultural differences should be carefully nurtured and preserved, they are something one should simply live with.

Though May is around the corner and the days are turning warmer, the sinking feeling in Dren's stomach is growing. Every day Copenhagen peacefully vibrates beside him, but back home people are still being killed, and he still doesn't know a thing about his father. It has been warm in Copenhagen these past few days, but Dren has been shivering lately and Lola cannot but notice that with each passing day he is becoming increasingly withdrawn, but she knows what to do. "Pack your things, we're going to Berlin," she says, and when Dren stares blankly at her, she adds, "Say hurray, man—I'm taking you to Berlin!" and she rolls her eyes with a cheerful laugh. Soon it will be Walpurgis Night and the traditional May Day demonstrations, something certainly not to be missed. They will stay, as in previous years, at the *Subversiv* in Prenzlauer Berg, right next to the Mauerpark, and, in a heartbeat, here they are, reader, already in Berlin, ten of them, stepping off the train, Max from the Berlin *Subversiv* is waiting for them at the Zoo station. He's got long green dreadlocks and a Palestinian kefiyah wrapped around his neck. He greets them all warmly, saying the others will be arriving from Italy later that day. *Subversiv* is dedicated to this kind of European underground network. They take the U-Bahn from the station to Prenzlauer Berg and spread out in the carriage. Dren is so excited he can barely breathe. The stations whizz by one after the other—Wittenbergplatz, Potsdamer Platz, Stadtmitte, Klosterstrasse, Alexanderplatz—then the U-Bahn surfaces and makes its way past the buildings, Dren keeps peering into all the windows.

Lola dozes off, smacking her lips in her sleep. He does not understand how she can let herself miss out on all this. He tries to shake her awake but Lola just smiles and Dren lets her be. Lola does not share his fascination. Berlin is Berlin. What's there to say? She can come and go whenever she wants, but now she's tired and she wants to sleep and that's that.

Later that day, having settled into Berlin's *Subversiv,* Lola is rested and perky again. The conversation over lunch at the long communal table in the kitchen becomes heated, Max is utterly inspired as he talks, he mentions the perfidious policies of the Red-Green government, the Fourth Reich, he speaks about countercultural awareness, about politics without parties, he talks about his own prescription for life, about direct action, about liberated territories and autonomous micro-regions. "Escalation!" he virtually shouts, "total radical escalation! That's what German autonomists are advocating!" Max is brilliant, and yet—Dren cannot sit still. He would rather take a little walk than sit here, because Berlin is over there, behind that wall, and it is beckoning to him. While people at the table hatch plans and elaborate tactics, he and Lola steal out into the sun and fresh air. Dren's heart is pounding, boom-boom, and it won't stop for the next two days. He is in Berlin, where he has always wanted to be, there should be no end to his happiness, and yet, that feeling in his stomach, that ongoing lump in his throat. . . . Just to dispel the cloud of dark thoughts that looms over him as dusk approaches, on their way back to *Subversiv* Dren stops to call home, in Prizren, from a phone booth in Schönhauser Allee, and he catches his breath when against all expectations, he gets through. He is beside himself. "It's ringing, Lola, it's ringing, I can't believe it." It rings several times and then he hears the sound of the receiver being picked up, that brief crackling of static, and finally a male voice which says in pure Serbian, "Yes? " He panics and drops the receiver in despair . . .

Fatmir Berishaj and Marija Pavlović appeared at the *Große Hände* Cultural Center on Sunday, the second day of May 1999. The organizer's idea was to present these two prominent ex-Yu writers that evening (given the bombastic title: "Serbia versus Kosovo: No Acceptance / No Repentance") as the civilized European face of Serbia and Kosovo. Unfortunately, however, things do not always work out the way the organizers wish or the way the printed program says. On that second day of May, Marija Pavlović was in a particularly bad mood. It was her birthday, and she had been drinking steadily since early morning, all alone, feeling sorry for herself. Here she was, fifty-eight, old age was creeping up on her, a time when she needed peace and quiet more than ever, and the only thing she could honestly say for herself was that she was a disaster on all counts: she came from a country and a city that had been bombed, she was getting old without a man by her side, she was stinking drunk day in and day out, her writing was uninspired, dull, routine. She was mediocre and forgotten and a failure—a plain old lush.

Early that evening, when she was due to go with Ulrike and Fatmir to that cultural, whatever it was, center, she was already as drunk as a skunk. As soon as they arrived she made a beeline for the bar and, ignoring her politely smiling hosts, tried to get a grip on herself by downing a double caipirinha, but she fell into a deeper and deeper blue funk.

Still, there was the program to get on with. Fatmir steps up onto the stage, Marija follows him, carrying her drink and, as if on purpose, trips over the cable on the way to her seat. The moderator jumps up to give her a hand, but she doesn't even fall, she just teeters awkwardly and drops her glass which provokes a lone but humiliatingly resounding snicker in the half-empty auditorium. Luckily, the moderator does not miss a beat, takes the floor, turns to her, avoiding her eyes as he speaks, introduces her briefly, and inaccurately, talking a bit in English and a bit in German; nobody understands anymore exactly what it is that he wants to say. The applause at the end is tepid, Marija's lips dry, the lights blinding. The moderator clears his throat and turns smilingly to Fatmir, suddenly he is less uncomfortable, now he is talking about the man and his work, speaking only in German, at length and accurately, Fatmir throws in the odd droll comment, also in German, the audience responds warmly and, after this fulsome introduction and all these superlatives, there is raptuous applause. Meanwhile, Fatmir Berishaj, that Klagenfurt rogue, that darling of the muses, critics, and nongovernmental sector, just smiles laconically. "One would think you'd written your Ph.D. on me," he says flatteringly at the end, to which the entire audience laughs politely, and Marija cannot stop herself from rolling her eyes. She is both nervous and tense and wishes she could be somewhere else. As Fatmir gets into his story about the tragedy of the Kosovo Albanians, Marija sinks deeper and deeper into her own thoughts. She is so tired that her whole body aches. She has hardly slept a wink for the last two nights. . . . First on Friday it was Walpurgis Night with all the wild goings-on in and around the park, the torches, stakes, blaring music, loud partying in the squat across the road which went on until the early hours of the morning, and then, yesterday, there was the May Day Parade, lines of people snaking all over Prenzlauer Berg, political slogans, flags, punkers, squatters, anarchists, labor trade unionists, organizations of Kurds, Turks, women, gays and lesbians, environmentalists, radical Maoists, everybody was there, and on the other side were the police and only the police, a proper army of robocops, Marija spent the whole day out in the streets, in the crowds, she came back to the apartment when night fell, by which time the street scene had become too violent, and anyway, there was a bottle of tequila waiting for her at home. She sat on the balcony and drank straight from the bottle, all around cars were in flames and shop windows were being smashed, right under her window the police had surrounded and isolated a demonstrator with green dreadlocks, Marija recognized him as one of the people living in the building across the way and watched from above as he lay splayed on the sidewalk, in a green army jacket, torn jeans and boots, a Palestinian scarf wrapped around his neck, she watched the cohorts of robocops push their way through the crowds of demonstators pouring in from all sides, and suddenly she got carried away, *that's* how drunk she was, revolution, revolution, "Fucking cop cunts!" she yelled in Serbian, brandishing the bottle at the police, "Fucking cowardly cunts!" she screamed even though nobody there understood a word except for a skinny, dark-haired guy who, in the middle of the angry crowd blinked straight at her as if he could not believe his ears, but the very next minute, jostled away in the mass of people, he disappeared behind the corner, far from Marija's sight, and from Fatmir Berishaj, whose face momentarily appeared on the balcony underneath hers, looking up at her from below in resigned astonishment . . .

Following Fatmir's lengthy introductory speech, which drew tears from many in the emotionally predisposed audience, the moderator turns triumphantly to Marija. "Is there anything that you would like to add to this?" he says, his voice now much steadier than before. "Please enlighten us with your personal view of this terrible plight of ethnic Albanians in Kosovo."

Only then does Marija snap out of her funk. She clears her throat. Then again. Then one more time. "Thank you," she says, her voice echoing irritatingly. "I couldn't agree more with Fatmir's detailed account of the position of the Albanian minority in Serbia and Yugoslavia, and I would like to stress that I deeply sympathize with the Albanian people. However, I feel the need to add that Albanians are, unfortunately, not the only victims of the Milošević regime."

She hears the invisible audience murmuring and squirming in their seats. "It is important to know that we are all victims," Marija adds. She feels like a deflated ball, a limp sack, an empty space. "And I mean all of us."

Sticky, salty beads of wet trickle down her cheeks into her mouth. Her stomach is burning, the acid is rising to her throat, making her nauseous. "We are all Albanians," she says.

Open shouts of indignation in the audience. "I am not," says the first voice cheerfully, and the audience bursts into laughter.

"This is rubbish," somebody else cries out.

"Serbian propaganda," shouts a third.

"No, she's just drunk," says a fourth and once again laughter fills the hall.

Marija blinks but does not see anything, or anybody. Her face is wet, gleaming with tears and perspiration.

"Indeed, Marija," Fatmir now jumps in—nothing can disturb his damned Klagenfurt equanimity, "we are all Albanians, but you know, as they say: some people just happen to be more Albanian than others."

The audience again explodes with laughter, and then applause, and Marija feels that it is more than she can bear, that she simply is not ready for this. She is not the type. Anyway, she is tired. Tired and old. She wipes away the sweat and the tears, pretends not to have heard Fatmir's remark, and turns to the impervious darkness behind the lights. "You don't seem to understand," she says to the invisible audience, "look what's happening all around you." But even she sees that it is too late to make amends and that everything has already gone downhill. "I am—" she tries to say, but is interrupted by laughter and whistles from the audience, she wants to say something more but can't. She is certain that if she speaks, the terrible, inhuman howl deep down inside her will come flying out. "I'm sorry," she somehow manages to mumble. "I cannot . . . I . . . I'm so sorry . . . ," and blinded by tears she gets up and heads for the edge of the stage. The clip mike falls onto the floor: the microphone crackles. Then suddenly it stops, it is pitch black and deathly silent as she heads for the green-and-red neon sign that says EXIT. It would be good if Ulrike could show up now and help her, but she is nowhere to be seen. Marija passes through the double doors. Now she is in the vast empty hall. She passes through some more double doors and here she is, outside, in the street, but there is nobody here either: the whole of Berlin is completely empty and belongs just to her.

And now, that constantly sinking feeling that Dren has had since he left Avnstrup is finally subsiding, he has not even thought of his father for two days, for two whole days he has simply been enjoying himself, but on Sunday here he is again in front of the phone booth in Schönhauser Allee, he wavers a bit, paces back and forth, musters up his courage, clasps the plastic phone card in his sweaty paw, shoves it into the slot, and slowly punches in the numbers, one by one. Again he gets a connection. It rings five whole times and then he hears a short *click* and that same voice saying in pure Serbian, "Yes?" Dren clenches his jaw, grinds his teeth, a wave of heat flushes his face, but this time he does not put down the receiver. "It's Dren," he says, also in Serbian, "Dren Kastrat, Anton Kastrat's son. I'm calling from abroad, from Germany. Who's that? Whom am I speaking to?" He strains to hear but again there is only an unnerving rustle, as if the receiver is being switched from one hand to the other. Then suddenly a crazy idea occurs to him—maybe it's their next-door neighbor and he is taking care of the apartment until everything blows over. "Uncle Marko," he says, suddenly hopeful, "is that you?"

The voice at the other end barks out a laugh. "Uncle Marko? No, I'm not Marko. "

Dren gulps. "Sorry, but I'm calling to see what's going on with my father." His voice is trembling. "Hello?" he says nervously.

"Who?" says the voice at the other end.

"My father," Dren says again. "Anton Kastrat. "He lives there."

"Aaaah," says the voice as if only now understanding, "well, why didn't you say so, man? To tell you the truth, as far as he's concerned, you have nothing to worry about anymore. But tell me, what's your name again—Dren? Well then, Dren, how are things in Krautland? What are you doing there?"

This guy is not from Prizren, Dren says to himself. Prizren Serbs don't talk like that. "That's none of your business," he says, clenching the receiver still tighter in his sweaty hand. "And why are you in my apartment anyway? What are you doing there? Where's my father?"

"Hey, hey, take it easy," says the voice. "Cool it," it says. "Truth be told, kiddo, your father is no longer with us," he declares slowly, with a smirk, taking obvious pleasure in doing so.

Dren turns ashen, his cheeks quiver. "I'm sorry?"

"Your father is no longer with us, I say," the voice repeats, considerably less patient now. "Do you understand Serbian, or what, damn it?"

Dren sees red. "Who are you?" he stammers. "Where is my father?" he stammers. "What are you doing in my apartment?" he yells. "What have you done with my father?" he yells.

The voice at the other end abruptly, implacably, cuts him short. "Now you listen to me, you little fairy," he hisses into the receiver. "We slit your old man's throat. He didn't struggle too much. It was fucking easy. The man was old. You get it now? So you just make sure you don't show up in Prizren, you motherfucking Shqiptar, or the same thing will happen to you! You get me?"

"But I," Dren starts to speak but then falls silent.

The voice at the other end laughs. "What's the matter," it asks mockingly, "cat got your tongue? "

"But," Dren stammers, "but . . ."

"Fuck it," says the voice, "that's how it is. Let me give you some advice," he adds, as Dren registers the soft beep in the receiver signaling that they will soon be cut off.

"Some well-meaning advice," says the voice. "Don't come back here, there's nothing for you here, no father, no house, nothing, so you just stay where you are, man, have a drink in our name in that Krautland of yours and tell all your people over there that Kosovo is sacred Serbian land and that . . . "

They are suddenly cut off and all Dren hears is a monotonous, flat tone.

"Babi. Dad," he says, pressing his brow against the receiver, "Babi."

All he feels is immense emptiness in his lungs, the aching void that is left when all bonds have broken.

He wanders aimlessly around Berlin, somehow even makes it down to the river, it looks dark and peaceful to him, he sits down on the farthest bench in the darkest corner of the riverfront and cries his heart out, helplessly banging his fists against the varnished wood beneath him, "Babi, Babi, Babi," then eventually he calms down: he finds the powerful rush of the water soothing, he could sit here for hours listening to it, it is late at night when he finally gets up and heads back. At first he walks slowly, placing one foot in front of the other. But step by step he feels lighter, tired and hungry and sadsadsad, but as light as a feather, and this lightness, Dren thinks to himself, wiping the tears from his face and walking faster and faster, this lightness: it must be freedom. *Real* freedom. Because now, in the end, there are no more limits to his life—"You have no father, you have no house, you have nothing"—that voice had been right, absolutely right: he had cut loose from everything a long time ago, the whole of time is Dren's time now and every space is his as well. And everywhere is home. And so he rushes back to Prenzlauer Berg, to Mauerpark, to *Subversiv*, to Lola, to everything that exists only because of him, and when he finally arrives, out of breath and soaked in sweat, he is suddenly stopped dead in his tracks by the sight of something utterly out of the ordinary for such a peaceful Sunday night: several police cars have blocked off the street and dozens of commandos, in full gear, are getting out of the vehicles. Dren retreats into the shadows, steals back into the park, follows the fencing, barely breathing. Out of nowhere Koni suddenly appears, scaring the life out of him; Koni had been hanging around in the park when it all started, when the commandos showed up and replaced the ordinary cops. And now, here they are, going into action: one commando group soundlessly enters the building's courtyard, another climbs onto the roof, a third, in gas masks, is by the door and at a silent signal storms inside, you can hear screaming, banging, things being overturned, lots of voices, followed by an explosion, thick smoke pours out of the building, people come running out of the front door, some are nabbed by the police, Dren frantically scans the scene for Lola, he does not see her, the others are getting away, running down the street and regrouping farther on. "Let's go," says Koni smiling, people are still jumping out of the squat's windows and through the doors, there are more of them than the police thought, most of them are carrying at least some sort of weapon, a rod or baseball bat or something, a number of them bring out the Plexiglas police shields they swiped in yesterday's clashes, Koni chuckles, "Come on, man, let's go, come on." He covers his face with a hankie, pulls up his hood, gives Dren his own cap, and since there is no sign of Lola, Dren follows Koni, pulls the cap down over his head to at least partially conceal his face, laughing to himself as he runs behind Koni. Koni's good mood is contagious, they zigzag their way, running, evading the cops like in a computer game. The air is saturated with tear gas. It stings his eyes, constricts his throat, makes him nauseous, but he keeps on moving. To his left he sees two cops trip up Koni, Dren escapes their grasp and runs as fast as his legs will carry him to the squatters' barricades, rocks fly overhead, raining down on the cops. Dren runs over to the squatters and is welcomed with applause and loud cheering. Lola is there, she's all red from her hair, "Dren," she cries out, "Dren, where have you been, you fuckin' cunt," hugging and kissing him. "Where have you been?" she cries. Dren wants to tell her that he has spoken to his father and that his father is fine. He doesn't want Lola to worry unnecessarily. He wants to tell her he loves her but he doesn't have time for any of that. The police have broken through the barricades. A rock flies at the windshield of a jeep that is heading straight for them. The driver loses control of the wheel. The vehicle starts careening dangerously and crashes into a tree. Several Italians quickly surround the jeep, demolish it, and try to yank off the doors, the cops inside are clearly in a panic. Outside a cop lunges at Lola, wrests her free from Dren's grasp, and drags her to the police van, with Lola thrashing, kicking, yelling and swearing in Danish, and when Dren jumps on top of him to defend her—she's all he's got left in life—another cop races over and whacks him in the back with his nightstick . . .

It is absolutely unbelievable how quickly Marija Pavlović sobered up after she'd had a good cry in that little square in front of the *Große Hände* Cultural Center. Considerably more clear-headed and calmer, she walked the surrounding deserted streets, though she did not know exactly where she was or where she was going. She was relieved to see more and more people around because now at least she could be sure that there is a life (after all!) apart from the world of Serbs and Albanians, apart from the lofty mission of the Center for Intercultural Dialogue, apart from the lights that bored straight into her eyes and that invisible, dark, mean audience. She chose the first restaurant that caught her eye. She took the corner table in the little trattoria and tried to enjoy her dinner, but when she finally headed for home she was so tired that she dozed off in the carriage of the U-Bahn and almost missed her stop. She jumped off the train at the last moment, could hardly wait to crawl into bed, but instead of the peace and quiet she was hoping for she found her normally quiet street amok with police cordons, smoke bombs, water hoses—bedlam. The police had finally decided to empty the squat across the way because of all the illegal activities going on there, at least that is how the tall, young, almost painfully handsome policeman explained it to her while Marija kept yawning in his face. And no, he did not let her through to her house: she pleaded with him, argued with him, even threatened him, but it was no use. And just when she began to despair, two young men with hoods and hats pulled down low appeared out of nowhere behind his back and in what was an incredible super slalom broke through the police lines and made straight for the positions held by the evicted squatters. The police-man was briefly distracted, and Marija, always adept at taking advantage of a moment of confusion, stole away, disappearing into the inky night, as if she had never even been there. Meanwhile, one of the two daredevils was tripped up and thrown into the police van, the other was somewhat luckier and managed to reach the squatters. But the very next moment, the police released tear gas, there was a terrible noise as the robocops overran the hope-lessly improvised barricades, and dozens of them appeared on the opposite side of the street, surrounding the squatters, grabbing and arresting them. In an effort to protect herself against the tear gas, Marija retreated far into the first doorway she found. Once the smoke started clearing up, she saw in the midst of this apocalyptic chaos a group of policemen bending over the same dark-haired young man who had earlier escaped their grasp. They kept thrashing away at him, but he just soundlessly curled up, his body jerking on the asphalt, trying to protect his head with his fists. Impulsively, Marija ran over to them. "Hey," she yelled. "Hey!" She hurled herself at the first police-man but only managed to hit his plastic shield, and he did not even notice. Then she heard the loud screech of car tires and out of the cloud of smoke emerged a police jeep, going in reverse, swerving uncontrollably all over the road. The police suddenly jumped to the side, somebody pulled her out of the way, she was thrown to the ground, scraping her elbows and hands, and when she looked up she saw the vehicle drive over the body of the beaten up young man, and even through all the noise and clamor, she could hear his bones cracking. She shouted something. She did not know exactly what or in which language, but shouting at a moving vehicle was senseless. Inherently deaf to all her shouts of warning, it nonchalantly caught the young man's body with its rear wheels and started to drag it down the road, leaving behind a trail of blood. The jeep then jumped in place, finally drove over the obstacle and, making a huge racket, headed for the exit to Schönhauser Allee. Marija dragged herself over to the young man, her elbows were smarting and her knee hurt so badly that she could not straighten it, but somehow she got herself over to him. He was alive. All that was left of his stomach was a lump of bloodied pulp, but he was alive, choking, spitting up blood, blinking furiously, as if struggling not to fall asleep. "There, there," she whispered, "sssh, sssh." She did not know what to do exactly, or what to say, how to help him, how to save him—she had never held a dying man in her arms before. That same instant, the young man wheezed loudly and clutched at her with his grazed, bloody hands. "There, there," Marija mumbled again, and then shouted: "Help! Help!" Dark blood gushed from the young man's stomach, soaking her pale spring dress. "Help! Somebody, help!" she kept yelling like crazy, but nobody saw her or heard her. A full-scale street battle was again raging. Somebody was even photographing it from nearby. Her eyes registered the white flash and, for just a moment, she was conscious of her disheveled hair and wild-eyed face. Good Lord, she thought. But, the eyes of the young man were already glassy and still. The squeeze of his hand went limp. Even the blood stopped bubbling out of his gaping mouth.

"Help," Marija sobbed. "Help!"

With a trembling hand she stroked the dead boy's head.

The ambulance arrived fifteen minutes later, only after all the squatters had been arrested and the street completely cleared of the crowd. If was, of course, too late for anything; the only thing they could still do was to certify death. Marija cried and cried on her knees, until they lifted her up and took her to the side. The dead boy was placed in a long, nontransparent, zippered body bag and removed. The ambulance drove away to the strident wail of its siren and Marija remained standing there, to the side, where they had left her, feeling empty, empty, empty . . . That same moment she felt a hand on her shoulder. She knew whose it was before even turning around.

Sure enough, it was Fatmir Berishaj's.

Marija and Fatmir spent the rest of the long night together. First they drank at Fatmir's, then at Marija's, she could not stop shaking, he was endlessly kind and gentle, daylight was just about to break outside, she was terrified at the thought of being alone, so they lay down together, as friends, in the morning darkness Marija listened to Fatmir's even breathing, she closed her eyes and surrendered herself to the warmth that coursed through her stomach and limbs. She drew closer and rested her head on his chest, he put his arm around her and laid his warm hand on her thigh, his large body calmed and warmed her, she drew closer still, smiled and kissed him on the cheek, he smiled in response, and they both fell asleep, virtually at the same moment.

It will soon transpire—once Marija Pavlović gets over the short-lived shock of having had a young man bleed to death in her arms—that the entire affair did not affect her that badly. Quite the opposite. Her longstanding depression vanished as if with the wave of a hand, and she drank considerably less than before. Indeed, the coming days were to bring her one surprise after another. Marija saw the fact that the dead young man was actually a Kosovo Albanian, a refugee from Prizren named Dren Kastrat, as an unfelicitous, improbable, and above all sad coincidence, but the media picked up on it, for them it was something quite different—sensational, the whole story reverberated like a bomb, and soon amateur photos appeared from somewhere showing the writer Marija Pavlović (so, a Serb) cradling the head of the dying young man, a victim of police brutality named Dren Kastrat (so, an Albanian), as she, dishevelled and covered in blood, calls for help, while street battles are raging in the background. And all this was happening not somewhere in the Balkans, but in the middle of Berlin. The picture was repeatedly shown on all the television stations. Marija unexpectedly became the focus of German and European public attention and thereby, albeit unintentionally, atoned several times over for the incident she had caused at the *Große Hände* Cultural Center. The media uproar over the tragic death of the young Albanian refused to die down, just like the succession of violent anti-police demonstrations that for months erupted all over Europe. CNN ran a story on the whole thing and *Der Spiegel* issued a center spread with an unusually moving series of pictures of the event; Marija Pavlović's fame and reputation received a new boost later that year, when Europe's most prestigious prize for documentary photography—the FOCUS Feature Photography Award—was awarded to the author of the moving series of photographs, entitled, appropriately, if for the uninitiated enigmatically, "Rootlessness."

Translated by Christina P. Zorić

Others

Bora Ćosić

THERE IS THIS IDEA OF A LITTLE PERSON, ATTRACTED BY THE OUTSIDE world, who can hardly wait to get out into the street and run down it. It is a misapprehension. To me, at the age of five, my family's move from Zagreb to Belgrade in 1937 was like a disaster. I could not understand my parents, why had they done that? Up until then, I had had my own little corner, my autonomous Kazakh republic in my parents' home, a single-story building surrounded by a garden, and I had no desire to leave it. In a space like that, a child can create his own Alpine peaks and Ukrainian plains; what more does he need? But then some rough-looking people come along, load all our chairs onto a big truck, and take them who knows where. To the corner of two noisy Belgrade streets, up to the third floor, with traffic roaring down below, into a throng of tenants and a pace of life I had never known before.

Any move is exile into another world, among strangers. Little Lukacs did not say hello when callers came to the house because he felt that he had not invited them, that they had nothing to do with him. Similarly, I had nothing to do with my parents' plans to change where we would live; nobody had ever asked me for my opinion. The soul of a child is just another one of those bundles they toss into the huge truck along with everything else, for it to be jostled around at will. I was a jostled child, a little soul transferred to a new garrison in our life, without any right of appeal. For a child is merely the smallest private in the military hierarchy of the family, and he must silently accept any order issued by higher authorities.

My mother unpacked our things in this new house of ours and arranged them in the new space, trying to re-create the same layout as before. But it was no use. The windows were not in the same place, the ceiling was a bit higher, there was always something to indicate that there was no going back to the way things were. My mother kept walking around these new rooms, bumping into armchairs and furniture; the proportions of our existence had changed, what should have been the same was found to be different.

I was glad that even the adults could see what had happened. That there had been a major painful change, like when people quickly move to a raft from a sinking ship. People who are moved to a different place look ship-wrecked to me. Wet and exhausted, they manage to reach the shore and then lie there on the sand, under the sun, trying to recover. This other place may even be an island of paradise, but it is new and it is foreign. And it takes time for us to understand how we wound up in this world of abundance. I can remember my mother sitting at the table, lost deep in thought, trying to figure out what needed to be done to re-create that previous arrangement of our life, and our fate.

I realized that there is also always another life somewhere nearby, one quite different from, almost the opposite of, our old one. As if the one we have contains its own opposite, and any kind of change will bring it out from its hidden depths. So these wardrobes, bookshelves, and Father's armchair all contained within them that other version, which was just waiting for a chance to come out.

The same proved to be true on the street. When I took my first walk with my mother, I realized that the familiar park, tram tracks, and small houses across the way were gone and instead there was now suddenly a river with lots of ships, and a huge area of flat land; it was as if another world, vast and unknown, had appeared. We had to take a deep breath, get ourselves to the main street, and, in so doing, find some sort of direction to the future. I thought that these must be the same houses from Zagreb, only seen from a different angle, under a different light, that everything in this city was made of old material, only reconstructed, like after an earthquake. The layout of the streets had simply changed in the process, and one had to relearn how to find one's way in this new town, and in this life. A little five-year-old does not know where to go anyway, but his mother ought to know, and I trusted that she would put me on the right road.

Then friends came to the house, my father's colleagues from work, cheerful and young, except there was something funny about the way they talked. Suddenly I understood only some of what until then had been a familiar language. It was as if I had found myself in a madhouse where everybody talked like me, only they didn't, as if there were two languages which collided when spoken; this was my first lesson on the differences, however small, between Serbian and Croatian. This new semi-language was spoken at the baker's, the butcher's, the perfume store where I went with my mother, but we continued speaking our way, in our language of before. I think they quietly laughed at us behind our backs. Then I wondered which of these two languages was the right one and who could explain it to us. Because there is always the official language of a place, a street, a house in that street, and slightly different kinds of speech.

I had two little friends, Russian girls. Their father was a watchmaker, their mother was always making tea which we drank out of a saucer, the Russian way. There were Russians everywhere in our new neighborhood, and they all did something special. They repaired watches, or did type-setting, or tuned pianos. I slowly began to understand that other kinds of people, even Russians, were needed to do these different jobs. The Russian women in the neighborhood made wonderful hats and mysterious lamp-shades for a completely new kind of lighting. They spoke in a funny way, like baby talk or when you're a bit tipsy. There were Hungarians, too. They mostly did water-main repairs and knew something about electricity. Life became different, confusing but fun. I was a little afraid that we would lose ourselves among these strangers, even my mother had started talking differently somehow, in that new Belgrade way.

Then I noticed that there were many different ways of speaking in one and the same town, and very different ways of behavior, too. A hairdresser who lived opposite us liked to go naked on the staircase, making girls scream with fear, or perhaps pleasure. A fat office worker from the floor above would go out on his balcony, drop his trousers, and loudly break wind to spite the tailor who lived across the way. My mother warned me to ignore it all, but I felt that everything around us had to be taken into account. I asked her how many different people there were in the world and why? The little republic of my room was splitting open on all sides, and the world came bursting into my life, though I had never invited it in. Now I understand little Lukacs; strangers are an irritation to any child, not just to the boy who was preparing to become Europe's greatest philosopher. Various ladies came calling on my mother in those days, relating countless stupid, boring events, and it went on for hours. Then, in the evening, the adults would sit down at our table and play cards, which to a small child was a very silly occupation anyway, but even worse was that these people were foreign, unfamiliar, some other kind of inhabitants of the times, simply incidental contemporaries of what was then my life.

Different, too, were the people who came to our door, asking for a crust of bread. My mother would offer them a bowl of soup and a spoon reserved for beggars—it was big and made of lead. They would sit on the staircase and eat their lunch, put aside for people who do not eat at tables with table-cloths, so there was this whole world of people who ate on staircases, in basements, in the street even, sitting on their crossed legs, and everyone looked upon them as foreign, as if there was an entire nation of the poor and the wretched, born in an unknown land. At the time, I didn't understand where this land was and how one got from there to here, to us. My mother always spoke to them very politely, as if they did not understand our language and spoke only their own, beggars' language. She spoke to them in short sentences, so that they could comprehend her better, as if they were sick in the head. Ordinary people cannot understand how a person can reach a point where he has to eat on the staircase, out of somebody else's plate, using a heavy, specially designated spoon made of lead. As if they suffer from some unknown illness, the illness of poverty, which they caught who knows where. As if poverty spreads like measles or whooping cough among hitherto healthy, normal folk. I enjoyed these people because they always joked with me when I appeared behind my mother's skirt at the door. And, once they had finished their soup, I expected them to perform for me, stand on their hands or play something on a comb. I asked my mother when would we be poor, like them, thinking that that would make us much more interesting both to ourselves and to others.

Then I began noticing the skinny students who would gather in the corner of our room, whispering with my young aunts, and later humming some melody, Russian perhaps. I thought it must be forbidden to sing such songs. At some point, my mother would take me out of the room, and I realized that somebody was constantly trying to remove me from the most interesting things in life, where others were having fun playing the most important roles. Now that I had finally taken an interest in the lives of others, I felt that they were forcibly trying to remove me to a separate room, and once they had done so, they could embark on their fascinating, secret other life behind closed doors. I did not know how to make them let me into that room of a different life, if only once in a while. Later I heard that in hidden corners and darkened rooms all over town, young people were reading aloud in hushed voices from soiled and heavily underlined books, making plans about who knows what and who knows against whom. So there were two utterly separate worlds, one that sat in cafés, strolled down the street, and worked in offices, and this other hidden world of secret circles that discussed how to take all this café- and office-sitting, all this senseless street-strolling, blow it up sky-high and hoist what was to me a meaningless red flag on top of the tallest building.

In the years leading up to the war I became increasingly introverted, a moody and taciturn child, as if I had my own cell of conspirators, my own circle of one, where I dreamed of carrying out a coup, the greatest one there is in life: growing up. Later, very particular kinds of people were to intrude—German occupying troops, Russian liberators—not just with their language but also with their appearance, customs, and views.

With the advent of communism, yet another kind of person appeared, uncommunicative and austere. Taking up their offices, commands, and ministries, these people were unapproachable—ordinary folk avoided them, and when they did have to deal with them, they assumed that recognizably ingratiating tone. The middle class has two extremes: either utter aloofness, or, when circumstances are dire, there is that pragmatic note, with all its false humility. And so in my youth, there appeared once more in our common history that element of persons unknown, people who were somewhat arrogant, seemingly self-assured but actually always tense, as if the war was not over and somebody might fire a gun at any moment from behind the corner. I knew some of these people, one of them preferred to sleep on the floor, another slept fully dressed, he just removed his boots, nothing else. I think these people were afraid that they were only temporary residents of our city, that an order would suddenly be issued, or a plane would drop a bomb, or something would happen, and so one shouldn't undress at night!

Later, this picture gradually changed, and that happened when one of these newcomers took my young aunt for his wife, and, as in many other families, we became a mixed household. Other people slowly became a part of our life, retaining that stern air and sometimes negative attitude to their newfound environment. Even some of the middle class now became this other kind of person; girls from good families, separated from the ordinary world, joined their colonels, chiefs, and ministers in an asylum of new finery, luxury, and vast privilege; a new class, revealed by Milovan Djilas, had embarked on its separate life. It is a time I remember as the empty capital, especially in the summer. A time when generals and their newly arrived missuses vacationed in secluded summer resorts, in settings full of delights envisaged only for the future, while the rest of the populace, impoverished and abandoned, plodded along those sweltering summer streets, where there was nothing. A feeling of discontent slowly began to grow among the people, the dream of equality had been shattered. Hell is other people. So declared not a reactionary but one of the foremost writers of the left, Jean-Paul Sartre.

It transpired (even for the young me) that each individual's fate had its own individual purpose, just as every human body had its own individual smell. It was the hallmark of my being, in the same way that my ideas could not be anybody else's.

From my earliest childhood I remember a kind of distrust on the part of others, which even a very young person feels when it is directed at him. In my first years at school, I noticed this differentness among these little people, each of whom was a continent unto himself, and it was hard to condense this miniature world into just a few rows of school benches. I had some strange subjects, some friends of my father's sent me a special little writing tablet from abroad, but instead of being black for use with chalk, mine was white, you could write on it with an ordinary pencil. That tablet was the object of huge envy at school, as was a little coat I got from some relatives in America. Inscribed on that little white board with its red lines, as if lifted from the banner of an admiral's ship, was my fate: separateness. But the most important thing was this: though I had started school a year early, I already knew how to read and write, and it was this that sealed my fate as an outcast. I was from another town, I came from the modest family of a shop assistant, but unfortunately I knew something the others didn't, and that made my schoolmates unspeakably furious. The chubby daughter of the president of a Belgrade municipality was in our class, she was driven to school in a luxurious car, her mouth was always caked with egg from breakfast, but it was me who was the object of their odium, me, the little gnome from out of town, who on the very first day knew all his letters. I was different from them, and they were different from me. My biography was inscribed on that tablet, made of unknown material, plastic probably, the biography of an alienated being, due partly to my own neurosis and partly to the general psychopathic image of the world. Because this is a crazy world; millions of ideas buzzing around in so many heads across the planet can only produce general schizophrenia, not a harmonized, unified system. "In the present social situation," Fernando Pessoa wrote, "however well-intentioned a group of people might be, however concerned they all are with combating social fictions and working for freedom, it is not possible for such a group to work together without the spontaneous creation amongst them of a tyranny, a new tyranny, in addition to that of the existing social fictions, without destroying in practice everything they love in theory, without involuntarily standing in the way of the very thing they wish to promote. What can be done? It's very simple. We should all work for the same end, but separately." To this, the acerbic wit of Vladimir Nabokov unknowingly added his May Day slogan: "Workers of the world, disunite!"

The individual human instance, including mine, has its own problem: there are more of others than there is of me. And so, in pursuing my destiny, I had to establish my Menshevik status, that of a minority. I, like every other individual, am the voice of the minority faction in the vast soviet of sameness. So no one in the galleries can use his own weak case to outvote that Lenin of collective views. Later, this feeling only grew. And my minority existence became increasingly difficult to declare in an assembly that felt very strongly about common stands. I, therefore, was seen as other, as a kind of renegade and dissident, unnecessary in every respect.

But the fact that I am in the minority, said the Croatian poet Miroslav Krleža, does not mean that I am not right. On the contrary, recent history teaches us exactly the opposite: the Bolshevik multitude is often wrong.

Translated by Christina P. Zorić

Sepulchral Saturday

Beqë Cufaj

I'LL NEVER KNOW WHY HE WANTED TO SEE ME ONE LAST TIME BEFORE HE passed away. The phone call came one Saturday morning at the end of summer. The calls from Brussels from my mother, brother, sister, and other relatives had changed in tone over the last six months. I started to shake whenever I saw one of their names on my cell phone display, realizing that his condition must have gotten worse. I knew there was no hope of improvement, no way back. The bitter end was gradually approaching and, with every visit, it became clear to me that my last reserves of optimism were nothing but denial. His illness was a constant presence in our minds. It spread slowly until it was foremost in the thoughts of everyone close to him. The whole family suffered because it was inexperienced in such calamities.

The call was different that morning because my father wanted to see me. He was now on his deathbed and had gasped to my brother: "Tell him, he should come around . . . if he can . . ."

I knew right away what his final wish would be about. My knees started to quiver. My whole body was sapped of strength. Yes, it was now time. Everything would be different after this day, after this trip. It was going to be a shock, and then endless mourning.

I had trouble collecting my thoughts. The last six months passed in front of me. The frequent train journeys, so different from the trips I usually made for professional reasons. The pacing back and forth in the ward. The many cigarette butts in the oval cement courtyard of the clinic. The intolerably sympathetic smiles of the nurses and staff. Greeting the other patients. The technical equipment that filled his room. The view of the park with its lofty oak trees and mown lawns.

How torturous these one-, two-, or three-day visits were! Despair spread throughout my being like the cancer cells in his body that was kept alive by the apparatus. Numerous injections a day, dozens per week, and hundreds a month. The parched, shriveled, and bent old man, whose eyes told me that he couldn't take it anymore, didn't want to carry on. The medication was numbing his brain, but I was relieved about this. At least he would be spared the terrible pain.

His words were confused. He would speak to his dead brothers, his mother, and to his father, who had died in the Vojvodina as a soldier in some army in the Second World War. My grandfather had passed away without ever having seen his youngest son.

It was all too much for me to bear in those months. Everyone around me, from close relatives to distant friends, seemed indifferent to the fact that this man to whom I owed my existence was in an appalling state on his departure from this world. Never more would he see the sky and the sunlight.

Everyone I knew called and visited, trying to comfort me and lift my spirits. Then they returned to their normal lives, their day-to-day routines. I had a hard time facing people when I went into town—the children, young women, seniors—some at work, others unemployed. The hospital was in the center of town, where people I didn't know were suffering and dying, just as he was.

Normal life with its everyday cares and concerns. This was my hell, my sorrow.

Waiting at home for a taxi to take me to the train station, I glanced at the window of my favorite bookstore. The poster that read: "Down with savings books, up with real books" was still hanging there.

The cream-colored Mercedes taxi stopped on the main street where I live, and I hurried over. It was ten o'clock, and my train was leaving in half an hour. The driver got out to meet me. He was the same guy who had driven me home from the station three nights before. The same phone number, 878, glared in big red letters across the hood, trunk, and side doors.

"I can't take the car any farther into the road you live on. It's a one-way street," he explained as I jumped in. This was the most important thing in his life at that moment. The noise of the motor died as I closed the door.

The driver was in his fifties. The black leather seats in the car smelled of stale cigarette smoke.

"No problem. I'm glad you could make it," I replied curtly, trying to muffle the quiver in my voice.

"Terrible weather, isn't it? The heat is enough to drive you mad," continued the taxi driver as we made our way to the train station. The temperature outside was the last thing that interested me. But how was he to know?

"You just have to get used to it," I declared with a shrug.

I couldn't see the driver's face from the backseat. Caught between visions of the past and the merciless present, I had no time to react to what he was saying. He was only talking, just trying to break the ice with the topic of the unusually high temperatures at that time of year, and about the town in which he'd spent his entire life and that he knew like the back of his hand, and about the changing times that were getting worse and worse . . .

"I don't think it's ever been as bad as it is today," he noted, winding down his monologue.

"How far are we from the train station?" I interrupted, wanting him to know that I was in a hurry.

"We're almost there. Don't worry," he said, going on, if I remember rightly, about the train station that had once been the pride of the town and which was now a magnet for all sorts of tramps and riffraff drinking cheap wine, to junkies sitting cross-legged on the pavement with their dogs and listening to music on CD players of dubious origin, and to asylum seekers from Africa and Asia ready to pounce on unattended suitcases. These impostors were quick to scatter and then reappear on the same spot.

"And the police do nothing about it. No wonder this country is going to the dogs. It's never been as bad as it is today . . ."

I glanced at the taxi meter, flipped open my wallet, and left a couple of bills on the front seat.

"Keep the change. Have a coffee on me," I blurted as I bolted from the car without saying good-bye.

It was still early in the afternoon, but the heat rising from the sidewalks was intolerable. I had to hustle to catch my train.

My fellow passengers all looked tired. You could see it in their eyes and in their sluggish movements. I felt ill at ease among them in the compartment. Anger was rising in my guts. "Calm down, not here. Swallow and count to ten," I would always say to myself.

"Why isn't the damn train moving?"

"What does it matter whether we get there a few minutes early or late? It doesn't change anything."

"OK, OK, let's count them again."

"No way! I told you already that you've already had more than your share. You've had three more than normal," she scolded angrily as she stared at the bottle of beer in his hand.

"Come on! That's not true. You can see I'm still completely sober."

"Look, I can prove it because I've got everything written down for every single day. And if ever you try and cheat, it's all here in black and white."

"Fuck it. Open the damn notebook and let's have a look."

"Here it is . . . One, two, three . . . eight, nine . . . And for today, I've got twelve recorded. That's three more than you had yesterday and a lot more than last week . . ."

The elderly lady with gold teeth attempted to distract her young grand-daughter from the conversation of the agitated couple, but the little girl was fascinated by it. She was captivated by their slurred speech, by their nasty words that she would never be allowed to use, and by their blurry eyes and sallow cheeks.

Every time she was about to ask a question, her grandmother would interrupt with the tale of the mermaid who went back home after saving her lover and his ship from the Cyclops on the stormy sea.

The train was still not moving. I looked out the window, seeing that the sky was now overcast. Heavy gray clouds had blotted out the sun that had been such a bother to the taxi driver. Soon there was thunder and light-ning, and a deluge of raindrops began flowing down the grimy window of the compartment. Outside there were people running for shelter. What a terrible day!

"Grandma, grandma! Look, there's the mermaid you told me about!"

"No, no, dear. That's not her. She wears white clothes. And she doesn't live here and doesn't travel by train." Her explanations seemed to be directed at all of us, rather than at the little girl.

"When's this damn train gonna get movin'?" slurred the drunk. He couldn't handle it anymore. He needed another beer.

"I gotta have it. You understan' me? Gimme a bottle!" he shouted.

"The whole compartment is going to stink of beer. And there's a child here, too," protested his wife in a low voice. "Read your newspaper. Look here, there's an article on the last page about a human head found in a plas-tic bag in a garbage bin at a subway stop. They say it belongs to a vagrant who went missing a couple of months ago."

"Excuse me, would you mind?" interrupted the elderly lady in an indig-nant tone.

"Come, dear. Let's go and freshen up," she continued, and took her grandchild by the hand, giving her perplexed neighbor a nasty stare.

"Jus' gimme one last beer and I'll leave you in peace and quiet. I promise."

"OK, but I promise *you*, this is the last one, even if we sit here until the day of judgment," she retorted.

"How can they do that? They've locked up all the washrooms," complained the elderly lady. "What am I supposed to do with my granddaughter?"

"But grandma, I don't have to go!" protested the little girl.

"Good God, I don't believe it!" muttered the old woman. She seemed to be expecting a reaction from me, but I said nothing. Nor did the fellow sitting next to me.

"They must be crazy!"

"Grandma, grandma! Why aren't they letting those people get onto the train? The mermaid with the little dog wants to get on, too!"

"I don't know, dear. Come and have a little sleep now. Hop onto my lap and dream about something nice until we arrive and meet your dad."

"Ladies and gentlemen! We apologize for the unforeseen delay caused by the inclement weather," echoed a metallic voice from the loudspeakers. "We hope to continue the journey as soon as possible. At the moment, we are waiting for the passengers from a connecting train. We regret any inconvenience caused by the increased volume of passengers on this train. Thank you for your understanding."

"What, you mean there are gonna be more people in this compartment?" complained the drunk.

My cell phone rang, jolting me back to reality. It was my brother wanting to know when I'd be arriving.

"He doesn't say anything anymore," he reported. "They've transferred him to the palliative care unit." I told him about the storm and the delay. Everyone in the compartment was staring at me. My foreign language confused them.

Not even the drunk made a comment. I could sense an expression of sympathy on the face of the elderly lady, in whose lap the little girl had fallen asleep. The quiver in my voice had no doubt betrayed me. Or maybe the tears in my eyes. The man next to me still showed no reaction.

I don't remember how long it took until we arrived at the second-to-last station before the Belgian border. By the last stop the compartment was empty. Everyone had gotten out, and I breathed a sigh of relief. Too many people in a cramped space. And too many inquisitive faces. Now that I was alone, I was free to return to thoughts of the father with whom I hadn't had much contact in the last few years.

To flee is betrayal, but to stay can be betrayal, too. That's more or less how Max Frisch put it. I hadn't known the quotation when I said good-bye to my father the day I set off on the long road of emigration to a world so different from his.

In spite of the distance, he continued to think about me, to worry about me while I was abroad. As for me, I felt no great need to talk to him about my life.

I had spent my childhood and teenage years very attached to him, but then I realized that I didn't need him anymore. I grew up in a country that constantly preached "Brotherhood and Unity" among the nations and national minorities, peoples and ethnic groups, between capitalism and socialism. But no one took it very seriously. Least of all my father.

He had his own way of interpreting and of practicing it. In Tito's Yugo-slavia, the Albanians were foreigners in their own land. They spoke a different language, had less access to education, and were behind the rest of the country in every respect. Their transition from a feudal peasant life in the countryside to the "emancipated" urban environment of socialism was for years a profound yet positive shock for everyone who had been used to peering from the peephole of a distant fortified tower.

My father, for his part, a lowly public servant in the incredibly compli-cated self-administration system of former Yugoslavia, admired the Tito regime in some respects, but dreamed simultaneously of another Albanian life. The dichotomy left us in a constant state of tension, caught between two poles. I later came to realize that I accepted everything I saw and expe-rienced at that time as completely normal. But I don't want to moralize here; that's not my way. After all, to distance oneself from moral interpreta-tions does not mean to act without a sense of morals.

I am grateful to the man—my father—who passed away that Saturday, for allowing me to see myself as an individual, devoid of extreme moral values.

When I was a child, he always proclaimed humanitarian beliefs such as respect for others, and tried to inculcate his beliefs in me. Sanctity in unusual circumstances. What was sacred to him, a Kosovar, was Alba-nia, where the political and social situation certainly merited the term "unusual." As a result, my family would secretly watch television from Albania, but when friends or relatives visited, the channel would be turned to Tito television. Some would regard this as inconsistent or even immoral, but it was normal for my father to prefer the forbidden fruits of Albanian television and, at the same time, to have a portrait of Tito hanging in our living room. Marshal Tito no doubt secretly enjoyed being able to watch the channel of the enemy.

My father remained true to his principles even after the fall of commu-nism and the outbreak of the Balkan Wars, although, older and resigned as he was, the sheer depth of the changes had shaken him. It was then that my problems with him began.

Everything he had preached was a shambles. His vision of sanctity, Alba-nia, proved to be morally depraved. The country we watched on television, now openly with friends and relatives, had no moral values to offer. On the other hand, Yugoslavia's erratic political evolution was leading increasingly to open assaults on us by the military.

The Albanians, who were the outsiders in that curious oasis of artificial friendship among the peoples, were the first to get beaten up. Slobodan Milošević sent in the tanks and, with an iron fist, robbed Kosovo of its autonomy.

Those were bad years. I got beaten up for the first time in my life, for no reason at all, just because I was Albanian. I was out in Prishtina with a friend, who now lives in Germany, too, when we were stopped by three Serbian policemen who wanted to see our ID. We showed them our papers and they began to batter us with the butts of their Kalashnikovs. I don't know what provoked the beating. The second incident took place a few months later. I was on a bus that was stopped by a Serbian patrol. The police divided the travelers into two groups. Serbs and all of the women were told to stay on the bus. The Albanian men, to whom I now belonged as a nineteen-year-old, were forced off. One by one we were kicked and struck with rifle butts. It is no pleasant experience being attacked. If you think you are strong enough, you hit back. If you don't, the rage wells up within you. The effect of this abuse increased when the Albanians were expelled from schools and universities. It all became quite normal. A whole people was being beaten up. It lasted for years. The anger and frustration within us evolved into irreparable hatred.

My father never spoke of anger. He was in a state of despair and warned us to be careful and to avoid danger. For my part, I was furious. I was furious at being the object of their hatred. And I began to include him in my anger because he would have none of my raging and my calls for rebellion.

He continued to preach humanistic values and didn't believe that things would actually come to war. Not in our part of the world. Milošević had more important tasks. Everything would be all right in the end. He shared this belief with many a Kosovar—and later a European—pacifist. I couldn't listen to their views any longer. Not because I was in favor of war. If I had been for war, I would have taken up arms myself. I preferred to leave my father and to forsake my country, and flee from all the preaching and hatred.

In Yugoslavia, war broke out in one part after the other. First of all in Slovenia, then in Croatia, Bosnia, and finally in Kosovo. These wars took my father by surprise. From May 1998 he was an internally displaced person in Kosovo, fleeing from one town to the next, from one village to the next, pursued by armed Serbs who, up to then, had only been beating people up. Now they were slaying them—indiscriminately, insanely. The regions of Drenica and Dukagjini were the worst affected. The world now knew what the Serbs were up to: ethnic cleansing of territory they were claiming as theirs. In Bosnia, they were responsible for hundreds of thousands of deaths. Now in Kosovo they were trying to kill tens of thousands. My father lost friends and relatives. One of his sons was wounded. My brother, who had believed in my father's moral values, now keeps a piece of shrapnel in a glass jar. A Belgian surgeon removed it from his leg in November 1998.

In the end, my father was driven out of Kosovo, together with a million other Albanians. I am eternally grateful to the country that took him in when he left Albania, the country of his dreams, or rather, of his nightmares. Western aircraft began to bomb Serbian positions, and at that moment I stopped squabbling over politics with my father. Others were carrying on the political debate—on land, sea, and air. The "Great Powers," as he would call them. Curious as it may seem, those were the most harmonious days we ever spent together.

When the West drove the Serbian forces out of Kosovo, my father and a million other Albanians returned. This was a relief for two reasons. Not only had taking care of my parents pushed me into debt, but also my father was convinced that Kosovo was where he truly belonged.

He took up residence in Kosovo once again, under the protection of the "Great Powers," and we got along without any problems. He led his life and I led mine. We began to see eye to eye on political issues. The foreign troops kept the peace and protected the Albanians from one another. Otherwise we would have been at one another's throats. They also protected the remaining Serbs from being beaten up—this time, by the Albanians. "All Kosovo Serbs who have not committed crimes, that is, who have not killed innocent children, women, men, and old people, must be free to return to their homes, and they will return someday." That was his conviction . . .

Everything seemed unchanged at the hospital. Twilight had already fallen over the town and the pale glow of the streetlamps on the road gave an odd tinge to my brother's skin and eyes. We walked in silence.

"He's been moved to another floor," my brother stated as we entered the building.

I pushed the button for the fifth floor. The ward looked exactly the same. For the first time, I noticed the faces of the two nurses at the reception desk. They were no doubt responsible for presiding over the last days of the dying patients.

The room was dark. My mother sat sobbing softly at his bedside. I went over to the two of them.

His eyes were closed and were drawn deep into their sockets. He had great difficulty breathing. The apparatus above the bed was different from what I had noticed on the other floor, and the smell was strange, too.

I took his limp hand in mine.

"He's here," whispered my mother to him in a faltering voice.

He opened his eyes and took my hand, squeezing it feebly, but as much as he was able. He stared at me and then his eyes closed again. My brother grasped my arm and led me out of the room.

I never heard what he said. I couldn't think clearly. Everything was confused.

This would be the last time I was to see my father. I knew this when I was leaving the hospital. It was the last time.

Outside, the incessant traffic circulated as usual. I could feel the thrumming pulse of the world around me. It was breathing. For the last six months I had found it so difficult to deal with all the stress—the hustle and bustle. Now I needed it. I longed to get back to it, to feel it engulf me.

Translated by Robert Elsie and Janice Mathie-Heck

Rain

Dimitré Dinev

SHE HAD PREDICTED THE RAIN THAT FELL AND MADE THE CORN SHOOT UP
high enough for a horse and rider to hide in it, and also the rain that
seemed to be composed not of drops but of transparent seams with which
heaven was trying to patch up the earth. And she had foretold the rain that
consisted of ice pellets big as walnuts, which destroyed the harvest, left blue
marks on their skin, and congealed all the words in their mouths, except
for the curses. She had also predicted the rain that blinded their eyes to
colors, extinguished all joy, befuddled their minds, and crept into their
souls, filling them with an antediluvian black sorrow, and driving people to
madness and suicide. In her unenviable life as a soothsayer, Parashkeva had
foretold and predicted all kinds of rain but she had not predicted this one.

It surprised the villagers one Monday. The village was situated in a
basin-shaped valley, flanked on three sides by steeply sloping mountains.
From a distance its white houses and red roofs resembled missing teeth.
The narrow, potholed road that led to the village ended there, and anyone
who wanted to get to the village or leave had to take it. Trees still grew on
two of the mountains; the third was treeless, for in the course of the centuries they had all been felled. The village cemetery ended at the foot of this
mountain. No one knew anymore exactly who had founded the village and
when, but they liked to tell stories about its beginnings. One of these stories had it that twenty-four women, Maenads from Dionysus's retinue, had
started the first settlement. Another legend said that twenty-four escaped
female slaves from all over the world had established it. And because there
were no men among them, they had turned to their gods, asking them to
change if not all their shadows, at least one of them, into a man. It's uncertain which of the gods the women had beseeched, but their prayers were
heard and a man was made to arise from the shadow of the leader of the
women. From this union a race came into being—young men and women
who possessed special abilities. They were fast, able to disguise themselves,

to mimic any voice, and they could pass into and return from the kingdom of the dead to obtain advice about the future. Some people thought that the story about the shadow should be interpreted metaphorically, that the women had actually laid siege to the roads and repeatedly kidnapped a couple of men who, after a year, began to look like shadows because of the services they had to perform.

Since its founding, the village had often been razed to the ground and rebuilt again. Members of various tribes and peoples looking for a happy place had settled there, praying to their capricious gods with little success, and eventually disappearing without a trace. Today the village lies in Bulgaria, and its weather-beaten houses accommodate the troubles of many Bulgarian, Turkish, and a smaller number of Roma families. The oldest and the most powerful families today are the Tshelebis and the Orlinovs. Their roots go back to the Middle Ages, and the history of the village is inseparably linked to that of these two clans. The two families have been carrying on a very serious, very ancient feud, which repeatedly resulted in a rift between the Muslims and Christians living in the village. This quarrel was actually preceded by a great friendship: the friendship between Abdul and Jassen. Both were very poor and had left the village when they were seventeen to go hunting for treasure. Seven years later they had returned on two prancing white horses. The horses' saddles alone were more valuable than the houses in which the young men had grown up. They had indeed found a treasure: a jar full of gold coins. Dividing half of the coins between themselves, they buried the other half in the forest for leaner days in the future. But capricious as fate will be, a shepherd had seen them burying the jar. He had taken the money and moved somewhere near the sea. There he became a merchant, and in gratitude he had a ram's horns gilded.

When the day came that the two friends went to fetch the money, they found the jar, but it was full of dried sheep turds. Each swore that he had nothing to do with the disappearance of the coins, which was indeed the honest truth. But how often on this earth has the truth ever managed to overshadow the glitter of gold? The feud between the two families grew from that day forward, and it continued no matter who reigned over the land. From then on, many barns on both sides were engulfed by fire, many lawsuits filed, and many burns and stab wounds inflicted.

Not until the end of the nineteenth century, when Osman and Ognjan were the families' heads, was there peace once more between the two clans. These two possessed that increasingly rare gift: common sense. They were good friends, just as their ancestors had once been. They built a school in the village and helped the poor, whether Muslim or Christian. They were even buried next to each other. The one in accordance with Muslim custom, the other with Christian rites. Ognjan, who outlived Osman, actually wanted to be buried in his friend's grave, but the relatives thought that was going too far. Yet in their lives as well as in their deaths the two friends were destined to achieve what heretofore no one had managed to accomplish: that Christians and Muslims not only live together in peace but also find their eternal rest together in peace. Ever since that time the village has had only one cemetery. And no matter whether, as time passed, there were more Christians or more Muslims, the crosses of the former rose next to the stone slabs of the latter.

When the Communists seized power, everything changed, the cemeteries, too. For, now up in heaven there was neither God nor Allah, but only the stars. Therefore only stars could mark the resting places of the dead, and the cemetery came more and more to resemble a dusty, weedy patch of heaven open to any proletarian. And all those who stayed in the country had to accept this new heaven. Many Turkish and several Bulgarian families left, but the Tshelebis stayed behind with their dead. As did the Orlinovs.

The quarrel between the two families flared up again in the 1950s. This time the reason wasn't gold, but love. A son of the Orlinovs seduced a daughter of the Tshelebis, and because no one approved of the relationship, he ran away with her. Both families sent people out to find them. They pursued the young lovers from one village to the next until they lost track of them. No one ever heard anything more from them. However, the two families had lots to say. Each blamed the other for the affair, and since a lot of anger had built up in the meantime because the Communists were treating the Turkish minority in the country worse than the Christians, the entire matter culminated in a mass brawl between Bulgarians and Turks. The police sent troops to the village, and many people were arrested; some were sent to work camps, among them the oldest son of the Tshelebis. From that moment on, the old feud came back to life. The years passed, communism collapsed, governments and regimes changed. Sometimes a Turk was elected mayor, another time a Bulgarian, but still the feud went on.

"There won't be any peace until Osman and Ognjan rise from the dead. Only the dead friends can put an end to this feud," Parashkeva's mother, the soothsayer Shelka, had prophesied. Meanwhile, since neither of the two friends nor anyone else had risen from the dead, no one believed the feud would ever end.

Now it was raining in the village. A rain that no one had expected, not even the soothsayer Parashkeva. The first day it rained the farmers put on their rubber boots and filled the tavern with loud banter and dirty footprints, drinking and enjoying this God-given day off. And the second day, too. The third day there was slightly less talk and more drinking. But no matter how much they drank, they remained sober as if the rain had diluted the schnapps. On the fourth day most of them stayed home, emptying out their cellars and carrying everything to the upper floors; it was evening by the time they got to the tavern, with spiderwebs in their hair, to down at least one glassful and curse the rain. Most of the villagers didn't lie down in their beds that night, for in the meantime the rain had forced its way through the shingles of many of their roofs and was dripping down into the rooms. That's why, when at around five o'clock a white stream came flowing past some of the houses, they didn't know at first whether what they were seeing was real or only a mirage. It took a while before the village idiot, Nesho, dared to dip his finger into the magic substance to taste it and shouted, "It's milk!"

They soon discovered that the downpour had swept away Gerassim's dairy, overturning the large milk cans. Several hours later there was a loud scream. It came from Kalina, Gerassim's wife. She was running around the farmyard, barefoot, dressed only in a nightgown, yelling at the top of her lungs for all the neighbors to come and help. Her two little daughters stood in the doorway of the house, crying. In the middle of the farmyard, on the wooden cover of the roofed-over well, stood a phonograph that was playing an old scratched record by Lili Ivanova. Gerassim stood next to the well, under a quince tree. He was wearing the white shirt and black trousers in which he had been married and that now gave off a smell of mothballs. He had climbed onto a broken-backed wooden chair and was in the process of soaping a piece of rope. On his feet gleamed the patent leather shoes a cheese dealer from Greece had once given him. A cigarette protruded from a corner of his mouth like a shaky finger pointing up into the sky. His sheepdog Balkan was circling the chair, growling and baring his teeth, and that was why none of the neighbors dared come near him. Many people had gathered around the fence, hidden under their umbrellas as if under large, charred sunflowers, wondering what they should do. Gerassim was not much liked. He was stingy, and for a long time they had wished him a little bad luck. But none of them wanted to see him dangling from the limb of a quince tree. Gerassim was just attaching the rope when the mayor arrived. He leapt out of his jeep and was the first to enter the farmyard.

"Help us, Hussein; I'll be grateful to you for the rest of my life," Kalina said and promptly threw herself upon him. By now the rain had thoroughly soaked her nightgown, making it possible to marvel at all the unusual features of her naked body. The outline of her mound of Venus stared at the mayor like a third reproachful eye. It distracted him and interfered with his thinking. The mayor didn't know where to look. At her or at Gerassim. At what made life sweet or what made it bitter. With a great effort he tore his gaze away from Kalina and turned it on Gerassim. "Come down, you crazy fool! Don't throw away your life so stupidly."

Gerassim spit out his cigarette, "To hell with life."

"We'll all help you rebuild your dairy," the mayor said, keeping a wary eye on the dog.

"To hell with your help. I'd rather eat dirt than accept help from some damned Turks," Gerassim said, pushing his head into the noose.

"Don't talk nonsense; get down right now."

"Don't come any closer. Or I'll set my dog on you!"

"Somebody fetch my gun so that I can shoot the rotten cur," the mayor yelled.

At that moment old Kina Orlinova walked into the farmyard leaning the weight of her eighty-three years on a cane. "They told me there's an idiot at Gerassim's house who's lost his respect for life. Are you the one, you little pisser?" they heard her croak.

"Fuck life, fuck the rain, fuck fate, fuck you all!" Gerassim yelled, but they could tell he was uncertain.

"Stop complaining. Better if you fuck your wife . . . Or better yet, go ahead, die and leave her behind, alone. The other men will fight over her," Kina said. There was loud laughter. They laughed on the road and in the farmyard, too; the old people laughed and the young ones, and Gerassim's children standing in the doorway laughed.

Gerassim looked at them all in surprise till his eyes fell on Kalina. Her nightgown was clinging to her like a second skin forged from the fog of many male dreams. He felt the rubbing at his neck and the rubbing in his trousers. He pulled his head out of the noose, climbed down off the chair, grabbed Kalina's hand, and went toward the house.

"I'll go get myself a rope, too, if that's how I can get to your wife," someone shouted.

"Let me know if you want a younger man," a second one piped up.

Gerassim showed them his middle finger and without turning around disappeared into the house with Kalina. Outside the people laughed and the mayor laughed, while Balkan, the sheepdog, just kept barking and barking.

The sixth day—if you could call it that, because it was so dark that not even the roosters dared to crow—passed without any unusual happenings.

Everyone was waiting with bated breath for the great flood of water from the mountains, and it was very quiet in the village. All you could hear were the dripping of the rain and the blows of Süleiman's adze, as he was turning his wooden fence into a raft. But toward noon something happened that surprised many of the villagers. The young widow Eliza turned up at the tavern. She had more reasons to hate the water than any of the others, because, a year ago, while she and her husband were on vacation, he had drowned in the sea. It seemed she had put aside her mourning garb and was wearing a light blue dress. Her entrance was greeted with appreciative whistles. But she only smiled and pointed with her painted fingernails at a bottle of schnapps. Her lipstick had already left smudges on the fourth glass, when she said, "I can't live another day without the sun. I'll take home the first man who can show me the sun this instant."

"You're just making fun of us. Give us an easier task," the men said, and many hats were thrown to the floor. Calmly she finished her glass of schnapps and, taking a mirror out of her pocket, saw in it a woman who was ready to take on whatever fate had in store. She applied more lipstick and left the tavern. On her way home she whistled every time she jumped over a puddle. Once there, she turned on the radio so as not to hear the rain, and began to pack a suitcase. She had packed twice before already, but each time she'd put in the wrong things, things that drew her back into her house. That's why she hadn't managed to leave. But this time, she promised the reflection in the mirror, she was going to do everything right. It was quiet in the house, as quiet as the ocean floor. And just as the ocean had swallowed up her husband, the house was swallowing up all her happiness and joy.

When it got dark, there was a knock on the door. She opened it. Outside stood Saprjan. He had lost his job at the coal mine two months earlier, and for two months his cigarette had been glowing below her window. "Now he's plucked up his courage," Eliza thought, and it made her smile. "Did you use up all your cigarettes?" she teased. He didn't answer. He just unbuttoned his shirt and showed her a blue sun tattooed on his chest. Eliza laughed and slammed the door in his face. She saw the open suitcase, and felt the loneliness of many nights streaming toward her from all the rooms, pushing its way into her throat, cutting off her laughter, and threatening to drown her. She opened the door again and looked at the man whose body was as wet as if he had just come out of the sea. Taking a deep breath, she thrust her hand through his curly hair, grabbing it the way you do a drowning man's, and pulled him into the house.

* * *

On the seventh day everyone in the village was awakened by a rumbling roar, so loud they thought one of the mountains had come down in a landslide and buried them. The earth shook and windowpanes rattled, but after that it was quiet. The villagers were so unaccustomed to the silence that they imagined they could hear other people's thoughts. Only gradually did they realize that the rain had stopped. Doors creaked open, boots splashed, people shouted to one another as if to make sure they were still alive. Gathering in small groups in the village square, they racked their brains over which of the houses might have collapsed, and if not that, what else might have been the cause of the tremendous roaring noise that had penetrated even into their deepest sleep. But they were surprised to find that not a single house had been flooded, or even swept away. And while they were all wondering whether God or Allah had performed this miracle, they saw the village idiot, Nesho, marching briskly toward them. He was carrying a wooden cross over one shoulder as if it were a weapon. He stopped in front of the mayor, saluted, and gave his report: "I respectfully wish to inform you that the cemetery has disappeared. Either it's been stolen, or the dead have simply cleared out."

At first the villagers had trouble believing him, especially the Christians. Because Nesho had often given them crazy information and caused misunderstandings. But the Muslims felt a madman like Nesho might well have been chosen by Allah to amuse himself, to toy with the fool's thoughts, or now and then to speak through his mouth. So the Muslims immediately marched off in the direction of the cemetery. The Bulgarians followed, some because they too were uncertain, a few out of curiosity, and still others because they were hoping to find a new reason to ridicule them. On the way, one of the Bulgarians recognized the cross that Nesho was carrying on his shoulder as the one that he had temporarily placed on his mother's grave two weeks earlier. Flushing red with rage, he ran after Nesho. A wild chase ensued to the amusement of the crowd; for Nesho did not want to give up his weapon, no matter what. After he had run twice around the group of villagers, Nesho turned down a side street, and leaping over several fences, left his pursuer behind, gasping for breath. The villagers were still laughing when they reached the end of the village. But suddenly their faces turned serious; the saliva dried in their mouths, their tongues stiffened. They grabbed at their mustaches and headscarves, seeking some hold. Because usually you could see the tombstones from the edge of the village. Yet no matter how they strained their eyes scanning the area, they couldn't see the cemetery. Not even the gate or the fences remained.

After having recovered somewhat from the shock, they decided to get to the bottom of this strange situation. Once they reached the spot where the cemetery had been, they saw that the cause of its disappearance was not of a magical nature but something quite normal, and they were all distinctly disappointed. Apparently an avalanche of soil and rocks had become detached from the mountainside and buried the cemetery. The villagers pondered what was to be done. That wasn't easy, for nothing like this had ever happened here before; nor had anyone ever heard of something like this happening anywhere else. But the longer they discussed it, the more significant their dead became. Most villagers felt that without graves the village would lose its memory, its history. Paradise, someone said, was the only place where there were no graves . . . or Hell, added another. But where on earth had there ever been a village without a cemetery?

"What will other people think?" "That we don't honor our dead?" "That we've devoured them?"—voices in the crowd were heard to say.

Suddenly, every single one of the dead had become very important, even for those villagers who had for many years neglected the graves of their dead relatives. And for that reason they unanimously rejected the mayor's suggestion that a symbolic resting place be erected for all Muslims and Christians. They called him an atheist and a Communist, and it would almost have come to blows if Mustafa Tshelebi and Momtshil Orlinov—the heads of the two most powerful families in the village—had not intervened.

Now all eyes were turned on them. Conforming to a very old, deeply rooted custom, the people calmed down and waited eagerly, because, since time immemorial, the words of the two clan heads carried more weight in the village than any of the country's laws. The Turks followed the Tshelebis and the Bulgarians the Orlinovs. And the former now looked to Mustafa, and the latter to Momtshil. Both men felt the burden put upon them by all these eyes—as well as a sense of abandonment by their families—as a result of their decision to take on the responsibility for so many living as well as dead souls. And moreover, they felt that this decision now linked them to each other more strongly than any blood ties ever could. And even though for seven years they had not spoken one word to each other, they now stepped off to one side and, lighting cigarettes, they conferred for some time in muted voices. The glowing tips of their cigarettes defined circles in the air and were eventually extinguished with a hiss in a puddle. At that point the two men stepped out in front of the crowd. "We owe our forefathers, if not everything, then at least the small favor of knowing where they are buried, so that we can visit them in the future, too," Mustafa began.

"We bury our dead so that their souls will find peace, for if they don't have a grave they will wander around on this earth and we must take the blame for that," Momtshil said.

"We have to dig out our cemetery, and the Muslims will arrange their graves in accordance with their custom and the Christians in accordance with theirs, so if not in life, then at least in the Hereafter, an understanding will prevail between the two," Mustafa said.

"But it's especially important for us to discover the graves of Osman and Ognjan and reconstruct them, for the entire village owes them a debt of gratitude," so spoke the two, and a sigh of relief passed through the crowd.

The following day two excavators arrived operated by two greasy-haired fellows with impertinent eyes and glib tongues. Almost the entire village had gathered at the buried cemetery to help with the digging. The owner of the general store, having sold all his picks and shovels, had to order more from the city. Slowly and evenly they removed the soil and carried it off. That's why it took two days before the first gravestones turned up. However, the landslide had swept down upon the cemetery with such force that it had torn most of the gravestones off their foundations, dragging them away, and erasing the demarcations between the graves. Very few graves were still recognizable. The trees and bushes that had grown up between some burial plots and which might have served as points of reference had been uprooted and swept away as well. And so most of the villagers were unable to find their family gravesites. Someone asked about a map of the cemetery, but there was none and had never been one. There was only a register of the dead, but that was incomplete because mice had nibbled on some of the pages. So they called together the oldest inhabitants, the same ones who were always called on to testify whenever an argument broke out about a piece of farmland and who knew more about the property lines than any cartographer. The old people tottered around a while, poking their sticks into the soil as if they wanted to test it, blinking, shrugging, and finally admitting that they couldn't be of any help. They knew how the land had been parceled out among the living but not among the dead.

So the villagers decided to dig up the dead and try to identify them by means of the items that had been buried with them. They also hoped to be able to tell from the position of the body whether it was a Muslim or a Christian. Even though the religious laws of both faiths forbade disturbing the eternal rest of the deceased, the clergymen of both congregations realized that this was a special case and gave their permission. Their faces reflected great humility and deep understanding at the mere thought of all the money they could earn because, after all, the disinterred bodies would have to be reburied. You could have sworn the two had never looked more spiritual.

Very carefully and lovingly the villagers began digging, and quite soon the first corpses came to light. It was somewhat easier for the Bulgarians to recognize their dead. Some could be identified by a necklace, a ring, or a mirror; others by their shoes or their clothing, which gave occasion for criticism of the quality of present-day shoes and materials. Others were identified by a pocket watch, a gold tooth, a prosthesis, or by the bottles of schnapps or wine that lay beside them, tempting quite a few tipplers to take a sip. In most cases whenever a corpse was recognized it was also possible to identify those lying to the right and left.

For the Turks it was much harder. Their burials were modest. For they buried their dead merely wrapped in a shroud. What was important were the words whispered in their ears before the ants and worms entered by that same pathway, and that their heads be turned to Mecca. Nothing else. A few words, a cloth—that was all that accompanied them to the Beyond. What more does the soul require? For if there really was another, a better place, then the shoemakers and tailors there would be better, too. So why take anything along from here? The earth consumed the bodies of the dead very rapidly, so that soon nothing remained but their bones. And that is why it was more difficult for the Turks in the village to recognize their graves. And quite a few hearts were filled with envy. There were arguments over several of the bones. Sometimes the Turks quarreled with one another, sometimes the Bulgarians did. Sometimes there were arguments between Turks and Bulgarians. One would hold a skull or another skeletal part up to his nose, claiming that a skull like that could never belong to a Bulgarian. Another, holding up a thighbone belonging to the same corpse, would insist that there could never have been such a slender Turk. They were on the point of attacking one another with the bones when someone suggested it would be better to take the bones to the soothsayer, Parashkeva, or to fetch her here so that she could consult the spirits. Everyone thought this a splendid suggestion—striking their foreheads, they wondered why they hadn't thought of it before.

The most impatient and those who had argued most vehemently immediately picked up a skull or a few bones and went to see her. So many bones piled up in her waiting room in the course of the next few hours that her family could no longer go to the toilet without having to jump over them. But for her grandchildren all this was a lot of fun. Her six-year-old granddaughter, Somiza, even managed to take a skull without being observed.

She ran through the village with it, scaring some of her girlfriends and making others jealous until she was caught by Entsho Gurbelov, a Roma, just as she was about to use it to crack open some walnuts.

Entsho was in a good mood. Two things were important to him: that his house be bigger than the mayor's and finding the grave of his deceased son. The first thing had started five years earlier and was turning into a tale without end. For no sooner did he have enough money to add another story, then the mayor also increased the height of his house. After all, he couldn't allow a Roma to loom over him. And for that reason neither of the houses as yet had a roof. The people made fun of the crazy Roma, but they ridiculed the mayor even more. And this pleased Entsho and made the quarrel quite worthwhile. As to the grave of his oldest son, with that he was more fortunate because he had already found it. Five years ago when his son died in an automobile accident, Entsho had placed a cassette player next to him in the grave that played his favorite music as the soil was filled in. Now he had found the cassette player again, and it made him so happy that he began to dance beside the grave holding the player. But the biggest surprise was that it still worked. He just had to put in new batteries and the villagers all heard it play the familiar songs. With the help of his son's grave Entsho was able to reconstruct the resting places of his entire clan; it didn't take him long at all. He had to turn the cassette over only once. And so now he was in a good mood and didn't scold little Somiza, but helped her bring the skull back where they needed it.

The news about what had happened in the village spread rapidly throughout the land, and the farther it spread the more incredible the rumors grew. Some said that in some village somewhere the dead had packed up their headstones, tombstones, crosses—in fact, the entire cemetery—and vanished. Others said the dead had done it to show their dissatisfaction with the deplorable state of affairs in the country, emigrating just like many of the living. Still others claimed that the dead had risen as at the Last Judgment and that they even had political ambitions.

In any case, the events had captured the interest of the public at large. Many television teams came to the village, increasing profits at the tavern, and for a few days even satisfying their own curiosity as well as that of the populace; the TV people promised that financial help would come as a result of their reportage and then left the villagers alone with their pile of bones. Only the mayor made use of the television reportage to promote himself politically, and Entsho, the Roma, who allowed them to film him standing proudly in front of his house, where he elucidated the advantages of burying people in accordance with Roma custom and also explained why his house did not yet have a roof. The other villagers found the media visit nothing more than a disruption because it delayed everything.

But gradually the peace and quiet Parashkeva needed to speak with the spirits of the dead returned. She was able to communicate with them only after sunset, which made everything more difficult, but the villagers were patient. First she made sure that all the skeletal remains that had accumulated in her house found their way back into the earth so that her family had room again for their everyday life. Only then did she go to the cemetery to deal on the spot with the remaining cases. Now and then a spirit would appear who was not missed by anyone, as for instance a Roman legionnaire who talked in a most vulgar fashion, and a Greek lute player who spoke in iambic verses. The other spirits showed their understanding of the situation and were accommodating. Gradually names were attached to the skeletons and things settled down at the cemetery.

The villagers were very grateful to Parashkeva and rewarded her so generously that, some time later, she was able to spend three weeks on Crete with her husband. Every night when she got home she spent a long time in front of an icon of the Holy Mother of God and without letting her husband's snoring distract her, she prayed fervently to be forgiven in case she had mixed up any of the skeletal remains, for she alone knew how capricious the spirits are and how they like to play tricks on people.

There were also some villagers who remained indifferent to all these events. One of these was the widow Eliza, who, ever since she'd discovered the sun on Saprjan's chest, preferred tracing its blue rays with her fingernails rather than spending time at the cemetery.

Gerassim didn't understand what all the excitement was about either, for if ever there was someone who had cause for complaint, it was he, because he had lost what mattered most—the dairy that made it possible for him to earn a living, that secured his existence—not some heap of bones. It surprised him how quickly the dead had become more important than the living, and he felt a bit of regret that he hadn't killed himself.

The Tshelebis and the Orlinovs were the most zealous in trying to introduce some order into the ranks of their dead. And distrusting Parashkeva's extrasensory powers, they relied rather on their own common sense, logic, and memories—all things that didn't necessarily make it easier to deal with the dead. In spite of that, they had identified most of the remains. But the most important ones were still missing: Osman and Ognjan, the two forebears who had ushered in the longest phase of peace between the two families. They had been buried side by side, and at some point their graves were found. But it was no longer certain who was buried on the right and who on the left, and since, back then, Ognjan had expressed the wish to be buried as simply as his friend Osman, Mustafa and Momtshil were now faced with two very similar piles of bones. Momtshil was almost sure that his forefather lay on the right. But to settle all doubt, he suggested to Mustafa that they take the aforementioned bones home and study them in greater detail and to include his mother in making a decision as well, because no one in the family was closer to that time period. Mustafa agreed. He in turn wanted to show the bones to his father. So each put his bones into a sack and went home.

First Momtshil thoroughly washed all the bones, then, covering the big table in the living room with pages from the newspaper *Arbeit,* he laid the bones out on the paper. Next he took out a bottle of schnapps, which had in the past afforded him many an inspiration, filled a glass, and drank it in little sips. Then he took the skull and began to look at it from all sides. "Dead or alive, man remains a puzzle," he thought as he drank his second glass. Carefully he began to feel his own head and discovered that its shape was completely different from that of the skull. A quiet doubt began to sprout in his heart. He was still holding the skull when his mother, Kina, came into the room.

"Help me," he said.

"No one can help you. Has a jackdaw sucked everything out of your brain or something?" she said and sat down on a chair that sighed as deeply as she did.

"Is this him?" Momtshil asked, holding the skull up to her eyes.

"Say his name, then you'll find out."

"Don't make fun of me."

"Then I'll tell you. That's not him. He breathed, lived, laughed, did a lot of good, and was respected by everyone. What you're holding isn't alive. It belongs under the ground and not on our table."

"But it's important."

"Only people are important. The dead belong to the dead, the living to the living."

"And it doesn't matter to you whether he'll be buried as a Muslim or not?"

"These days there are lots of things that don't matter to me anymore, but it wouldn't have mattered to him either. They say he had expressed the wish to share a grave with Osman, but in those days they didn't dare to do that sort of thing."

"They say that he was big and strong," Momtshil said after a while.

"So they say."

At that, Momtshil jumped up and laid the bones out on the floor so that they formed the shape of a human skeleton and lay down next to it. His ancestor came up to his shoulder. "Look, this can't have been him," he shouted jubilantly.

"Enough of this nonsense now. I have more important things to do," Kina said and left her son to himself. Momtshil got up, put the bones back into the sack, and went over to Mustafa's.

In the meantime Mustafa had had a few anxious moments. He had also washed his bones, but then he left them unattended for a short while, and his senile mother had tossed one of the bones to the dog. It wasn't easy to get the bone back. The dog even bit his arm and he had to punish the animal. But now all the bones were lying together again on a white cloth that covered the table, and Mustafa kept looking back and forth at them and at a photo that had been taken of his forebear in Istanbul. The longer he looked the more uneasy he felt because he could see absolutely no resemblance between the two. His father was no help either, for he had only glanced briefly at the skeletal remains, shaken his head, and gone back to bed. Then the dog began to bark in the courtyard. Mustafa peered out and saw Momtshil standing outside the door, a sack over his shoulder. He asked him to come in, called to his wife, Emel, to make two coffees, and led him over to the table.

"I think I've got the wrong one," Momtshil said.

"Me too," Mustafa said, taking the sack from the hands of his guest. He took out the bones and placed them next to the others. The two sat down on the sofa, lit cigarettes, and watched the smoke rather than looking in each other's eyes. Emel came, served them two steaming cups of coffee, and disappeared as quietly as the steam. Outside a hen called to her chicks, the dog barked briefly at a shadow. The two men, slurping their coffee and dragging intermittently on their cigarettes, squinted at the bones. The coffee burned their tongues, smoke got in their eyes, and one by one the moments turned to ash. "The longer I look at them, the less certain I become," said the one.

"I can't tell anything about these bones either. They look so much alike," said the other.

"Yes, like twin brothers," said the first one.

"Why not bury them in the same grave? First as Muslims, then as Christians," the second suggested.

"I've thought about that too," the first one admitted.

"Let's do it first thing tomorrow morning," said the second one.

"Good. Tomorrow," said the first one.

"Can I leave them at your house overnight?" the second asked, gesturing with his head toward the bones.

"They won't run away," the first one said.

The other didn't say anything for a long while, long enough to give his eyes time to take in all the things around him. "It's really odd, but this is the first time I've been in your house," he said.

"It's been seven years since we last spoke to each other," the first one said.

"Back then your hair was still black," the other said.

"And you still had hair on your head," the first one replied.

"Here we are, talking with each other," the second one said.

"And you are my guest," the first one said.

"And it's all because of the rain," the second one said.

"Thanks to the disaster it caused," the first one answered.

"I hope we won't wait for the next misfortune," the second one said as he got up.

"Life will tell," the first one said.

"Yes, that's how it is," the other agreed. And for the first time their eyes met.

The entire way back Momtshil thought about what he should tell his family back home, weighing and testing each word, but he simply couldn't decide which word should be the first to cross his burned tongue.

Translated by Margot Bettauer Dembo

Three Monologues About Others

Slavenka Drakulić

1

Mira V., 41 yrs. old, mother of Verica V., 10 yrs. old.
Statement to school psychologist

I know, I know why you've called me in. Her teacher says Verica hasn't spoken a word for a week. She just sits there, silent as silent can be. She does her homework, she writes on the blackboard when she's called, but when the teacher asks her something she doesn't open her mouth. The child has been struck dumb. Her teacher phoned me the other day, she said she didn't know what to do with her and asked me why Verica was refusing to speak. She's an excellent student, after all. And I said "Miss" (I almost said Comrade, like we used to at school in my day), "Miss," I said, "she doesn't talk at home either. Not about what she had for lunch, not thank you, not please—nothing, not a word! You're an educated woman, you read the papers, you watch television. You know that Verica's father was arrested. You know all that." "Yes," she said, "I know of the case. But I'm worried about Verica. She needs help. Because if this goes on much longer, she'll have to see a doctor."

Well, it did go on, both at home and at school. I say to her, "Verica, honey, tell Mommy what's the matter." But she just looks at me with those big dark eyes of hers and then goes off to her room, shuts herself in, and puts her music on loud, too loud. I can see that the child is in a state of shock and that it's my responsibility, who else's, to tell her why her father is in prison. I can think of a few other people who should be sitting in prison, but they're not. There you are. We were just unlucky, that's all. But I can't tell her that. I mean, it's no explanation. So I sit in the kitchen, crying. My kid is losing it, the police have taken my husband away, what's going to happen to us? I don't know where to go, where to turn. What have I done

to deserve this? It's no use thinking now about what might have been ...
I'm sorry, I can't stop crying. I can't go on like this. I'm at my wit's end. Tell
me, how can I explain it to her, how? What should I tell her? How can she
understand what's happened? She wasn't born until after the war.

Thanks for the glass of water. I feel better now.

Where do I start? With Verica's birth? The war? Or that wretched television? The TV is always on in our house. He watches the news and sports
programs, I watch those, what do you call them, soaps. Verica watches
cartoons and music shows—once she's done her homework, of course. We
were watching TV that day. Actually I was pottering around in the kitchen
when I heard them announce a film about Srebrenica. I didn't pay any
attention. I'm not interested. I'd rather forget about the war, about Srebrenica and everything. My husband sometimes wakes up in the middle of the
night, screaming; once he was drenched in sweat, I barely managed to calm
him down. I peer into the living room. He's sitting on the couch, stock still,
staring at the screen as if he'd just seen a ghost. Some soldiers are leading
a bunch of young men away, five or six of them, their hands tied behind
their backs. I take a closer look and think I see him, my husband, in camouflage uniform! But I'm not sure. I still don't suspect anything. I look at
the TV, then at him, his eyes are blank, there's a strange expression on his
face. Then I recognize his voice, he's swearing, and then there are gunshots.
They're shooting them. The young men keel over. The worst was seeing him
kick one of the dead men on the ground, a boy.

He turns off the TV. "I'm done for. Damn those motherfuckers. I'm
finished," he says, dropping his head into his hands. I reach for his arm.
"What's finished?" I ask. He pushes me away, real rough. I think he's going
to hit me. I turn around and there's Verica. I realize she's been standing
at the door of her room the whole time and has seen everything. She is
standing there staring at us, white as a sheet. Tears are streaming down her
face. "Verica," I shout, as if she's far away. "Verica!" There are only a few
feet between us. He jumps up and steps toward her. She slams the door in
his face and locks herself in her room. I hear the key turn. He starts banging furiously on her door. "Open the door," he yells. "Open it right now!"
I scream at him, "Leave her alone. Leave the child alone!" and I pull him
back to the couch. He's so worked up I'm scared he's going to beat the daylights out of her. Why he threw himself at her door that way I don't know. I
suppose he felt bad that his daughter had seen him on TV like that. That's
what I think.

And then he simply collapsed, as if all the strength had suddenly gone
out of him. He flopped onto the couch like an empty sack. I felt sorry for

him. I took a bottle of brandy from the shelf, I figured a drop or two would do him good, calm him down maybe. He took a slug and lit a cigarette. I took a slug myself, you bet I did

So we're sitting there, drinking, neither of us saying a word. What was there to say?

Early the next morning the doorbell rings. We knew it was the police, that they had come for him. He's in prison now. Waiting to go on trial. I'm sure you know that. Verica hasn't said a word since seeing that clip on TV.

It's not that I want to defend my husband. He can do that on his own in court. But . . .

Verica was born in 1995, after the war, in the fall. We came here from Knin, from the Krajina region. I'm a refugee. I fled ahead of Operation Storm. I was already heavily pregnant, about to give birth. My husband had left Knin earlier. He was a captain in the Yugoslav People's Army, the JNA. And then a commander in the Serbian Autonomous Region of Krajina. He had come here earlier and signed up as a volunteer, with the Scorpions, I guess. What do I know? He never talked about these things, about where he went and what he did. He sent money home regularly. That's what we lived on. He'd always been a soldier, he didn't know anything else. I was a cashier at the department store in Knin, until Storm.

We'd already put a roof up and almost finished the house. There was just a bit left to be done. I was thirty already. I couldn't put off having a baby. We figured the war was sure to end . . . No, no, I couldn't stay there. Later we managed to sell the house to some Croats, decent people. They paid us for it. Just enough for us to be able to settle down here. When I think about what happened to others, we did OK. At least that's what I thought until a week ago.

He wasn't with the volunteers for long, a year maybe. And everything would have been fine if it hadn't been for that TV program. If Verica hadn't seen him on it . . . Verica and everybody else.

My husband isn't a bad man. I'm not saying he's not guilty. He killed, and for that he has to take responsibility. But I wish somebody could tell me how to explain to a child born after the war that it was wartime and that people kill in wars. If you judge her father then you've got to judge the war. That's what I think, anyhow. Not all wars are the same, for instance it's different if you're defending yourself. Or if you're defending your country, it should be different. So how did her father come to shoot, to kill some-body? Lots of other people killed, but they were lucky, nobody filmed them doing it. And now they're keeping their mouths shut and their heads down. And nobody will ever know what they did. I know that those young men shot dead in the film were civilians not soldiers, and that's why he has to go on trial. I say, I'm not defending him. There's no excuse for him shooting civilians, and some of them, they say, were minors, kids. Though when I remember Knin, they shot at us too, and we were civilians, nobody asked who was or wasn't a civilian. I mean, it's not easy to understand how the war began, how it happened to us. How did those young men, those Muslims from Srebrenica, become our enemies? How did the Croats in Krajina become our enemies? What turned her father into a killer? Why doesn't her teacher explain that to her? She should know how better than us. Verica's father will be convicted, but what about the politicians who started the war, what about the generals? From what I can see, they're all doing fine. Nobody's arresting them. As if there had been no war. But they'll have to talk about it because my husband can't be the only one to blame or those hundred or so small fry who may be put on trial here one day.

I see now that it's no good keeping quiet about these things. I, for one, know how it was. I was born in 1965, and I remember that the others, the Croats, Muslims, Albanians, whoever, weren't our enemies. We lived together, went to school together, married each other. But I don't know how to tell Verica what changed so much that her father . . . No, I can't, I can't talk about it anymore. It's easier for me if he goes on trial. It wasn't easy for him either, living with those ghosts of his who haunted him at night. But why doesn't Verica talk to me? I'm her mother after all. It wasn't me who went to war. I'm not to blame! I don't really know. Maybe her silence is also my fault. My husband was a soldier. In wartime. I never asked any questions. I just kept my head down and listened to him, to the politicians, to the big guys. When Verica was born I hoped I'd forget all about it. What's the war got to do with me, I thought. Plenty, I see now.

2

Josip P., 32 yrs. old, unaired radio interview

I volunteered, I was seventeen when the war broke out in Slavonia, where I'm from. I'd just finished my sophomore year in high school. All my friends, from school, from my neighborhood, had signed up as volunteers. I mean, what else could I do? I couldn't be the only one to stay behind. But I found it weird, we all did . . . because we'd grown up with the Serbs, gone to school with them, to tell you the truth, we didn't know who was what and we didn't really care either.

Until push came to shove . . .

At first it was more like Boy Scout camp. We didn't have uniforms or weapons.

In the daytime, we'd practice with a couple of rifles and then at night we'd go home. Later, when things heated up, the operations we carried out were for real. I didn't realize it was a war, or even what war was until a school friend of mine got killed. He was the first in our group to be killed, Luka was his name. He was scrawny and small and awkward somehow. He wasn't good at running. He was killed in action. A bullet in the stomach. When he was hit we dragged him to safety. We had already taken up our positions. The hospital was far away. I told the commander that I would take him to the hospital, that I had to try and save him. He was my school friend. He told me to take the car. We put him in the back of the Zastava and set off. The driver was an older guy from the brigade, a guy named Damir. He drove like a maniac to get us there as fast as he could; the road was pocked with ruts. The car was bouncing all over the place. My friend Luka cried out that we should just leave him, that there was no point in taking him to the hospital. He knew he was finished. "Quiet. Save your strength. You're not finished until you're finished," I shouted at him. It was awful watching him suffer like that. Pale as death, as they say, sweat pouring off his forehead, the splotch of blood getting bigger and bigger . . .

It took us two hours to get to the hospital. The building was half-demolished. A young doctor, barely older than us, immediately gave him a shot, morphine I guess. For the pain. He examined the wound and told me there was no point operating on Luka. "The guy hasn't got a chance, he's lost too much blood. You just stay here by his side," he told me. "It won't be long."

Luka died quietly. He simply fell asleep.

For me, that was the beginning of the war. Everything before that—the tanks, the shelling, the wounded, the dead—that was nothing! Because sitting there in that wreck of a hospital, holding Luka's hand, I could feel something inside me change. I felt this growing anger at the people who had done this. Because I had known him. His death changed me. It definitely changed me.

Later, others told me the same thing, that something inside them had snapped when a friend, a relative, or a neighbor was killed. At first you feel this blinding fury, like you're going to explode, and all you want to do is grab a gun or a bomb and go after them.

We had to keep an eye out for guys like that. A couple of times we lost men stupidly. Human beings aren't made of stone. They can go crazy, and once that happens you can't stop them.

After that first violent reaction, I felt kind of indifferent. No, not indifferent, that's not the right word . . . I don't know, it's more that you just don't feel anything. Like you're not a person anymore. You're a robot. You turn into a killing machine. That's the worst of it.

I'm telling you all this because of Marko, so you'll understand, and maybe I will too, how it happened. Marko was a Serb, but he was one of a dozen of us from the neighborhood who had all signed up together in the war. His best friend was Ante. One day, Ante's parents, Ankica and Marijan—I knew them both really well—were found dead in their house. Their throats slit. I don't know anymore how or why what happened later happened, if somebody said that they'd seen Marko at Ante's house or if Ante simply heard that Marko had been there. Anyway, the rest of us suspected Marko of the killing. Though when I think about it today, I'm not so sure anymore.

Here's how it went.

I remember we all got together that day in the ruins of our elementary school. We drank and horsed around a bit . . . then Ante asked Marko, really loud, so we could all hear: "Are you my best friend?" "Of course I am," Marko replied. "And did the two of us grow up together like brothers?" Ante pressed on. Suddenly we all fell silent and listened. We found it strange, unnatural somehow, and waited to see where this was going. "Yes, we did," said Marko. "Did you eat at my house a million times? Do you remember that you moved in with us when your mother was in the hospital for an operation?" "Of course I remember, how could I forget," said Marko, becoming visibly uneasy now.

"So why did you slaughter my parents? How could you?" says Ante.

Silence. We all turned and looked at Marko. Nobody said a word. Marko looked first at Ante, then at us, as if we'd gone crazy. He looked surprised at first, and then scared. It was already late in the day. Scorching hot, the sun streaming in through the broken windows, the air heavy. I could feel a lump in my throat.

"It wasn't me," Marko said very seriously, looking Ante straight in the eye. Ante leaped up and smacked him hard in the face. "Liar!" he screamed. Marko wiped the blood from his mouth. "You've got to believe me. I'd never do a thing like that. We're friends," he said, still quietly.

But Marko's words just seemed to infuriate Ante even more. "I do, huh? I've got to believe you? No, I don't got to do anything, understood?" Ante roared. "My parents were killed. If you didn't do it then it must have been one of your people!" Marko still kept a grip on himself. He was still trying to talk, to calm Ante down, who was already clearly beside himself.

The rest of us formed a circle around the two of them.

"They're not my people, you're my people. Am I fighting on your side or theirs? How can you think that I could kill Auntie Ankica and Uncle Marijan? They were like parents to me," said Marko.

And then Ante broke down. Tall, big, his head shaven, he cried like a baby. Then he started hitting Marko, shouting: "Admit it, you slit their throats! Admit it!" He shouted and cried, lashing out blindly at Marko. Marko said nothing. He didn't try to defend himself. I remember thinking that was odd. Why wasn't he defending himself if he was innocent? But at the time I still didn't know that you can't defend yourself from being a Serb. Ante was our friend, but Marko was our friend, too. Ante seemed to go completely berserk. Who wouldn't? I would have done the same if I had found my parents lying dead on the floor in a pool of blood. "Admit it," he sobbed, "admit it. I'll kill you!" "I didn't do it," Marko sobbed. "How can you even think I'd do something like that?"

I don't know how long it all lasted. At one point, Marko fell to the ground. He realized how serious it was when one after the other of us joined in with Ante. First Tomo started kicking him in the ribs, then Pero. Then all of us went for him, as if we'd lost our minds or something. To this day I don't really know what happened. I guess we poured all our anger and helplessness and fear into those punches and kicks. That whole dumb war. I cried, the others cried too, I remember. And Marko, his face covered in blood, sobbed: "I didn't do it, I didn't, I didn't" . . . but nobody was listening to him anymore. We punched and kicked him to a pulp.

The air reeked of dust, burning, and sweat. And of blood. I can't forget the sickly sweet smell of Marko's blood. Then Ante did something I'll never forget as long as I live. The memory of it haunts me sometimes, and I can still see them as if they were here in front of me right now. He loomed over Marko, grabbed his jaw with both hands, and suddenly ripped it off in one go. He must have had superhuman strength at that moment. Marko let out a strange sound, something between a howl and a sob. I once heard a wounded dog make a sound like that. And I heard something else. I heard the bone crack. I'll never forget that sound, it was so different from all the other sounds and noises. I saw Ante holding Marko's jaw in his hand. Marko was wheezing, choking on his own blood, blood spurting from his gaping wound.

We left him there in the ruins. We never spoke of him again. Not long after, Ante was killed. He threw himself into battle after that incident. It's a miracle he lived even that one month after Marko died. But he wasn't right in the head anymore.

Only three of our group survived the war. We don't see each other anymore, except by chance. Why would we? The prewar days have been forgotten; as for the war . . .

The only thing that troubles me is Marko. He claimed to the end that he was innocent. Maybe he didn't kill Ante's parents, after all? Maybe we were wrong not to believe him. He was our friend. How could we not believe him? Just because he was a different ethnicity. It's like we'd been infected by the madness. When I think about it today, yes, war is like a kind of madness. That's why I drink, I drink and hold my tongue. I don't know what made me tell you all this now. I guess it had to come out or it would've choked me to death. Maybe it would be better if it had. Who cares about me, anyway? Even I don't care about myself anymore.

3

Fahrudin M., 55 yrs. old
Statement to the social worker re adoption application

I remember it as if it was yesterday, December 18, 1992. The Serbs had taken up their positions, ringing the town, shelling us day and night, you couldn't go anywhere. We were trapped like mice. There was no food, no gas, no medicine. I was on duty that night. I worked at the hospital in maintenance, repairing minor breakdowns on the various machines, feeding the furnace when needed, that sort of thing. Mind you, we weren't heating at the time because there was no coal. At first I used wood, but how are you going to heat such a huge concrete building with wood? Later there was no wood to be found anywhere, people had cut down all the trees in the street, the parks, around the school. So it was cold in the wards upstairs, they covered the patients with blankets, clothing, whatever they could find. I brought in some old blankets myself. One day Muniba, the cleaning woman, came by. She used to come down to the basement to see me, bring a cigarette or two, if she had them. The doctors and nurses upstairs would get them as thank yous. To give them their due, they would share them, they would. So one day, Muniba and I are sitting there, smoking, and I ask her what's new, because she knew which doctors and nurses were on duty, and if there was anybody upstairs I knew. A neighbor of mine wound up on the operating table not long ago, they had to cut off his leg. He'd been hit by shrapnel. I had to tell his wife . . .

So, there's Muniba, smoking, not saying anything. And I see she's worried. I ask her how her husband is doing. I knew he had a weak heart. Her daughter had some kind of illness, too, a woman's thing, I think. She says,

"He's fine, everybody's fine, but it's not good! It's not good, Fahro," she says to me. "Don't think about it. The times being what they are, let's just get out of this alive. Yes," Muniba says to me, "and times are bad when a mother abandons her newborn child. She just ran off and left him. Young, barely sixteen, a kid herself. She thinks it'll be easier for her to survive without a baby. Maybe it will be, you can't blame her. Then again, not even a cat abandons its newborn kittens, she looks after them. I go to her room today and see that the bed is empty, and she's just had a baby. So I ask, where is she, has she suddenly died or what? 'Died my foot!' says nurse Nena. 'The Serbian whore legged it!' You know that new driver, well it seems that he takes people over to the Serbian side, for money. He's got connections, apparently he knows the Serbian commander. They went to school together. Somebody must have paid to get her out of here."

"And so, what, she left the baby behind?" I ask. "A baby boy, two days old, feisty, hungry, crying. They gave the poor little thing to a woman who'd just had a baby, to breastfeed. Thank goodness the woman is still here, but she's being discharged tomorrow. Now they don't know what to do, who will take care of him. He'll freeze. He'll die of hunger. None of our people want to take him. He's not just an orphan and a bastard, he's a Serbian orphan and bastard!"

I have to admit, I winced. Something troubled me. No woman abandons a newborn baby just like that. So I say to Muniba, "Take me to see him." "What's there to see? You're no wet nurse," she says surprised. "It's nighttime, nobody will know. Come on, do this for me," I say. So she takes me up to the room, it's freezing cold, there's plastic covering the window, and the little tyke is fast asleep, all wrapped up. He's tiny, no bigger than a loaf of bread. You can barely see him. I stand there looking at him, thinking. My wife and I could take the child in, why not? We have two daughters. They're big already. Things don't look good for the poor little orphan. What nurse Nena said somehow troubled me.

The next morning I light a small fire, I have some twigs and kindling in the house. I wake up Amira. She makes us some coffee, *Divka,* that coffee substitute. We still had a little left, not much though. It's not real coffee, but it smells like it, so for a minute you can pretend it's the real thing. Anyway, we always have a cup in the morning. So I say to her, "Listen Amira, there's this tiny baby boy in the hospital. His mother's abandoned him and gone off to her own people. He'll die if nobody takes him home, but everybody's afraid to take him in because his mother's a Serb."

Her back is turned to me. She's silent, washing something. I can see she's thinking.

She doesn't say anything. "There's a war on. Times are hard. We're already going without. And a baby needs . . ." she says after a long silence. It's not that the baby is Serbian. I know her. My Amira is a good person, as good as they come. When she turns around, I see she's crying. "How would we manage?" she says. She's right, I think, but don't say anything. The four of us in a one-room shack, with only two beds. It's temporary accommodation. Our own house was destroyed. "We'll manage somehow. He'll have what we have," I say. I've got to admit, I was a bit scared. I mean what would people say? So I ask her, "Aren't you afraid what people will say?" "What's there to say? A child is a child. It's not to blame if its mother is a Serb. It's a sin to let it die. He's a human being, after all. We can't think only of ourselves."

My heart raced! I embrace Amira.

The next day I bring the baby home. The hospital is glad to be rid of him, but I see them shaking their heads, surprised. At home, it's a celebration! My girls are crying one moment, laughing the next. They carry him around. They've already found a baby bottle somewhere and are heating up the milk. The baby waves its little hands, smiling. I swear to Allah, so tiny and already smiling, you can hardly believe your eyes. I give him my finger to hold and he squeezes it, like a real little man. I'm happy. "You're going to live, my son," I whisper to him.

So there we are, he'll be seven in a couple of months. He's growing like blazes. He's a happy little boy. It's time to send him to school. That's why I'm here. The school says I have to get his papers in order first, with his full name and the names of the parents, and everything.

You know what people are like. They say all sorts of things. I've been called a traitor, a Muslim raising a Serbian child. They said I was crazy. They said all sorts of things. One person even spat at me full throttle. Others turned away when they saw me. Never mind, it's their loss not mine. Who cares who his mother was? He's a child, a human being, as my Amira says. He needs to be cared for. I've got to say, though, there are also some good people around. They come to the house, bring the boy presents. The children play with him, just as they should.

The war is over and he's survived. What really worries me, though, is that the kids will give him a hard time at school. But what can you do? That's life. Just so long as he's alive and well.

Meho—that's his name, after my late father—is our pride and joy. So I want to adopt him if I can. It wouldn't be good for him to go to some other family, we're his family, right?

Translated by Christina P. Zorić

The Other Questions

Aleksandar Hemon

1. Who Is That?

In March 1969 I was exactly four and a half years old. My father was in Leningrad, in pursuit of his advanced electrical engineering degree. My mother was in labor, attended to by a council of her women friends. I spent the evening orbiting around Mother, but when she felt the baby pushing out, I was sent to bed and ordered to sleep. I defied the order and monitored the developments through the keyhole. My mother had her hands on her basketball-shaped belly, huffing and crying, but the council did not seem too worried. Naturally, I was terrified, for even if I knew that there was a baby in her stomach (for that is what I had been told), I still didn't know how exactly it all worked, what was going to happen to her. So when she was urgently taken to the hospital in obvious pain, I was left behind with a mess of terror-provoking thoughts countered by my grandmother, who soothed me by claiming that my mother would not die, that she would come back with a brother or sister. I did not want a brother or sister; I wanted my mother to come back; I wanted everything to be the way it used to be. The way it used to be was that the world harmoniously belonged to me; indeed, the world was me.

But nothing has ever been nor can it ever be the way it used to be. A couple of days later, I went to retrieve my mother from the hospital with a couple of adults, whose names and faces have sunk to the sandy bottom of an aging mind—all I know about them is that neither of them was my father, who was still in the USSR. On our way home, I shared the back seat with my mother and a bundle of wrapped-up stuff they claimed was alive and was in fact my sister. The alleged sister's face was seriously crumpled, containing no facial expression, except for an ugly, indefinable grimace. Moreover, her face was dark, as though she were soot-coated. And when I traced my finger across her cheek, a pale line appeared under the soot.

"She is filthy," I announced to the adults, but none of them acknowledged the problem. From thereon in, it would be hard for me to get my needs and thoughts heard.

Thus my alleged sister's arrival marked the beginning of a tormentful, lonely period. Droves of people came to our home to lean over her and produce ridiculous sounds. Few of them paid any attention to me, while the attention they paid to her was wholly, infuriatingly undeserved: she did nothing but sleep and cry and undergo frequent diaper changes. On the other hand, I could already read, not to mention speak, and I knew all kinds of interesting things: I could recognize flags of various countries, I could easily classify animal sounds: doggie says: *Av, av;* cow says: *Moo.* I had knowledge, I had ideas, I knew who I was. I was myself, a person.

For a while, as painful as her existence was to me, she was but a new thing, like a new piece of furniture or a plant in a large pot, something you had to get around to get to Mother. Over time, however, I realized that she was going to stay and be a permanent obstacle, that her presence in my life was going to be lasting, and that Mother's love would never reach the pre-sister levels. Not only did she impinge upon my world, she obliviously asserted herself—despite not having a self at all—into its very center so it was now entirely organized around her. In our house, in my life, in my mother's life, every day, all the time, forever, she was there—the soot-skinned not-me, the other.

Therefore I tried to get rid of her as soon as I had a chance. One afternoon, Mother left her alone with me for a few minutes to pick up the phone. My father was still in Russia, and for all I know she could have been talking to him. She did talk for a while, out of my sight, while I watched the little creature, her unreadable face, her absolute absence of thought or personality, her manifest insubstantiality, her unearned, unapproved (by me) presence. I started choking her, pressing my thumbs against her windpipe, as seen on television. She was soft and warm, alive, and I was holding her existence in my hands. I felt her neck under my fingers, she was squirming for life, I was causing her pain.

Suddenly I recognized that I should not be doing what I was doing, I should not be killing her, because she was my little sister and I loved her. But the body is always ahead of the thought and for another moment I kept the pressure until she started vomiting. In an instant I was terrified with the possibility of losing her: her name was Kristina, I was her brother, and I wanted her to live so I could love her more. Though I knew how I could end her life, I did not know how I could stop her from dying. It is so much easier to kill someone than keep them alive for love.

My mother heard her cries, dropped the phone, and ran to her aid. She picked her up, calmed her down, wiped off the vomit, made her inhale and breathe, then demanded an explanation from me. My just-discovered love for my sister and the related feeling of guilt did not at all displace my self-protective instincts: I bold-facedly stated that she had started crying and that I had merely put my hand over her mouth to prevent her from bothering Mother. I shamelessly claimed good intentions coupled with ignorance, a proven way to get out of trouble and deny responsibility, and so I was forgiven. I never tried to kill Kristina again and kept loving her, but I was no doubt monitored for a while.

The memory of that murder attempt is the first one in which I can see myself from the point of view outside myself, and what I see is myself *and* my sister. Never would I be alone in the world, never again would I have it exclusively for myself. Never again would my selfhood be a sovereign territory devoid of the presence of others.

2. Who Are We?

When I was growing up in Sarajevo in the early seventies, the dominant social concept among the kids was *raja*. If one had any friends at all, one had a *raja*, but normally the *raja* was defined by the part of town or the building complex one lived in. Each *raja* had a generational hierarchy: the *velika raja* were the older boys whose responsibilities included protecting the *mala raja*—the smaller kids—from abuse or pocket-emptying by some other *raja*, but whose rights included unconditional obedience, whereby the little ones could always be deployed to buy cigarettes, naked-lady magazines, even condoms, or volunteer their heads for the *velika raja*'s merciless filliping practice—my head was often submitted to a cannonade of the dreaded *mazzolas*. Many *rajas* were defined by and named after their leader, usually the strongest, toughest kid. We feared Ćiza's *raja*, for example, whose leader Ćiza was a well-known *jalijaš*, a street-punk. Normally, we would never see Ćiza, who was old enough to be constantly invested in various forms of petty crime, but his younger brother Zeko was his deputy, and it was he whom we feared most.

My *raja* was a lesser one, as we had no leader. We were defined by a playground—which we called the *Park*—between two symmetrical, identically constructed buildings in which we lived. In the geopolitics of our neighborhood (known back then as *Stara stanica*—the Old Train Station) we were known as the *Parkaši*. The *Park* did not only contain playing equipment—a slide, three swings, a sandbox, a merry-go-round—there were benches as well, which served as goals when we played football. There were also, most importantly, the bushes where we had our *loga*—our base, the place where we could escape from marauding Ćiza's *raja*, where we hoarded things stolen from our parents or pilfered from other, weaker kids. The *Park* was our rightful domain, our sovereign territory, which no stranger, let alone a member of another *raja*, could trespass—any foreigner was subject to a punitive attack. Once we waged a successful campaign against a bunch of teenagers who mistakenly thought that our *Park* was a good place for smoking, drinking, and mutual fondling. We threw rocks and wet sand wrapped in paper at them, we charged collectively at the weak, isolated ones, breaking long sticks against their legs, while they helplessly swung their short arms. Occasionally, some other *raja* would try to invade and take control of the *Park* and we would fight a war—heads were cracked, bodies bruised, all and any of us always risking a grievous bodily injury. Only when Zeko and his troopers—our more powerful nemesis—came to the *Park* we had to stand back and watch them swing on our swings, slide on our slides, make sand castles of our sand, while we could do nothing but imagine a revenge deferred into an indefinite future.

Now it seems to me that when I was not in school or reading, I was involved in some collective project of my *raja*. Besides protecting the sovereignty of the *Park* and waging various wars, we spent time at one another's homes, swapped comic books and football stickers, sneaked together into the nearby movie theater (*Kino Arena*), had meals with one another's families, and attended one another's birthday parties. My primary loyalty was to my *raja* and any other collective affiliation was entirely abstract and absurd. Yes, we were all Yugoslavs and pioneers, and we all loved Tito and our country, but for them I would not have gone to war and taken blows, as I had frequently done for my *raja*. Alternative identities, like the ethnicity of any of us, were wholly irrelevant. To the extent we were aware of ethnic identity in one another, it was related to the old-fashioned customs practiced by our grandparents, fantastically unrelated to our daily operations, let alone our struggle against the oppression we suffered from Zeko and his cohorts.

Once I went, with most of my *raja*, to Almir's birthday party. Almir was somewhat older than me, therefore an authority on many things I knew nothing about, including the explosive properties of the insulation material we called "glass wool"—on one occasion I repeatedly ducked as he threw a handful of "glass wool" wrapped in paper, like a hand grenade, promising a detonation that never came. Almir was also old enough to be getting into rock music, so at his party he played *Bijelo dugme,* the Sarajevan rock band that was scaring the living daylights out of our parents at the time, what with their hairy looks and antisocial, antisocialist, asinine music. Other than that it was birthday business as usual: we ate sandwiches, drank juice, watched Almir blow out the candles on the cake, gave him his presents.

For his birthday party, Almir was boyishly, neatly dressed, which on that occasion meant a wool sweater with black and orange stripes, somewhat fluffy and comparatively resplendent—our socialist-Yugoslavia clothes were determinedly drab. The sweater visibly belonged to someplace else, so I asked him where it came from. It came from Istanbul, he said. Where-upon I quipped: "So you are a Turk." It was supposed to be a funny joke, but nobody laughed; what's worse, nobody thought it was a joke. My point was that a foreign sweater made him a kind of foreigner, a teasing possible only because it was manifestly and obviously and unquestionably untrue. The failed joke entirely changed the mood of the party: to my utter sur-prise Almir started crying rather inconsolably, while everyone looked at me admonishingly. I begged them to explain what it was that I had said, and when they didn't, or couldn't, I tried to explain how the joke was sup-posed to have worked, digging thereby a deeper hole for myself. Let me not go through all of the steps of the descent into a disaster—before long the party was over; everyone went home and everyone knew that I ruined it.

Subsequently, my parents explained to me that "Turk" was (and still is) a derogatory, racist word for a Bosnian Muslim. (Many years later, I would recall, yet again, my inadvertent insult, watching the footage of General Ratko Mladić speaking to a Serb camera upon entering Srebrenica—"This is the latest victory in a five-hundred-year long war against the Turks," Mladić said.) After Almir's birthday party, I learned that such a word, such dis-course, existed. Moreover, it seemed that everyone knew about it before me. What I said *othered* Almir, it made him feel excluded from the group I was unimpeachably part of, whatever group it was. Yet my joke was supposed to be about the flimsiness of difference—as we belonged to the same *raja*, having fought many wars together, the sweater established a momentary, evanescent difference. Almir was teasable exactly because—self-evidently— there was no lasting, essential difference. But the moment you point at a difference, you enter, regardless of your age, an already existing system of differences, a network of identities, all of them ultimately arbitrary and unrelated to your intentions, none of them a matter of your choice. The moment you *other* someone, you *other* yourself. When I idiotically pointed at Almir's nonexistent difference, I expelled myself from my *raja*.

Part of growing up is learning to develop loyalties to abstractions: the state, the nation, the idea. Therefore, you have to be trained to recognize and care about differences, you have to be instructed what constitutes identities, you have to declare your loyalty to an abstraction-based community that transcends, indeed erases, your individuality, including your right to free association with other individuals. *Raja* is no longer possible as a social unit, loyalty to it—the "we" so concrete that I could (still) provide a list of names that constituted it—no longer acceptable as a serious commitment.

I cannot honestly claim that my insult was directly related to the fact that our wars and the golden days of our sovereignty ended soon thereafter. At some point all the conflicts with other *rajas* were resolved by playing football, which we were not all that good at. We still could not beat Zeko and his team, because they had the power to determine what constituted a foul or a goal, so we did not dare foul them and when we scored a goal it was always denied.

As for Almir, he didn't play soccer well enough, and he got even more into *Bijelo dugme,* a band I would forever hate. Soon, he reached a point in his life when girls were accessible to him. He started leading a life different from our childhood lives, becoming someone other than ourselves well before we could. Now I don't know where he is or what happened to him. We no longer belong to "us."

3. Us vs. Them

In December of 1993, my sister and my parents arrived as refugees in Hamilton, Ontario. In the first couple of months, my parents attended English language courses, while my sister worked at Taco Bell, which she called Taco Hell. Things were very complicated for them, what with the language my parents could not really speak, the generic shock of displacement, and a climate that was extremely unfriendly to random human interactions. For my parents, finding a job was a frightening operation of major proportions, but Hamilton is a steel-mill town teeming with immigrants, where many of the natives are first-generation Canadians and therefore generally friendly and supportive of their new compatriots. Soon enough my parents did find work—Father at a steel mill, Mother as a superintendent in a large apartment building, in which many of the tenants were foreign-born.

Yet within months, my parents started cataloging the differences between us and them—we being Bosnians or ex-Yugoslavs, they being purely Canadian. That list of differences, theoretically endless, included items like sour cream (our sour cream was creamier and tastier and much better than theirs); smile (they smile, but don't really mean it); babies (they do not bundle up their babies in the severe cold); wet hair (they go out with their hair wet, exposing themselves to the possibility of lethal brain inflammation); clothes (their clothes fall apart after you wash them a few times), etc. My parents, of course, were not the only ones obsessing over the differences; indeed their social life at the beginning of their Canadian residence largely consisted of meeting people from the old country and exchanging and discussing the perceived dissimilarities. Once I listened to a family friend in what could fairly be called astonishment as he outlined a substrata of differences proceeding from his observation that we like to simmer our food for a long time (*sarma* being a perfect example), while they just dip it in extremely hot oil and cook it in a blink. Our simmering proclivities were reflective of our love of eating and, by extension and obviously, of our love of life, while they did not really know how to live, which pointed at the ultimate, transcendental difference—we had a soul, and they didn't. The fact that they had no interest in committing atrocities either and that we were at the center of a brutal, bloody war, which under no circumstances could be construed as love of life, did not at all trouble the good analyst.

Over time, my parents stopped compulsively examining the differences, which could have been simply because they ran out of examples. I like to think, however, it was because they were socially integrated, not least because the family expanded with more immigration and subsequent marriages and procreation, so we now included a significant number of native Canadians, let alone naturalized ones. It has become harder to talk about us and them now that we have met and married some of them—the clarity and the greater significance of differences were always contingent upon the absence of contact and proportional to the distance. You could theorize Canadians only if you did not know them or meet them, for then the vehicles of comparisons were the ideal Canadians, the exact counterprojection of "us." They were the not-us, we were the not-them.

The primary reason for this spontaneous theoretical differentiation was, I believe, rooted in the instinct of self-legitimization, which requires a constant presence of otherness. In a situation in which my parents felt displaced and therefore inferior to those who were always already at home, the constant comparison was a way to equate themselves rhetorically with Canadians. We were equal to them because we could compare ourselves to them. We were as legitimate as they were because our ways were at least as good as theirs, if not even better—take our sour cream or the philosophical simmering of *sarma*.

But the self-legitimization could only be *collective* for my parents and their friends, partly because that was the indelible mode carried over from the old country, where the dominant ideologies in the past couple of centuries have been collective-based and where the only way to be legitimate was to belong to an identifiable, self-legitimizing group—a greater, if more abstract, *raja*. Neither did it help that an alternative, individual self-legitimization—say, defining and identifying yourself as a professor—was not available to them, since their professional lives or distinguished careers disintegrated in the process of displacement.

The funny thing is that the need for collective self-legitimization fits snugly into the neoliberal discourse of multiculturalism, according to which cultures and the related identities can be seen, recognized, and subsequently benevolently respected only within the network of differences, within the otherness-based epistemology. Multiculturalism is nothing if not the idea of a lot of *others* living happily together, tolerating and learning about one another, thereby learning about themselves. In the neoliberal discourse, every culture is equally legitimate as long as it is capable of self-legitimization. Differences are essentially required for legitimacy: as long as we know who we are and who we are not, we are as legitimate as they are. In the multicultural world there are a lot of *them* (which ought not to be a problem as long as they stay within their cultural confines, loyal to their roots), but there is no hierarchy of cultures, except as measured by the levels of tolerance in the culture—which, incidentally, keeps Western democracies high above everyone else. And where the tolerance level is high, diversity can be celebrated and mind-expanding ethnic food could be explored, opening up an exciting, utopian possibility of understanding and consuming the exotic purity of otherness. A nice American lady, unthreatened by my articulate otherness, once earnestly told me: "It is *so* neat to be from other cultures," as though the "other cultures" was an Edenic archipelago in the Pacific, unspoiled by the troubles of advanced civilizations, home to many a soul-soothing spa. I had no heart to tell her that I was really, painfully, happily complicated.

4. That's Me

The situation of immigration and displacement leads to a kind of self-othering as well. On the one hand, there is a tenuous relationship with the past, with the self that used to exist and operate in a different context, where the qualities that constituted us were self-evident and therefore in no need of constant negotiation. Displacement is a metaphysical crisis, whereby you have to reassert your presence in the world within the new metaphysical context. My parents did it by constantly comparing themselves to Canadians, and mostly favorably—precisely because they felt inferior and metaphysically shaky. By means of systematic nostalgia they established themselves, in their own minds, as stable and at least equal. On the other hand, there is the inescapable reality of the self transformed by immigration and displacement—whoever we used to be, we are now split between *us-here* (say, in Canada) and *us-there* (say, in Bosnia). Because *we-here* still see the present us as consistent with the previous us, now largely living over there in Bosnia, we cannot help but see ourselves from the point of view of *us-there,* from which we very much look like Canadians (or Americans or Germans). In other words, as far as their friends in Sarajevo are concerned, my parents, despite their strenuous efforts at differentiation, are at least partly Canadian and they cannot help but know it. They have become *them* and they can see that because they remained *us* all along.

Furthermore, there is the pressure of integration, which goes hand in hand with a vision of the possible life, the life they could live if they were perfectly Canadian. Every day, my parents see the Canadians living what in the parlance of displacement is called *normal life,* which is fundamentally unavailable to them despite the integrationist promises (far more fulfillable in Canada, and even in the US, than in the xenophobic Europe). They are much closer to it than any of *us* back home, so they can imagine themselves living a *normal* Canadian *life*—they can see themselves as others, not least because they have spent so much time and mind on comparison. Nonetheless, they can never be *them.*

The best theoretical expostulation on the subject above is a Bosnian joke, which loses some of its punch in translation but retains an exceptional (and typical) clarity of thought:

Mujo left Bosnia and immigrated to the United States, to Chicago. He wrote regularly to Suljo, trying to persuade him to visit America, but Suljo kept declining, reluctant to leave his friends and his *kafana.** After years of pressuring, Mujo finally persuades him to come. Suljo crosses the ocean and Mujo waits for him at the airport in a huge Cadillac.

"Whose car is this?" asks Suljo.

"It's mine, of course," Mujo says.

"That is a great car," Suljo says. "You've done well for yourself."

They drive downtown and Mujo says, "See that building over there, a hundred floors high?"

"I see it," Suljo says.

"Well, that's my building."

---

* A neighborhood coffee shop and bar

"Nice," Suljo says.

"And see that bank on the ground floor?"

"I see it."

"That's my bank. When I need money I go there and just take as much as I want. And see the Rolls Royce parked in front of it?"

"I see it."

"That's my Rolls Royce. I have many banks and a Rolls Royce parked in front of each of them."

"Congratulations," Suljo says. "That's very nice."

They drive out of the city to the suburbs, where houses have grand lawns and the streets are lined with old trees. Mujo points at a house, as big and white as a hospital.

"See that house? That's my house," Mujo says. "And see the pool, Olympic size, by the house? That's my pool. I swim there every morning."

There is a gorgeous, curvaceous woman sunbathing by the pool, and there are a boy and a girl happily swimming in it.

"See that woman? That's my wife. And those beautiful children are my children."

"Very nice," Suljo says. "But who is that brawny, suntanned young man massaging your wife and kissing her neck?"

"Well," Mujo says, "that's me."

5. Who Are They?

There is also a neoconservative approach to otherness: others are fine and tolerable as long as they are not trying to join us illegally. If they are here already, they need to maintain reasonable neatness, adapt to our ways of life, the successful standards of which have long been established by us or, as some like to believe, by the US. The distance of others from us, their essential un-neatness, is measured by their relation to free market and democracy. The un-neat others always remind us who we truly are—we are not *them* and never will be. Some of them want to be us—who wouldn't?—and might become us, if they listen to what we tell them. And many of them hate us.

George W. Bush, in a speech to the faculty and students of an Iowa college in January 2000, succinctly summed up the neoconservative philosophy of otherness in his own inimitably idiotic, yet remarkably precise, way: "When I was coming up, it was a dangerous world and you knew exactly who they were. It was us versus them and it was clear who them was. Today, we are not so sure who the they are, but we know they're there."

And then they neatly arrived by planes on September 11, 2001, and now they are everywhere, and every once in a while we round them up, take them to Guantanamo Bay on secret flights or, alternatively, demand they declare they are not *them*. And once the war against *them* is won, we will be triumphantly alone in the world.

6. What Are You?

Here is a story I like to tell. I read it in a Canadian newspaper, but I have told it so many times that it occasionally feels as though I made it up.

A Canadian professor of political science went to Bosnia during the war. He was born somewhere in the former Yugoslavia, but his parents immigrated to Canada when he was a child, which is to say that he had a recognizably South-Slav name. In Bosnia, he was equipped with a Canadian passport and a UNPROFOR* pass, he went around with armed, blue-helmeted escorts, fully protected from the war so he could research it. With his Canadian passport and a UNPROFOR pass, he went through many checkpoints. Once he was stopped somewhere and the curiosity of the soldiers manning the checkpoint was tickled by the incongruity of a South-Slav name in a Canadian passport, so they asked him: "What are you?" His adrenaline was no doubt high, he must have been profoundly uncomfortable, if not a bit terrified and confused, so he said: "I am a professor." To the patriotic warriors at the checkpoint, his answer must have bespoken a refreshing, childlike innocence, for they most certainly did not ask him about his profession. They must have laughed, or told stories about him after they let him go.

To be at all comprehensible as a unit of humanity to the ethnically brave men at the checkpoint he had to have a defined—indeed a self-evident—ethnic identification; the professor's ethnicity was the only epistemologically and ontologically relevant information. What he knew or did not know in the field of political science and pedagogy was fantastically, hysterically irrelevant in the part of the world carved up by various, simultaneous systems of ethnic otherness—which, as a matter of fact, makes it no different than any other part of the world. The professor had to define himself in relation to some "other" but he could not think of any otherness at the moment, unless in his mind the required "others" were firefighters or waiters or high-wire acrobats.

He had to return to Canada to be a professor again. Except when he ran into my parents, for whom he was a perfect specimen of one of *them*.

---

* UN Protection Force, deployed for "peacekeeping"

7. What Am I?

My sister worked in Sarajevo after the war, equipped with a Canadian passport. Because of the nature of her work as a political analyst, she encountered a lot of foreign and domestic politicians and officials. Brandishing a somewhat ethnically confusing name, she was often asked, both by the locals and foreigners: "What are you?" My sister is tough and cheeky (having survived an assassination attempt very early in her life) so she would immediately ask back: "And why do you ask?" They asked, of course, because they needed to know what her ethnicity was so they could know what she was thinking, which ethnic group she was really representing in the given situation. To them, she was irrelevant as a sovereign individual, even more so as a woman, while her education or ability to think for herself could never overcome or transcend her ethnically defined modes of thought. She was bound by her roots, as they like to call that sort of thing in sensitive, multiculturalist societies.

The question was, obviously, deeply racist, so some of the culturally sensitive foreigners would initially be embarrassed by her counterquestion, but after some hesitation they would press on, while the Bosniaks, the Serbs, the Croats would just press on without hesitation—my sister's knowledge, her very existence, was incomprehensible until she declared herself. Finally, she would say: "I am Bosnian," which is not an ethnicity, but one of her two citizenships—a deeply unsatisfying answer to the bureaucrats of Bosnia, bravely manning government desks and fattening up at expensive restaurants.

Instructed by my sister's experiences, I am often tempted to answer proudly: "I am a writer," when asked: "What are you?" Yet I don't, because it is not only pretentiously silly but also inaccurate—I am a writer only at the time of writing. So I say I am complicated; I say I am nothing if not an entanglement of unanswerable questions, a cluster of others; I say it is too early to tell.

Cinema Volta

Drago Jančar

AT AN UNSPECIFIED DATE IN THE FALL OF 1909 THESE SEVEN PEOPLE CAME together for the first time: Janez Rebec, the owner of the movie theater Salone Edison, which contemporaries said was "*il più elegante salone di Trieste*"; Anton Mahnič and his wife, Katarina, who together had been showing films in Istria and today's Slovenia for several years; their two colleagues František Novák from Piran and Giuseppe Caris from Trieste; James Joyce, an English teacher at the Berlitz Language School in Trieste, along with his friend Nicolò Vidacovich, a Trieste lawyer.

Joyce, an Irishman, told those present that he knew of a city of five hundred thousand people that didn't have a single movie theater, whereas Trieste in those days had twenty-one. "Where's that?" the people around the table asked in amazement. Joyce didn't reveal his secret right away because it just seemed too precious. But he did tell them afterward that the city was of course in Ireland. They consulted a map of Ireland and Joyce pointed to Dublin, then to Belfast and Cork. If they could manage to open a movie theater in Dublin, then they could quickly extend the network to other cities that were thirsting just as much for the new art of moving pictures. Joyce said that, to start with, he was prepared to arrange for what was necessary in Dublin, which was where he came from and which he knew well, in order to open a movie theater there, if, of course, the gentlemen for their part were ready to put money into this plan. Janez Rebec and his colleagues had another theater going by the name of Volta, besides the Salone Edison in Trieste, and another movie house by the same name of Volta in Bucharest; they warmed up to the English teacher's scheme and on October 18 signed a contract with him, which Joyce's biographer John McCourt describes as a fascinating document that demonstrates that James Joyce was a genuine businessman and, in spite of his chronic poverty, knew how to handle money. Joyce, to be sure, only put up his knowledge and familiarity with the Irish situation for a project that guaranteed him 10 percent of ticket sales, whereas Rebec and the other partners had invested considerable sums.

The new partners went to work on the project with great delight. The most optimistic among them was Joyce, who recorded in a letter that it was possible to earn a lot of money in movies, writing that "some movie theater owners have become millionaires." He had every reason to assume this, because at that point the new art form was positively the coming thing; new films were shown in numerous Trieste movie theaters, mainly French ones, about Aladdin and the magic lamp (*Aladino, ovvero La lampada meravigliosa*) and Sleeping Beauty (*La bella addormentata*), and the film with the remarkable title, *The Nihilist* (*Dal socialismo al nihilismo*), and filmed operas like *Faust, The Magic Flute, Don Giovanni,* and *Otello.* That's how things were in the entire grand monarchy and all over Europe: people streamed to the movie theaters, and you could absolutely predict that success was assured with the opening of the first and only movie theater in Dublin. Only Joyce's brother Stanislaus was somewhat skeptical; he felt the cinema was marked by American corruption and doubted whether this new invention could work in Dublin, of all places. And he was proved to be correct.

James Joyce, who went from Trieste to Dublin that same month, had done his work well: in Mary Street he found premises at a reasonable price and took care of good publicity in the newspapers. The Cinematograph Volta in Dublin was ceremonially opened on December 20, 1909. On the program were *The Enchanted Castle* and the tragic story of Beatrice Cenci; later they showed *Suor Angelica* and a film titled *How to Pay Bills Easily!,* which the partners probably hadn't looked at closely enough in light of what was to follow. After some initial box-office success the Cinematograph Volta in Dublin began a downward slide; unpaid bills piled up; the partners rushed between Dublin and Trieste with new film after new film, but the number of viewers kept sinking; the income from ticket sales was no longer able to cover costs. Even films like *Crocodile Hunting* and *Quo Vadis?* were not able to get the Irish enthused enough to stream into the cinema and save the project. Rebec, Novák, and Caris informed Joyce in April 1910 that the venture had failed. Mahnič had gone to Dublin that same month to sell the movie house at a loss. The only one who hadn't lost anything in the enterprise was James Joyce, who hadn't invested a thing except the initial idea.

I'm not recounting this unusual, little-known, but in its way amusing, story out of interest in the organizational and mercantile abilities of the great author, nor am I doing so out of interest in talking about the beginnings of film as art form and the film industry in Europe. No, this story seems fascinating to me because of something else. Joyce reported his entrepreneurial adventure rather precisely in numerous letters but at no point does he mention that governmental or bureaucratic obstacles stood in his way. Neither is there a word about this in the very exact and extensive biographies of the partners that are concerned with every detail of this enterprise. A group of ambitious people at the beginning of the twentieth century opens several movie theaters, not only in their own city but in Bucharest and Dublin. Apparently they were not troubled by any customs barriers, tax restrictions, special state regulations, or national or ideological prejudices, but were united by their delight in the new art form—and of course by its possible benefits—and at the same time understood Europe to be absolutely obvious as an open setting wherein one could feel equally at home in Trieste, Bucharest, or Dublin.

If this Trieste group, which had come together there at the beginning of the twentieth century, could listen to us roughly one hundred years later talking about an Old and a New Europe and discussing the problems of integrating new EU member states, those gentlemen would probably have been quite astonished. It would be necessary to explain to them that Bucharest now lies at the other end of the world and that it belongs to the New Europe that is slowly being absorbed into the Old Europe. You'd have to tell them, too, that Janez Rebec would have been locked up for sure if he'd tried to use his money to set up a Cinema Volta there during the last fifty years. But even if he'd only tried to do it in Dublin he'd have had to surmount a veritable mass of administrative, tax, and other obstacles. The language they communicated in back then was doubtless Italian, but other languages were taken for granted for any and all, at least English, German, Slovenian, and Croatian. They would probably have considered us idiots if we'd told them anything about a multicultural society and the need for tolerance and understanding toward the Others, or about "being an Other." Or if we'd served up the famous political cliché about intercultural dialogue in the search for a common European identity. Or else they would have felt that *they* were the idiots because they wouldn't have been able to understand our new language at all. The differentness, the linguistic, national, and cultural identities, even European identity, and their exchange of goods and ideas, together with what today is called "multiculturalism"—all this was so taken for granted at the beginning of the twentieth century, so self-evident that no special term for it was necessary. When I told an acquaintance of mine the story about Cinema Volta, about its rise and sad end, he said Joyce and his troops were surely genuine oddballs. Were they really? Aren't we, who talk about respect toward differences today and at the same time deliberate as to how we can create a common world of ideas, aren't we the real oddballs?

Of course I don't mean to say that the Europe of 1909 was a proper Arcadia, a paradise of openness and joy where new cinemas sprouted up like mushrooms; but nonetheless the spirit of national and humane tolerance wafted over its open landscapes. I'm also not of the opinion that Trieste in that year was the ideal harbor for human longings and mutual understanding. It was just at that time that ideas of salvation in an even better world sprang up everywhere in Europe. But they were still in an embryonic state; nobody knew at the time what kinds of monsters were soon to develop from them. These thoughts were not wrong in principle, but the problem was that they excluded all other social and cultural ideas and that almost all of them imagined they could be put into practice as a march on seats of power, a march on Rome, on Berlin, or on Moscow. Many nationalists, anarchists, and various other social reformers had already gathered together in 1909 around the circle which was concerned with spreading Volta movie theaters around Europe so that people could laugh at moving pictures, or grow reflective or sentimental watching them; they gathered around those oddballs who expected to make some money from useless things like films—let alone art films. To put it into the language of film dramaturges: you'd have to characterize this state of affairs as that of an exposition in which the audience does not yet know in which direction history will take its course. It's not unlikely that the English teacher James Joyce anticipated history's dissolution and soon afterward quit that lively, multilingual, and multicultural Babylon on the seashore that goes by the name of Trieste. We know today that history indeed took a wrong turn, strictly speaking a completely wrong turn.

World reformers, who understood the world so differently from the Trieste film crowd, thought that the confusion of languages was not only totally unnecessary but also a great disadvantage. *Our* language, *our* culture, *our* party, *our* doctrine, *our* social unity—soon very different film images replaced the multiplicity which that part of Europe had coped with very well until then, had dealt with, educated itself with, had fun with, and had also discussed the Cinema Volta with. What followed was a broad-shouldered guy in a black uniform who theatrically proclaimed the superiority of the one culture and language and the inferiority of others, whether he announced it in a black uniform and from a podium before a huge mass of people or from a cockpit after the harvest while naked above the waist; his Trieste newspaper said that Slavic foreign language bugs had proliferated in the city Italians called home. And of course, he said, you knew what to do with bugs . . . Fewer and fewer films like *La bella addormentata* were shown in the Cinema Volta; instead you saw more and more images of young people marching and singing, *"Giovanezza, giovanezza / Primavera di bellezza . . ."* (Youth, youth / Springtime of beauty . . .).

At the other end of Europe, in a more distant, magnificent port city, in St. Petersburg, armed workers and peasants marched across the screens; a few years later, when the city was called Leningrad, songs of workers' victories reverberated there, laughing girls harvested wheat, lads with rolled-up sleeves pushed wheelbarrows onto piles of earth. Nobody was interested in films like *The Enchanted Castle* or *Suor Angelica* anymore. Soon there was no place in Europe for that group of people in Trieste clustered around the Cinema Volta. You had to declare your allegiance: to which nation, to which race, to which party, to which ideology . . . No need to go any further because we all know how it ended: the men who wanted to make the world function according to their rules soon dominated everything—people and the economy, art and culture—and had made film into a compliant propaganda tool. What followed was an insane century of ideologies, with its masses in Europe's squares, revolutions, parades, and animated speeches captured on film—but also with its prison cells, trials, deportations, concentration camps, assassinations, and massacres. The story of the Cinema Volta, with its beautiful beginning, ends in scenes offstage of naked death's domination that were never shot by any movie camera.

The second story, where the author of these words himself appears, has an idyllic beginning, too. It relates how, one nice sunny day in 1978, a lady friend and I went for a drive on a red gravel road not far from Trieste, and we suddenly found ourselves in one of the most extraordinary villages I have ever seen, Oprtalj. We walked the perfectly empty streets; only the wind came around the corners, and we wandered out onto a large, curving terrace with a superb view over abandoned vineyards and fallow fields. The wind tousled my companion's hair, just like in a film. If you're in a poetic mood, even the sight of empty streets, abandoned vineyards, and fallow fields can be magnificent. It was October, and the leaves were whirling up—driven by the bora, the autumnal downdraft the weather brings from the continent over the karst and Istria. I said, "Hey, this is the terrace where they'd sit around after their day's work. Maybe they'd have a glass or two of malvasia, play cards, and a quintet of local musicians would play Istrian songs on Sundays in the corner over there. And all that's left now is the raging bora."

I don't know about today, but when we used to go on forays around Istria at the end of the seventies there were only seventeen people left of the five hundred who had called the place home around the end of the war. Almost everybody had left the village in a gigantic exodus that signified the end of the battles that were initially cultural ones, then fights with fascistic power, and then military skirmishes among nationalities—until everything gave way to new revolutionary violence. All that was left were the empty streets of Oprtalj, fallow fields, abandoned vineyards, and the eternal bora; its melancholy howling and beating against the window shutters told of the impermanence of history and also of its consequences. It told us that there are always new political maps being drawn in the landscape, which is why people come and go, but the landscape itself remains, whether settled or uninhabited, whether the fields are tilled or overgrown with weeds and maquis.

And just like the Italians departed Istria after the Second World War, so, too, did tens of thousands of Slovenes evacuate Trieste after the First World War to save themselves from the swelling tide of Mussolini's Blackshirts who burned down the Slovenian cultural center in the middle of the city, with its theater, its cultural clubs, and cafés. And a bit farther down the road to the unoccupied town of Oprtalj lies the Brioni Archipelago at the end of Istria, a beautiful paradise of islands where captains of industry, ambassadors, and dictators, big and little, used to live. A TV documentary showed my childhood hero in his white marshal's uniform strolling on the deck of the good ship *Galeb*, leaning over the rail, looking thoughtfully off into the distance, maybe spotting dolphins, maybe snapping a picture. I think today that he probably didn't discover a single dolphin. Just an hour by ship south of Brioni lies the island of Gli Otok—no doubt he saw it once, although he probably was wondering what was going on there. In that horrible, high-security gulag for political prisoners in Communist Yugoslavia.

In short: ever since the military expedition of the Hapsburg Archduke Ferdinand Maximilian Joseph left from Trieste toward the end of the nineteenth century to set him up as emperor in distant Mexico, this outlier in the Mediterranean, this sleeve jutting very deeply into the European continent, has been the stage for bloody dramas, for national and ideological battles that have left deserted cities and villages behind and flushed away entire rivers of displaced persons. That was the drama that was played out in this corner of the world in the twentieth century; it had begun much earlier with the so-called *Kulturkampf* in which none of the participants expected the consequences to be so uncivilized and violent as they turned out. It was but one step from love of *Heimat* to brute force against one's neighbors who spoke a different language; the next step was to go from ideas of how to save society to concentration camps. Trieste, a cosmopolitan city of trade and communication, was also one of sheer, unbelievable, interpersonal narrowness; Trieste, the city and site with a truly cosmopolitan literature, was also the city of the roughest nationalistic altercations. The beautiful paradise of Istria and its coasts formed the backdrop for human intolerance and violence.

Back then in the abandoned village of Oprtalj, I didn't have the slightest inkling that the history of resettlement, ethnic cleansing, and completely deserted regions would be repeated; that new maps would be drawn that intrude on people's fates and change their lives dramatically. The large state that had collapsed bequeathed new gaping holes: small, idyllic Danube towns, deserted Bosnian villages amid green forests, the terrible desolation I observed with horror on another trip from Dalmatia into the heart of Croatia left by "Operation Storm." There was no dearth of evidence on film; every day the television brought into our living rooms pictures of crouching soldiers running toward the edge of the city and pointing at targets to hit, pictures of refugees and destroyed homes.

On that trip somebody I knew from Croatia explained to me the difference between a Croatian and a Serbian house. I thought that people were not only fighting because of linguistic and cultural differences but also maybe because they had different architectural traditions. But I was wrong. Housing construction was no different, at least not in the way there were differences in language, religion, or historical tradition. Serbs and Croats built twentieth-century houses the same way; since the tourist boom started in Dalmatia, they're just as unnecessarily large and replete with all kinds of little towers and fairy-tale porticos.

The difference did not lie in their construction but in their remains.

A Serbian house had a roof that was almost entirely untouched, whereas the rest of it was almost completely destroyed. The reason was, as my acquaintance explained, that our people had blown up the foundations;

the house simply collapsed, and if real specialists were on the job, the roof was almost perfectly preserved. On the other hand, a Croatian house was destroyed from above: in that way the roof was completely wiped out. This was because of the famous artillery of the famous Yugoslav National Army, which was advancing on Zadar. The shells hit the roofs of Croatian houses, the Serbian ones remained intact; the artillerymen in the Yugoslav Army didn't simply blaze away at anything. They nevertheless had to retreat when the Croatian Army arrived, and it had excellent demolition experts.

And even this has become merely history, because the majority of those houses have been rebuilt in the meantime. Now and then tourists relieve their boredom by pointing out a ruin from their car window on their way to the warm sea: hey, look, there was a raging war here fifteen years ago. Why again?

Now, at the beginning of a new century, it seems to us once again that these are dramas long past; they are other people's confusions and other people's lost and displaced lives. Peace activists and human rights advocates, but also politicians, TV commentators, and newspaper columnists, reiterate the magic words that are supposed to protect us from the spell of intolerance and violence. "Multiculturalism" and "the Others," respect for "being different," respect for minorities. When I once said in public that multiculturalism is a concept that belonged in agronomics, I reaped nothing but malevolent stares. A civilized, that is, a curious and creative person is by definition multicultural and cannot exist in a cultural autarchy. And you can broadcast clichés about the Other all you want: they will have no effect if we have not learned to deal with human, linguistic, cultural, and creative differences. After all that we've seen in twentieth-century movie theaters, after all we've seen, heard, and felt in our own lives, we cannot really reenter any history at all with the same innocent naturalness that belonged to the Cinema Volta and its protagonists. We will never be able to reenter that self-evident world of ideas about a common European economic and cultural space where people of different languages, professions, and talents created, at the beginning of the last century, the European movie-theater project.

Their venture was a fiasco solely from a financial standpoint, but everyone quickly recovered. Those who came afterward were faced with a Europe that had suffered moral, intellectual, and physical collapse. And we, who were convinced there would never be another war based on national or ideological conflicts, never any war at all, were forced to experience how "Serbian" and "Croatian" houses came about at the end of the past century out of linguistic and cultural differences.

Maybe our eternal hopes that this now really has come to an end make us look a little ridiculous: our hope that if we work hard in our stories, articles, and books about the Other—as if literature doesn't deal exclusively with the Other anyway; our hope that if we make an effort at the beginning of the new century to fill the pot of sweet togetherness with new contents and old stories and to smash the jug of the twentieth century.

Janez Rebec, the owner of the movie theater Salone Edison, "*il più elegante salone di Trieste*"; Anton Mahnič and his wife, Katarina, who together showed films in Istria and today's Slovenia for several years; their two colleagues František Novák from Piran and Giuseppe Caris from Trieste; the Trieste lawyer Nicolò Vidacovich, and the English teacher James Joyce— they at any rate would not understand us. The aforementioned lady and the aforementioned gentlemen, who met together in Trieste in October 1909 because of art and business, because of flickering, moving pictures on the screen in a dark room, would have found it trivial to talk about the matter at all.

Translated by Gerald Chapple

Where Other People Live

Miljenko Jergović

MY FATHER, TWO OF MY MATERNAL UNCLES, AND I ALL WENT TO THE SAME high school in Sarajevo. Before World War II, when the three of them attended, it was called the First High School for Boys. After the war, when schools turned co-ed, it simply became the First High School. In 1984, just before I graduated, the school changed its name a third time. It was called Heroes and Revolutionaries of the First High School. It was given its fourth name during the recent war, when it became the First Bosniak High School. Although it had been almost fifty years since my older uncle enrolled in the high school, in 1934, the inside of the building had not changed, as my grandmother, who attended parent-teacher meetings there in both his day and mine, was able to observe. The same teacher who taught the history of art to my younger uncle and to my father, who had enrolled five or six years later, was also to teach me. When the old schoolteacher died at the start of my sophomore year, all three of us went to his funeral.

From its inception in the 1880s, it had always been an elite school. After a lot of trouble, Bosnia's only Nobel Prize–winning writer, Ivo Andrić, graduated from the school, later talking about it with abhorrence and a faint whiff of distaste. That is probably why Andrić's name was never mentioned at school ceremonies when the principal would list all the illustrious figures who had attended our school. In my day its greatest alumni were considered to be Communist revolutionaries and the assassins of the Austro-Hungarian heir to the throne, Franz Ferdinand. Gavrilo Princip, the man who actually shot the archduke and his pregnant wife, did not attend our school, but his close collaborators did.

Our teachers repeatedly told us how we should look up to these shining examples. We lived in a socialist society where shining examples were held in high esteem. This included our parents and uncles, who were often hailed as examples of the ancient virtues of sacrifice and heroism.

There was my father, for instance, a top student, one of the best of his generation. And there was also my younger uncle, who was to represent the Yugoslav metallurgical industry in the Soviet Union and become a man of the world. The two of them were often mentioned. My older uncle, who had been a better student than both his brothers, was not mentioned. He was not a shining example. Most Yugoslavs had someone like him in their family, someone they did not talk about. As in a fairy tale, at least one of the three sons was not a shining example.

My older uncle was a straight A student. He corresponded with foreign friends in Latin, solved unsolvable mathematical problems, played the guitar, and wrote an essay about Paul Valéry. Blond and blue-eyed, tall and frail, in photographs he looked like a young aristocrat straight out of a Thomas Mann novel, who at the end of the book would die of, say, meningitis or tuberculosis, but it would be no ordinary death, no, it would symbolize the fate of a family or of an entire generation. That is what my older uncle may have looked like, but there was nothing Mann-like about his life, except that on his no longer existing headstone I would have gladly engraved the words with which Serenus Zeitblom, doctor of philosophy, bid farewell to his friend, the composer Adrian Leverkühn: "A lonely man folds his hands and says: may God have mercy on your poor soul, my friend, my homeland."

But I am not quite certain that I know what my older uncle's homeland was. What is more certain is that I myself have no homeland. So I am not sure what such an epitaph on his invisible grave would actually mean.

My older uncle's homeland might have looked like this: he was born in Usora, a small town in central Bosnia, where his father, my grandfather, was the stationmaster; he grew up along the rail tracks built by Austria-Hungary, often changing friends and landscapes; he learned Slovenian from his father—a Slovene by origin, his mother tongue was Croatian, but he started speaking German before either of the two. He learned it from his grandfather, my great-grandfather, a senior railway official, who was an ethnic German from the Banat region, born in a small town in what is today Romania, and educated in Budapest and Vienna. He, too, had spent his whole working life along the tracks of the Bosnian railway.

So, you see, my older uncle, and perhaps here I should say that his name was Mladen because it is too confusing to continue without names, lived in a complex environment and complicated linguistic situation. And you are about to learn just how complicated and to appreciate how language can determine a person's fate. Mladen's grandfather Karlo was proud of his German roots and until the day he died spoke only German to his four children. He never uttered a word of Croatian to them. His sons-in-law, two Croats and Mladen's Slovene father, all spoke perfect German, but to them he spoke in Croatian. With his grandchildren he spoke both languages, but only after they had addressed him first in German. If they greeted him in Croatian, Grandpa Karlo, or Otata as they called him, would pretend not to hear them.

They say that Sunday family lunches were something to behold. There was a strict linguistic protocol, today found probably only at European Union headquarters, but nobody ever wondered why. Otata Karlo felt very strongly about his Germanness and about his select position among men, and they all had to respect that. In return, nobody, least of all him, stopped them from being who they were or from speaking whatever language they wished amongst themselves. Otata was fond of his sons-in-law, did not mind that they were not German, and was proud of their occupations. For him, belonging to the railroads was like belonging to a secret organization, a Masonic lodge, whose members take a different view of the world and have a different role to play. A German railroad man and a Croatian railroad man were like brothers who understood each other better than any compatriot. Otata Karlo was a leftist and at the turn of the twentieth century he wound up in jail and then lost his job for supporting a railway workers' strike. It would not have been such a scandal had he not been the stationmaster and a German living amongst the wild Slavs, so he was severely punished by the powers of king and empire for betraying his national origins and his position in society.

But ideological issues were never discussed at home. Unless they concerned upbringing, wherein everybody had the same rights, regardless of religion or status. The poor little land of Bosnia, where in the 1920s and 1930s almost 90 percent of the population was completely illiterate, where typhoid and cholera epidemics were recurrent and endemic syphilis ran rampant and was passed on from generation to generation, like a sinister tradition, this Bosnia was an ideal place for Otata Karlo and his ideas. He never thought of returning to Banat or moving to Vienna or Germany. Though he was German, Germany was a foreign country to him. If we asked him about it, he would say that he could never live there because "other people live over there." To this day I have not heard a better definition of what is not one's homeland.

My uncle Mladen was closer to his grandfather than the other grandchildren, but he could not be said to look like him. Old Karlo had dark hair, a long gray beard and was on the short side; judging by his photographs he looked more like a Romanian rabbi, or at the very least a Jewish scholar, than a German. Mladen, on the other hand, got his Nordic blue eyes, height, and bearing not from his mother's German side but from his father's line of Slovene peasants from around Tolmin. Looking at the faded black-and-white photos of the two of them makes me wonder how their lives would have turned out had Mladen not learned German so easily, not enjoyed listening to his grandfather play the violin, not sat so near him at Sunday lunch. I wonder what would have happened had the old man hated the Slav in his grandson just a little bit.

In the courtyard of the building where my family had been living since the early 1930s, there was a big new Ashkenazi synagogue. Everybody, not just the Jews, called it Temple. People who had come to work in Sarajevo at the will and pleasure of the emperor and king, Franz Joseph, and who had stayed on, like Otata Karlo and my Slovene grandfather, came here to pray. Previously, in the days of Turkish rule, Sephardic Spanish Jews had lived in our city and there were no Ashkenazi. The Sephardics were mostly poor and because they distrusted the new occupying authorities, would not let the Ashkenazi newcomers into their temple. In a way, they did not believe that these people, too, were Jewish, and so they called them, like their imperial and royal protectors, Krauts. Eventually, a second, Ashkenazi or, as they called it, Kraut synagogue, had to be built and everybody called it Temple.

At the very start of the war, a day after the Ustashas took power, a mob broke into the synagogue, smashing everything in sight. They were not people in uniform. They were ordinary, ever so civilian folk. Among them were city bums and bullies, small-time crooks and better class citizens, and Roma, the very same people who only a few days later would find themselves being transported alongside Sarajevo's Jews to the concentration camps.

My Slovene grandfather, Franjo was his name, watched the temple being destroyed from his window. Grandma Olga tried to pull him away so that nobody would see him, but, despite his fear, he stayed by the window. It was a measure of his courage.

At the time, their son Mladen was in his third year of high school. They had taught him that what was happening was wrong. They told him that Pavelić was bad and Hitler mad and that he was bound to lose the war in the end. They, along with Otata Karlo, taught him everything that, from today's perspective, would seem important and necessary to know. But they also told him, of course, that he should never ever, no matter what, speak his mind about either Hitler or Pavelić. And that he should steer clear of people who protested against the new, Ustasha authorities. My grandparents, like their parents and our entire wider family, were against any opposition to the authorities on principle. There's nothing we can do about it. It's not up to us to change the state. You'll just wind up in jail, that's all.

They told Mladen to stay away from members of the Ustasha Youth, not to attend their events or gatherings, and, if asked, to say that he felt German not Croat. Who knows whether he ever had to tell anybody that he was German in order to avoid the consequences of being Croat; certainly, his knowledge of German and of some of the finer skills that the German race is famous for, such as their mastery of fencing or the violin bow, helped him to be increasingly perceived as somebody who was not a Croat and therefore could not be an Ustasha.

When he graduated from high school a year later, Mladen was planning to study in Zagreb or Vienna. We had lots of relatives in Vienna, they were not poor, and he could stay with them. It would have been a bit harder in Zagreb. He wanted to study forestry, because Otata had always told him that it was crazy to be in Bosnia and not live amidst the woods.

But in the early summer of 1942, he suddenly received his call-up papers, written in both German and Croatian as per the regulations of a united Europe. The unit Mladen was assigned to was part of the Wehrmacht, not the Croatian army, and only Sarajevo's finest, usually of German or Austrian descent, were sent there.

There were two possibilities: Mladen could either report for duty and go to war, or run off and join the partisans. Not for a moment did his parents, my grandfather Franjo and grandmother Olga, doubt that Hitler would lose the war and that Pavelić would finish with a rope around his neck. I know I have said this before, but it bears repeating: never, not for a single day, not for a single hour, did Franjo think that the people who had destroyed the temple and carted away our Jewish neighbors could win the war. Though he was not religious, he believed that evil could never win out. He was not a Communist, but his father-in-law, Otata Karlo, was a bit of one, and the partisans to whom Mladen would be escaping from his German draft papers certainly were. To join them would place him, in every respect, on the side of justice.

My grandparents knew that, but all the same they sent their son, my older uncle, to the Germans not the partisans. They figured that with them he would stand a better chance of surviving. He would spend a few months in boot camp, by which time Hitler would have lost the war. They figured wrong, however, because fourteen months later my older uncle was killed fighting the partisans. It was his unit's first battle and he was its first and last casualty. Several days later, the entire unit, along with its command, crossed over to the partisans. After the war, in the summer of 1945, four of Mladen's wartime comrades came to see his parents. They were now part of the liberation army and Franjo and Olga were the parents of a dead enemy soldier. After her son died, my grandmother never went to Mass again, she stopped crossing herself, stopped celebrating Christmas and Easter and when, at the age of fifteen, I asked her if there was a God, she replied: "For some there is, for some there isn't."

"And for you?"

"There isn't."

"And for me?"

"That you have to work out for yourself."

While his grandson was fighting as a German soldier, Otata Karlo was living in his house in Ilidža on the southern outskirts of Sarajevo, which at night was the target of various, mainly drunken, marauding troops. When the Ustashas set off on their nocturnal rampages, killing and plundering Serbian houses, Otata would take in the neighbors, sometimes as many as fifty at a time. And when the Ustashas came to search the house, he would stand at the door, with his beard and his scowl, and tell them in Croatian: "This is a German house. You're not stepping foot in here!"

No matter how drunk they were, they would turn on their heels and leave without a word. The look of hatred on his face as he watched them leave made him almost unrecognizable. He was like a different man. A terrible man. Somebody once told me that I had inherited that look of his.

Sarajevo was liberated in April 1945. A couple of months later they came to take Otata away to a holding camp from where he was to be deported, along with his German compatriots, to Germany. It was a kilometer-and-a-half-long walk to the train station in Ilidža. He was flanked by two partisans, while a third kept prodding him in the back with the barrel of his rifle. The man knew him from before the war, he knew exactly who and what Otata Karlo was, but he got a kick out of pushing him around a bit. That's how it is in life. You never know who will be carted off to a concentration camp, when or why. Only that people seldom think it will be them.

But when they reached the train station, Otata's Serb neighbors had already gathered in front of the cattle cars being used by the partisans to transport their victims to the camps. They shouted that he could be German ten times over but for four years he had saved them from the Ustashas and they were not going to let comrade Karlo go; if he went, they went. The partisans tried to disperse the crowd, rifle butts cut through the air, a few heads were bashed, but the harder they hit, the more stubborn the people became.

That day they returned Otata Karlo home and never came back for him again, even though he was a German and, along with other Yugoslav Germans, was slated for deportation to Germany. Who knows whether he would have made it there alive. It can be said that his life was saved by the very people whose own lives he had saved. Like in a fairy tale, his good deeds were rewarded. Otata died fifteen years later, at the start of the decade in which I was born.

His daughters were not treated as Germans in Yugoslavia, because they were married to Slavs. His only son, Rudolf, known as Nano to everybody except his sisters and mistress, who all called him Rudi, was not considered German either and so was not carted off to the camp. What were the criteria used by Yugoslav Communists when sending Germans off to the camps after the war and what, from their viewpoint, defined someone as being German? That is a question I have been unable to answer to this day. Our Nano looked more German than his father, he carried his last name, never Croaticized it or gave it a phonetic spelling, he had a library full of German books, went to concerts of classical music, spoke German with his friends, strolled the streets of Sarajevo's Baščaršija bazaar with relatives from Vienna and their lovely girlfriends, all of them Austrian, but the partisans did not consider him German. Why not? Probably because, with their policeman's sixth sense, they figured that our family's Germanness had ended with Otata Karlo and that Rudolf was uninterested in his roots. That sufficed for the partisans to spare a person from the camps and, in this respect, Communist concentration camps could not be compared with German or Ustasha camps.

After the liberation of Sarajevo, my younger uncle Dragan and my father were mobilized by the partisans and fought in one of the bloodiest battles of the end of the war, somewhere around the Croatian town of Karlovac. They were still high school students when they were sent to war and demobilized partisans when they actually graduated. My uncle later studied metallurgy and my father medicine. Both made a success of their professions and became respected members of society. And both carried family stigmas in their hearts and minds, and in their names, which were registered in their police files. My uncle's was his brother, who had died as a German soldier, while for my father it was his mother and her two sisters, who were very active in the Ustasha youth movement in Sarajevo, as a result of which after the war his mother was sentenced to prison and her sisters immigrated to Argentina.

My uncle and father joined the League of Communists, whose loyal members they remained until the break-up of Yugoslavia. As did my mother, who had been only a year old when her brother was killed. But even she was told on occasion, when it was deemed necessary, that her brother had fought on the wrong side in the war. She felt a little guilty about it. As did her younger brother. As did her future husband, my father, because of his mother and aunts.

This sense of guilt marked their lives and shaped their identity. It is a part of my own identity although I have never felt guilt myself, just as I have never felt the Germanness of my great-grandfather Otata Karlo or the Sloveneness of my grandfather Franjo. My case, I know now, is rather more complicated, because my identity consists more of what I am not than of what I am.

In the summer of 1993, with Sarajevo under siege from Mladić's and Karadžić's tanks, I left the city in a US military plane that was transporting aid relief and foreign and local journalists to Split. I thought I might be leaving forever. I was simply trying to save my neck, that's all. My parents, who had divorced many years earlier, stayed behind, each on their own. It struck me that I might never see them again. But, after seventeen months of war and siege, I was saving my life. I was doing what my older uncle had not been able to do. I was running away from my war.

I knew that I was going to Zagreb, to Croatia. Even though it was the land of my language, even though I am Croatian, I went there the way Otata Karlo would have gone to Germany. But I did not know it at the time. In saving my neck I never thought about how those "other people" live in Croatia, where I was a foreigner, just as Otata was a foreigner in Germany. He was a German whose Germanness was reflected in and could only exist in the context of non-Germans, in his daily contact with others, in the peculiar linguistic ceremonies that formed part of Sunday family lunches, in his arrogant behavior toward the Croatian fascists who wanted to search his house. My Croatianness was Bosnian and even more than that it was a carpetbagger's. That was the name given to people who, in the days of Emperor Franz Joseph, had come from different parts of the monarchy to settle in Sarajevo. They, with their different cultures and languages, created a non-national identity, whose cultural substrate was stronger than their sense of national belonging. In my case, and in the case of my family, this means that we are Bosnian Croats whose identity is defined by Slav, German, Italian, and who knows what other nations of the former monarchy. Without Austria-Hungary I would never have been born, because my parents would never have been born, because their parents would never have been born, because the parents of their parents would never have met . . . In that respect, my birth was a political project.

Once in Croatia, in the land of those "other people," I realized that I could spend my entire life here and even be happy, but I would never be one of them. If I used the word *we*, it would usually be a false *we*, the kind of *we* that makes one wince. So I prefer to say *them* and *me* rather than *we*. When talking about myself I will usually say things that people don't like hearing, things that they would never say themselves because they do not want to be different. It does not matter whether the difference is positive or negative; as soon as there is a difference, as soon as you in any way stand out from the crowd, it invites antagonism.

At the time of my arrival, Croatia was, ethnically speaking, a highly homogeneous country, with Croats and Catholics accounting for 90 percent of the population, most of them extremely hostile to anyone who belonged to a minority. This hostility was at the heart of the state's ideology, but it was also shaped by the fact that there was a war raging in the country and that one-third of its territory had been occupied. The role of occupier was played by the former Yugoslav People's Army, and the role of local traitors by members of the Serbian national minority. But members of the small Croatian Muslim community were also seen as enemies because at the time, and that was in the autumn of 1993, the Croats had launched attacks against Muslim regions in Bosnia and Herzegovina. Other non-national enemies included atheists, who were a reminder of forty years of Communist rule, and also probably of the people's own hypocrisy in matters of religion and God. As long as it had been the desired social norm, people negated religion en masse, but now that times had changed, they rushed to church, again en masse.

Yet people reveled in their various hatreds and enmities. That is nothing new either: no emotion is as all-embracing and fulfilling as hatred, and nothing but hatred can grow from a private to a public, societal emotion. In the nineties, during the time of President Franjo Tudjman, Croatia was very much a country of hatred. That hatred was mostly directed inward, against parts of its own society, against its own culture, history, identity, language . . . In Croatia even words were hated if they did not sound Croatian enough. And sounds could often be deceptive. If there was no object to pin their hate on, then people focused on things unrelated to minorities or other identities.

At such times, you can find all sorts of justification for wanting to be with the majority. Especially if you have come from a besieged city, if you are there all on your own, a subtenant, an intellectual proletarian . . . After all, Sarajevo was under siege from a people who were hated with a passion in Croatia at the time. So why wouldn't you acquiesce to such hatred, to being accepted as a member of society, to switching, as is only fair, from being an exile to being situated in society? If we abstract the moral norms that would speak against it, and such norms are always problematic if raised by an individual who opposes society, and if we forget that hatred also presumes a certain intellectual and social effort—which does not come easily to everyone—then it is genuinely difficult to find a reason why a person who arrived from Sarajevo in 1993 should speak out against the prevailing mood in the city and country where he has just arrived. I am not so vain that I have to be different at any cost. And I know that such differences are not conducive to particularly good living conditions.

So the reason I reduced every *we* to *I*—why, during that long season of hatred, I wanted to be the exception even though it gave me no moral pleasure or satisfaction to be so—had to do with how my own identity had been formed, an identity which in different ways had been shaped by what I was not and who I was not. My great-grandfather was a Banat German living in Sarajevo who spoke Croatian laced with a lot of Turkish words typical of Bosnian Muslims. He hid his Serb neighbors from the Ustashas not because he was a good or selfless man, at least not primarily for that reason, but because they formed an important part of his world, for what kind of German would he have been had they not been Serbs? He probably did not know what it meant to be German where there were no Serbs (Croats, Bosnians, Muslims, Jews . . .). From his point of view and mine, hatred in a multinational community is the same thing as self-hatred. That is why my Croatianness was substantially different from that of the people I found when I arrived in Zagreb, and even from my friends. Because while they rejected hatred for intellectual and moral reasons, or simply because that is how they had been brought up, I rejected it because it threatened me. Although I am a Croat, it threatened the Serb and the Bosniak (Muslim) in me.

My younger uncle Dragan, who was to become a well-known metallurgist and trade representative of Bosnia's heavy industry in the Soviet Union, was born in Kakanj, yet another of the little towns where my grandfather Franjo had worked as a stationmaster. The majority population in Kakanj was Muslim, and when Dragan went to school he was the only Christian in his class. In the 1930s, religion was a compulsory subject in all schools in the Kingdom of Yugoslavia and so my uncle had to learn to believe in God from a tender age and under unusual circumstances. For their first class of the day, all the children would go for instruction to the Islamic teacher in the nearby mosque, while Dragan stayed behind on his own in the classroom because there was no Catholic catechism teacher in the school, and the local priest, who could stand in for him when needed, had no idea that there was a little baptized sheep waiting for him in the school. And so, sitting alone within the four white walls of his classroom, staring at the blackboard and the photograph of King Aleksandar Karadjordjević hanging on the wall, my uncle felt the kind of desperate, confusing loneliness that makes even adults flee towns and countries where they are the minority for towns and countries where they will be the majority.

But instead of moving away with his family or letting his son be taught to believe in God by the parish priest while the rest of the boy's classmates were being taught by the local *hodja,* Dragan's father, my grandfather Franjo, told the teacher that since he did not want his son to be separated from the other children the boy might as well go with them to Islamic religious classes. It was an unusual but not unlawful request, and no one had anything against it.

That was how Dragan completed all four years of the *mekteb,* the Muslim primary school, and so even though he had been christened a Catholic, he knew the rules of Muslim prayer from a tender age and firsthand. It made him no less of what he was ethnically or religiously, but it did distinguish him from others of his faith and nation. The important thing here is not so much that he finished the *mekteb,* as that he came from a family that was prepared to send their child there because they did not want him to be left sitting alone in his classroom, deprived of what the school and the place gave all the other children.

The difference, however, lies not in a multinational versus a more homogeneous society, but in the attitude to differences. We can revel in hatred and use it to shape our identity, or we can live without it. If we do not hate, then we necessarily look to others and they necessarily become part of our identity. Otata Karlo knew that when he refused to go to Germany, because other kinds of Germans lived there. How would he communicate with them, how would they understand one another, how could a German like him live in Germany except in conflict and opposition?

In my novels and stories, I have written about my great-grandfather, the Banat German and his family, about my uncle who died an enemy soldier, about my grandparents who sent him to that enemy army, and about other important and not so important figures from my childhood. I mixed fact and fiction, brought them to life and extended their lives. I have told their stories many times in many places and forms. Even the story I am telling now, which unfortunately allows for no inventions, has already been told several times before. I cannot detach myself from it and I cannot let my uncle, whose grave has long since disappeared in the grass of a village cemetery somewhere in Slavonia, lie among millions of Hitler's soldiers. He is a part of my identity, of the guilty conscience that is passed on from one generation to the next, just as I add to my own national identity. I am such and such a Croat, apart from being such and such a person. Collective national and even religious identity often is not encapsulated in a name. Often, to be a Catholic goes against the widely held notion and identity of Catholics.

I thought that after the death of Franjo Tudjman and the implosion of the nationalist oligarchy in Croatia, the differences between us would, with time, fade, and that my notoriety among the national elite would simply disappear into the mists of the past, evaporate, like all other hatreds which had started evaporating with the end of the war. After all, this was a time when Croatia had started to clasp to its bosom dissidents from the nineties, honoring them with national decorations and attestations of exemplary patriotic conduct. Nationalistic pathos turned into the pathos of collective Europeanization, which might be just as irritating but at least is easier to live with. Flying next to the Croatian flag now is the flag of the European Union, even though Croatia is not a member. Perhaps this, too, is a reflection of some kind of colonial allegiance, a fragmented, schizophrenic identity, or maybe it is just that there are three flagpoles in front of every public institution and it would be silly to fly a flag on only one of them. The three flagpoles date from the days when the Yugoslav flag was flown from the middle pole, with the Croatian and Communist Party flags flanking it on either side. Today, the European flag flies next to the Croatian, and on the third flagpole is usually the contrived flag of some town or county . . .

But flags do not determine our lives. Yesterday's banner of nationalism may be today's flag of freedom. And vice versa. Just look at how much the importance of the American flag has changed in the five or six years of the Bush administration. My older uncle wrote a postcard to my aunt in Sarajevo, saying: "It's Sunday, a day off, the camp-ground is deserted, the German flag is flying. We sold ours." Though not entirely clear, this was his only political statement. After the war, the surviving members of his family could console themselves with these words, though actually they do not mean very much. We are people who do not really know which flag is ours. Those who did know also knew that hatred is sweetest when indulged under a flag. Why else would flags be waved so fervently at soccer games or at the Olympics? Our flags are there to humiliate the losers more than to celebrate the winners. Everybody knows it. The best-known Croatian soccer song says: "Tough luck, go rot, Croatia's the world title got." Why would anybody have to go and rot just because Croatia is world champion? Anybody who even asks such a question is probably not a true-blue Croat.

A year after the fall of nationalist rule, during the coalition government led by Social Democrat Ivica Račan, whose Europeanism brought a sigh of relief to all of Europe, including Croatia's first neighbors, I was at a film festival in Istria held in a small ancient hilltop town once almost entirely inhabited by Italians, who, when Istria became part of Yugoslavia, were given a choice by the Communists to either become Italian or stay Yugoslav and so, with suitcases in hand, they left, only to spend years in Italian refugee camps, never to see their Istrian homes again—well, this festival in this little town was a kind of cultural but also social and political testimonial to a new, anti-nationalist Croatia. It was attended, of course, by the new minister of culture, dubbed the "Croatian Malraux" by his supporters and sidekicks, a title he readily accepted since in Croatia, and generally in the former Yugoslavia and the Balkans, it is both customary and desirable to call one's top figures after famous foreigners, be it Franz Beckenbauer, Emperor Haile Selassie, or Shakespeare, it doesn't matter. Our minister of culture, this Croatian Malraux, had previously worked as a lexicographer, in other words he had mostly lazed about, or, having dealt with the couple of lexicographical entries placed on his desk that day, gone off to some coffeehouse to indulge in intellectual debate. I did not like the way he ran the ministry, and I had written a newspaper article to that effect, one that, admittedly, wasn't kind, but was far kinder than what I had written about Tudjman's nationalists.

The article was far from my mind that afternoon when I walked up to the café table where, seated in the shade of the huge Slav tree was a collection of film directors, producers, and general practitioner intellectuals, along with Minister Malraux. I knew these people, the minister included, and merely wanted to say hello the way I would on any day.

"Beat it, you piece of Bosnian garbage, go back to where you came from or we'll pack you off ourselves!" cried Malraux.

I wasn't too angry because the minister was obviously still recovering from a long and busy night, which had left him with a hangover well into the afternoon. Still, I stopped and stared at the famous director, who had been blacklisted in Tudjman's day and his films banned from television. He had been a major dissident, almost like Kundera if not more so. The man lowered his eyes and said nothing. He had to be careful around the hung-over minister because he wanted to make another movie and in Croatia that meant getting money from the state. The producer, too, lowered his eyes, this young man of promise, this fighter against all forms of nationalism and apologist for love among nations, and then one by one, so did the others, all dissidents from Tudjman's time, until I, having stood there waiting too long, turned on my heel and, to the shouts of the Croatian Malraux, walked away, down the Istrian hill.

I went, and am still, a happy man, because unlike Otata Karlo, I was not taken away by two men with a third prodding me in the kidney. That is the important nuance in our identities and because of it we live where we do, although we are not part of the majority. Happiness keeps us here and happiness, I am deeply convinced, has often cost us our lives. At peace with what we are, and with a sense of what we are not, we represent identities that no word, no passport, no identity card or permit can define. The masses know what they are from their coat of arms, flag, and name, and they chant it, while we are left with our long, confusing explanations, novels, and movies, stories both fictional and not, the need to visit a village in Romanian Banat where there are no more Germans but where the horizon has not changed since Otata Karlo was a boy, we are left with deserted little towns in Bulgaria, Ukraine, Poland, inhabited by people who quite literally went up in smoke, we are left with blurred memories, the feeling that we are one thing today and another tomorrow, that our hymns and state borders keep slipping away from us, we are left with remorse, a long and painful sense of guilt because our relative lived and died as an enemy and that makes us somewhat of an enemy ourselves, we are left with faith in what we hide behind our language, with the truth that our homeland is no more, and maybe never even existed, because for us every inch of land is a foreign country.

Translated by Christina P. Zorić

History of the Other

Ismail Kadare

1

There is a lot of talk about the Other nowadays. And, as so often happens when old themes and conversations are rehashed after a phase of oblivion, we tend to believe that it—the Other one—is the object of our attention for the first time.

In actual fact, all of the fuss and focus on the Other likely goes way back. It is no doubt just as old as human sexuality, fear, and death. The history of the Other probably began one day when a caveman returned horror-struck to his companions, reporting that he had seen something awful, something amazing, something that left him speechless. His fellow cavemen burst out: "What was it? *Qu'est-ce que c'était ça? Shto eto bylo? Was war es? Ç'ështe ajo?* Who's there? Stand, and reveal yourself!"

Primitive man was not particularly good at articulating his experiences in words. He had not seen a bolt of lightning, a wild beast, or a volcano, but something worse: a being that was like him, but was not him, with a body that was similar to his and of the same origin. But instead of attracting him, it became something that he profoundly feared, abhorred, and rejected.

For the first time, caveman found himself face to face with the Other. The interrogations continued in the cavern. Explanations were demanded, questions asked, replies awaited. "Show yourself! *Halte et explique toi! Stoy i obyavis! Steh und gib dich kund! Qëndro e shfaqu.* Stand, and reveal yourself!"

2

That episode goes so far back into history that we ought best mirror it with the following incident that took place one evening on June 22, 1602.

It was a premiere at the Globe Theatre in London, and the audience teemed to see the tale of a certain Hamlet who was about to slay his father in revenge. Not entirely new material, it must be said. It had already been performed on stage two or three times. The house was full, and indeed all of London was ablaze with rumors and gossip, just as it was every time performances like these were given. "Another of those tedious stories! Same old stuff. No, quite the contrary! This one is different. It's a masterpiece. It takes place at the Royal Court of Denmark. The author has changed all the names to avoid any diplomatic repercussions. I've heard that it begins with a ghost. Really? I love ghosts. No, I can't stand them, and my wife will be hysterical. She is very high-strung, you know."

The audience could barely wait for the performance to begin. And so it did, and was just as had been rumored. It was a foggy night out on the walls of the fortress of the King of Denmark. A silent watchman was on duty. Someone approaches in the mist, and the famous exchange takes place between the soldiers:

"Who's there? Nay, answer me: Stand, and reveal yourself!"

Much has been said and written about the opening scene of Shakespeare's *Hamlet*. Many scholars believe that the tense atmosphere and the harsh tone of the suspicious guards were designed to underline the fear that had spread through Denmark with the appearance of the king's ghost. Other experts have been surprised that such a masterpiece of world theater should have such a banal beginning—a simple exchange between sentinels. T. S. Eliot held that this was done on purpose. The grave tone of the line was to prepare the audience for the appearance of the ghost.

The exchange between the two sentinels is not unlike the one that took place two million years ago at the entrance to the cavern. The ghost about to enter the scene is essentially the same one that we love to discuss today: the Other. And his appearance is indeed "otherly." Nothing on earth could be more otherly and unnerving for human beings than the ghost of a dead man. Its skin, its hair, its eyes, the length of its arms and legs, its movements, its voice, its silence—everything is different. But this is only the start. It goes much deeper than this, from outward appearance to the very core of its being. The ghost is otherly because of its dual nature; it is both dead and alive at the same time. But it is different in many other ways, too. For example: in the knowledge it possesses, in its view of the world, in the enigmas it unravels, in the messages it conveys. In short, it is otherly in every sense of the word. It knows what we do not know, it sees what we do not see. It appears in the real world but looks unreal to many, or it appears in an unreal world that looks real.

At any rate, it looks dangerous, both when it seemingly comes to our assistance and when it looms with threats and wrath. The ghost of Hamlet's father on the parapets of the castle of Elsinor seems to appear in order to demand justice, to compensate for crimes committed. But in the final analysis, all that remains is a tally of murders and a pile of bodies.

Are we to believe it? This is Hamlet's big question, and ours, too. Thus we witness the call of one of the sentinels: "Stand, and reveal yourself!" It is our desperate appeal, our fear at the very start of the drama. "Do not hide from us any longer, reveal yourself!"

<h1 style="text-align:center">3</h1>

People are not indifferent to the ghost of the Other, and never have been. They may be petrified at seeing a snake or a tiger or when experiencing an earthquake, but never when confronted with their own image. Sirens sound when rivers overflow their banks or when wild animals are on the loose, but this is nothing compared to the real alarm expressed for something bearing man's image. People are better armed and prepared for this type of encounter than for anything else. They made themselves ready with long tales, books, music, symbols, walls, gates, and, more than anything else, weapons. Armies were deployed at borders; spies crept deep into enemy territory; sentinels held watch in lofty towers, ready to cry out: "Stand, and reveal yourself!"

When being instructed in the history of their country, schoolchildren have to learn all sorts of things: the dates of important events and the names of famous heroes as well as fair but faithless damsels. They learn and learn until, in the end, they discover that the spice of the dough in which this history is kneaded is the Other. Without it, the songs of their heroes would be boring, their victories shallow, and their celebrations meaningless. In brief: were it not for him, our lives would be pale, bungled, and senseless.

Wretched columns of prisoners of war marching, heads bowed, past their victors; the flags and banners of the foe seized with the soldiers and taken as trophies; vanquished commanders and kings shuffling by in shackles—all of these are unforgettable images of victory in battle.

The annals of history have recorded one curious war—that between the Hittites and the Hurrites. The main problem was not fighting the enemy, but finding him in the desert. The Hittite army set out, but of its return—if there was one—we know nothing. Nor do we know what occurred in that desert—who won and who lost. What was particularly disturbing at the time was that the Other was not to be found. He simply vanished in the desert, in contradiction to the laws of nature. They at least wanted to see their foe, to touch him, and have a go at him.

To avoid the Hittite-Hurrite problem—or let us say, the sheer disappointment—the Communist countries took pains to make the Other known and evident in their propaganda, films, and plays. They organized witch hunts and trials with living foes so that the Other would be present and visible in flesh and blood. Reveal yourself!

To stage the unmasking of the Other as effectively as possible, everyone had to await their downfall with great anticipation. In Communist terminology, this was called "holding high the revolutionary spirit"—in effect, fomenting unflagging hatred, fanning the flames to annihilate the Other.

To achieve this, the image of the Other was never allowed to be forgotten or questioned.

In other words, the Other—the source of all conflict and war—was ubiquitous. It was in our skin, in our language (barbarian, as the Greeks would say), in our religion, and in our ideas, doctrines, and civilization. The virus of its discord penetrated where one would least expect it—into our own families and political clans, tarnishing and destroying blood ties. It even managed to achieve the impossible: to infect the love between two human beings. This was perhaps its greatest victory.

4

There is something tragic, something fatal in this state of things. To put it simply, can there be an answer to the question: "Why such hatred, why so many wars, why does everything else lead to exhaustion and subside except for it?" The question may seem rather naive.

We believe that, with the passing of the centuries, humankind has acquired a certain degree of wisdom. And one could have hoped, now that the evil has been recognized, that it would look back at the foibles of the past with contempt and venture forth to a better future. But exactly the opposite has taken place before our very eyes. We see that humankind has stooped to such a level of folly that, as Karl Popper would say, it reminds us of two parties brandishing thousands and thousands of atomic weapons in their hands. Popper described them as two duelists who have come, armed not with a pistol to shoot the Other, but with five thousand pistols.

In view of the current state of things that has not changed at all as I write these lines, we have no right to regard such a question as naive.

But let us continue. Could all of this have been avoided? Where was the mistake? Is there hope that something could change?

War has been interpreted as the continuation of politics by other means, and politics is said to be a continuation of economics, and so on. Then there was the discourse on the dark side of human nature. Our world, with everything that takes place in it, is being observed through the lenses of billions and billions of cameras—that is, through the eyes and in the minds of billions of human beings. In other words, every human being has a geography and history of his own—a routine that he observes day and night, every minute and every hour. And these billions of individual visions, these billions of essences of the Other, offer a potential for catastrophe on a cosmic scale.

We must be careful with thought patterns that go beyond the capacities that nature has bestowed on our brains. We must return to a clearer vision of things dictated to us by our own human condition—that is, by our limitations. In this situation, we cannot avoid the simple question: "Is there hope that something could change?"

Of course there is. However nebulous the ghost on the parapets of Hamlet's castle was, those who saw it or imagined they saw it—the sentinels, the companions of the prince, even Prince Hamlet himself—dared to cry out: "Stand, and reveal yourself!"

This should be the focus of our discussions here at this forum on the Other. But let us return safely to the annals of history, where things perhaps took their start.

In the beginning, the records of history were ocular, if one may say so. It was the eye that was startled or frightened by the appearance of the Other, firstly by the color of his skin and then by everything else. The human eye is closely linked to the ear. It was the language of the Other that disturbed the ancient Greeks. They had no hesitation in calling it barbaric, and barbaric were the people who spoke it. Then that most eminent and, at the same time, most dangerous part of the human body, took over: the brain. It was disturbed not only by the skin and language of the Other, but by things that could not be seen by eyes or heard by ears—by the tales within it, its myths, beliefs, customs, memories, and fears. It was not only race and language that defined the Other. It was something more, something equally dramatic, something that escalated and attained the tragic. Whole nations were set on collision courses. Their customs and doctrines clashed, as did finally their civilizations.

What began with eyes and ears went much further than one would have expected.

5

It cannot be said that humankind was indifferent to the danger. In one way or another, if not directly then indirectly, it strove to find antidotes. The search for criteria to define the Other was an attempt to hold back evil. Beyond appearance and language, which made the Other easily recognizable in a primitive sort of way, people began searching for something more profound, something deeper in the body. And many nations, independent of one another, began to concentrate their attention on blood. It is not particularly clear why the distinction was made in something that, in itself, shows no distinction—something that is in fact quite the opposite. To look for a distinguishing feature where it is masterfully concealed could be regarded as a probe into evil or, possibly, as a questioning of the very evil intent within.

Blood has always fascinated human beings. As a result, much symbolic, mythical, and often fatal significance has been attached to it. The earliest interpretations of it can be seen in the first primitive models, full of fantasy, of future genetics. It was a twist of fate that made the ancient Greeks, for example, understand that blood that had left the human body could never return to it (quite true until the invention of transfusions). Their inability to get blood back into the body was interpreted symbolically as the irreversibility of fate in general.

Another such twist was what were called blood ties, which, according to our ancestors, explained affection among members of a family, a tribe, or a whole clan. It was no great leap from here to the concept of the purity or impurity of blood and all the repercussions this concept spurred, and then to the "taking of blood." Herein, too, lies the origin of repentance and the guilty conscience, emotions dealt with so masterfully in Greek tragedy.

Treating blood as an element of identification, as a sort of identity card for a tribe, clan, or whole nation, had two tragic consequences: firstly, crimes committed in the name of purity of blood, and secondly, crimes committed in vendetta, or blood feuding. We encounter both consequences in Homeric verse and even more evidently in Greek theater. But in the following centuries, the Greeks would be surpassed by far, and in the Holocaust carried out against European Jews in the mid-twentieth century, matters would reach their zenith.

6

The chronicle of the Other was to need, and, it seems, will always need new sustenance. The fear of the ancient Hittites not to be able to find the Hurrites has been repeated over and over in the chronicles of history. It is a fact that if the Other did not exist, he would have to be found, have to be invented.

Civil wars involving parties looking the same, speaking the same language, cherishing the same customs and, although hard to prove, having the same blood, were just as savage, or more so, than other wars. Divergent ideas always sufficed to stir up hatred and bloodletting. Religious beliefs, too.

A curious connection arose between blood and doctrinal ties. Although the Nazis were fascinated by the mysticism of blood, as long as it was directed against the Jews and other peoples considered undesirable in their eyes, they did not hesitate to trample on this ideal when it came to attesting to their loyalty to Nazi doctrine and to the Führer. Communist dictators, for their part, rivaled one another in betraying their own relatives in the name of Party loyalty. A whole lofty wall of propaganda surrounded the new socialist family, artistically fashioned by a never-ending stream of films, poems, and plays of a demonic age.

Although the horrors are lamented time and again, nothing stops them from being repeated. Never in the history of mankind has there been more research devoted to combating the Other, to inventing and devising shields and weapons.

The old question, posed at the entrance to the cavern, is repeated again and again.

7

"A specter is haunting Europe, the specter of communism." With these words begins the *Communist Manifesto* of Marx and Engels. One is reminded of the beginning of *Hamlet*. Just as the sentinels in the Danish castle once did, many people at the time of the publication of the manifesto certainly wondered: "What is this specter? This ghost?" And then a second question followed: "Why has it come? What is its message?"

Hamlet's ghost rose to denounce a crime and, of course, to seek revenge. The *Communist Manifesto* also denounced a crime and called for revolution—in other words, for revenge. This time, the crime and the revolution that was called for to punish it were of a global nature. The revenge, as one could imagine, was to be appalling.

Events unfolded as predicted. They are part of the history of the Other and constitute one of the most somber periods in the annals of mankind: millions of victims, prisons, torture, and endless anguish. Not too long ago, after much deliberation, the Council of Europe called on the former Communist countries to denounce the crimes committed under communism. For years now, opinions on this subject have clashed, even when the Communist empires still existed.

At that time, in particular after the death of Stalin, a certain consensus was reached to explain away the tragedies that had taken place. The formula that was used was designed to appease and placate. It was more of a justification than anything. Stalin was made the guilty party. In other words, communism was in essence just and fair, but had been degraded and ruined. Stalin was the one with blood on his hands, and Lenin remained on his pedestal.

No one was actually relieved by this explanation, in particular when the full truth was revealed and it was discovered that Stalin had merely been acting on orders from Lenin. The latter was the root of the evil, for he had been as brutal as his successor and perhaps more ruthless.

The formula was altered. Now both were the bad guys, and Trotsky, too, whom they had purged and eliminated. With them in the boat were their successors, big and small: Mao Zedong, Nicolae Ceaușescu, Walter Ulbricht, Enver Hoxha, and Fidel Castro, among others. Marx however was left untouched, a consolation.

If we were to paraphrase the first sentence of the *Communist Manifesto*, we might say that a question is haunting Europe. Will the guilt ever reach Marx himself? Composure, impartiality, and levelheadedness are required for an answer. As proponents of the world of letters, we writers, more than others, may be permitted the freedom to search for literary analogies, especially in view of the fact that, at the start of his *Communist Manifesto*, Marx seems to allude to Shakespeare's ghost. The latter appears on the parapets of the Danish castle to convey a message, and Marx appeared before the fortresses of Europe to proclaim the specter of communism. The messages and programs are similar. A crime is denounced; injustice must be done away with. A crime was committed by the bourgeoisie against the working peoples of the world and consequently revenge must be had—the overthrow of the bourgeoisie and the installation of the dictatorship of the proletariat.

This is the essence. It is now easier to answer the question as to whether the roots of communism were guilty in themselves or merely the leaves of the plant when they began to discolor.

The age-old question as to whether we should believe a message brought by a ghost (any ghost that appears before us) can be answered clearly in the case of Marx. His analysis of capital—that is, his investigation of the crime—is precise and convincing. But this is where the problem begins.

The medieval ghost that appeared in the Danish castle to persuade Hamlet to take revenge (and at the same time to overthrow the usurper, etc., etc.) added one condition. It demanded that he exercise restraint in his vengeance.

The concept is not a new one. It derives neither from Shakespeare, nor from Saxo Grammaticus, upon whom the playwright relied for his material, nor from the Icelandic sagas, upon which Saxo Grammaticus relied. The concept is as old as the world itself. Show restraint! Do not go overboard in your vengeance. This maxim can be found in the oral literature, legends, customary law, and poetic chronicles of most of the peoples on earth. It is implicit in the Homeric epics, the ancient Greek tragedies, even in the roots of Greek civilization (the gods of Olympus punished the Greeks when they went too far in their vengeance against the Trojans). It is one of the most progressive concepts the human race has ever produced.

Is it possible that Karl Marx, who spent his whole life involved in the overthrow of the bourgeoisie and its replacement by the dictatorship of the proletariat, could have been unaware of this maxim? Should he not have suspected that this great upheaval—the most fundamental in the history of mankind—would be accompanied by rivers of blood, by devastation, horror, and vengeance as had never been seen before on this planet?

We can safely assume that Marx was aware of this, just as was any uneducated singer of epic songs or any grandmother rocking her grandchildren to sleep with fairy tales. It is by no means a nasty insinuation, but simply a logical conclusion that Marx knew this very well. But he preferred to shut his eyes and let the havoc be wreaked.

There are a couple of paragraphs somewhere in Marx's work where he does deal with the "issue" (excessive violence), but they make things worse instead of better. They are incredibly naive, to say the least. It is easy to see that these paragraphs were added to wash his hands of the matter, in the manner of Pontius Pilate. Here he simply asks the working class to show some restraint in their exercise of vengeance. But the request is spurious. Marx suggested that the proletariat should not exert its rage on the dozen or so billionaires occupying key positions in the capitalist world, but should send them off to spend their remaining days as pensioners on a desert island.

It is difficult not to ask the question: "Mr. Marx, were you really so naive as not to know that when the capitalist world was overthrown, it was not simply a dozen or so billionaires who fell victim to wrath and vengeance, but millions of officials serving that social order: endless courtiers, bankers, judges, clergymen, merchants, policemen, civil servants, farmers, artists, soldiers, pimps, and scoundrels?" This is exactly what happened in all the Communist countries where tens of millions of people were snuffed out by the vehement hurricane of class struggle.

Karl Marx should not have devoted simply a couple of obscure and rarely read paragraphs—but the core of his work—to what the Danish ghost demanded. What he ought to have written was a "Second Manifesto" to begin as follows: "A specter of retaliation is haunting Europe, that of the victory of communism, the specter of unbridled revenge."

With this second proclamation, Karl Marx would not have held back all the crimes to come, but he could at least have saved some of the people from the fury of blind revenge.

The history of the Other would then have been quite different.

Translated by Robert Elsie and Janice Mathie-Heck

A Simple Truth

Fatos Kongoli

THE SUBJECT THAT HAS BEEN PROPOSED IS ONE ABOUT WHICH MANY PEO-
ple have written, without the final word ever having been said. One feels
uneasy about it. One is small and powerless to change anything, excluded
from the game in which other, mightier participants have long set the pace.
In our region of the world, old and new enmities have always surfaced and
there is nothing for it but to fear the worst.

Is this a fatality that we must simply accept? What would happen if
NATO and the international community were to withdraw from the
region? Would there be a new bloodbath? Will the peoples of the region
ever understand one another? Will they feel hatred forever, always waiting
for an opportunity to lunge at the others' throats?

The answer I wish to give to these questions is: no! It is for this reason,
despite a certain pessimism that I cannot deny, that I decided to contribute
to this anthology. It is a platform for me to communicate with colleagues
from the other countries of southeastern Europe in the hope that this dialogue will not be restricted simply to us.

"Southeastern Europe," as far as I am aware, is synonymous with "the
Balkans," both terms being used to describe the countries of the peninsula.
The complexities and confusion already begin here. For example, it is due
to the bad reputation that the Balkans have brought with them from history—the "comic opera penned in blood"—that the Hungarians, despite
their traditional ties to the region, refuse to call their land a Balkan country.
Indeed, if you want to insult a Romanian, all you need to do is tell him that
he is from the Balkans. The only reason the Slovenes did not object to being
classified as Balkan in the early 1990s was the prospect of receiving financial assistance from the West. It then became more acceptable to speak of
southeastern Europe as "the Balkans, together with Hungary." Or "the Balkans, together with Hungary, together with Romania." The central Balkans,
the folk museum of Europe, contained the others. Albania belonged to this
group, That was certain.

However, contemporary political realities are quite different. The political map of southeastern Europe has become much smaller. Greece was always part of a united Europe. Slovenia and Hungary joined later, and then came Romania and Bulgaria. As a result, the political map of the remaining part, the core of the Balkans, has shrunk. Those who managed to change their status and get into the great European family are rightfully happy about it. They have achieved their objective of being called "Europeans."

This is a subject of its own—the satisfaction and sense of superiority felt by those who are now part of the great European family, contrasting—may I venture to state without wishing to insult anyone who regards the term as inappropriate—with a sense of inferiority on the part of those who are still in the Balkans, which are, as we know, both part of Europe and not Europe at all.

Let us be frank. Being part of a united Europe in the early years of the third millennium means being a member of one of the richest clubs on the planet. However, the rest of the countries that want to get away from the political Balkans as quickly as possible and join the club with its blue flags will not necessarily be miraculously endowed with prosperity the day after their accession. But one thing is sure. Countries that are accepted into the club will from then on be living in a region of peace, freedom, and democracy. It was in 1998 that I first crossed an open border. I was staying at the Marguerite Yourcenar Writers' Residence in the northeast of France, and the Belgian border was only about ten minutes away. It was an overwhelming experience for me. No border checks, no customs officials, and, most of all, no weapons to be seen. As the citizen of a deeply traumatized country in the blood-drenched Balkans, after half a century of absolute isolation from the rest of the world, it was almost unbelievable. Why could it not be like this in our part of Europe, too? I wondered naively. Would the time ever come in southeastern Europe when borders would cease to be hurdles and impediments, between which the reciprocal wrath of nations and peoples infects like wounds?

Though much has improved in the Balkans in terms of mentality, and there have been many fundamental changes in a positive direction compared to even the recent past, I still suspect that we have not yet reached our destination, and many challenges await us on our way. We are full of prejudices in a reality in which our past is holding our present and our future hostage. The geographical borders are probably the least of our problems. More of a burden are the borders within ourselves. It is hard for us to suppress the barriers in our minds that exclude other peoples.

A few years ago—I believe it was in 2001—I had the pleasure of meeting a certain S.K., a Greek professor who lived in Brussels. We were together at a workshop held in the southern Albanian town of Saranda. I cannot remember exactly what the workshop was about, but it was concerned with language and national identity.

I had accepted the invitation more for personal than for educative reasons. I had not been to Saranda, the pearl of the Albanian Riviera, for years. I noticed S.K. out on the hotel terrace having coffee before the start of the workshop. He was a short, stubby fellow with a balding head and was dressed in a sand-colored suit with no tie. I thought I recognized his face, and that he was an Albanian.

The participants at the workshop were all well educated, and came from a variety of countries. I studied the program during the opening speech in the auditorium and noted that I was the only writer among all the scholars, historians, and linguists. I thus felt a little out of my element, listening to the lectures, one after another. Most of the guests read from their papers with a good deal of solemnity, imposed no doubt by the importance and the seemingly sacred character of the subject matter. Perhaps for this reason more of the participants were in suits and ties. I felt a bit awkward in my jeans and jacket.

I had in fact just come back from a conference of Balkan writers in Thessaloniki in Greece. All participants there had received a questionnaire with four standard questions on it. The first question was: "Do you think, with your writing, that you are serving your national identity?" This was quite a normal question under the circumstances, but because it was so simply worded, I was unsure of myself and set it aside. The second question was: "Do you think that all writers from the region have a common Balkan identity?" This question made me feel more awkward, because I had never really thought about the matter. I went on to the third question: "What, in your opinion, is the difference between writing history and writing literature?" I did not have to reflect long on this one. I scrawled on the photocopy: "Works of history by reputable and objective scholars—and not by individuals with manipulative agendas—if well written, give me the same pleasure as an action-packed novel." The main difference between history and literature, in my view, is in the way the material is dealt with. One is a science; the other is not. To put it briefly: the subject matter of literature is humankind. I was reminded of Maxim Gorky's saying that literature was a net in which the human soul was caught up. The subject matter of history is quite different from this. It is not interested in people as beings, in the human soul, although it can be misused to exert influence on people and their souls, just as in literature. On this point there was a similarity. They had a common effect, both positive and negative.

After the fall of the Berlin Wall and the collapse of the Eastern European dictatorships one after the other (Albania was at the very end of the line in 1992), public debate resumed with new vigor and within the new reality on a number of themes, such as the concept of the nation and its historical destiny, identity, crises of identity for the individual and societies, and national identity. Media outlets around the world continue to devote much of their time to these topics.

As a simple newspaper reader, these discussions and debates caught my attention. In the course of time, they left a bitter taste in my mouth in our new democratic era. I am not referring here to historical objectivities, interpretations of events, scholarly precision, or other such aspects about which I don't feel qualified to pass judgment. I am referring rather to pedantic teachers who cannot abstract themselves from the subject matter they have taught all their lives and who are caught up in a vicious circle of arguments. No more good can be expected of them today than yesterday. They crouch in the same trenches and shoot off shells with the same clichés and stereotypes as in the past. Their tone is often malicious, with an unmistakable twinge of mockery toward their neighbors. And one thing is particularly worrisome. Their "patriotic" writings were, and still are, well received by their readers.

I do not wish to dwell any longer on this prevalent phenomenon in our region, but do wish to focus somewhat on the region itself. What I find shocking is the fact that communities under certain circumstances—and the Balkan countries are eloquent examples of this—tend to crucify and even physically annihilate anyone daring to slaughter their "sacred cows"—anyone who endeavors to uncover the bitter truth or to find solutions that conflict with traditionally accepted beliefs. Under pressure from certain forces such as politics and the media, these communities often do not even notice that those sacred values have lost their meaning and have disintegrated into empty phrases to be misused in power struggles and for the agendas of certain groups or individuals. They are waved in front of these communities like banners on a battlefield, at a time when freedom and democracy in the countries of the Western Balkans are still very fragile—not to speak of all the other problems they face. Unemployment, corruption, and human trafficking are ubiquitous. Most people live in poverty in this region, and they are receptive to such themes, which are propagated by devious-minded individuals.

Such were my thoughts in Saranda as I studied the grave expressions on the faces of those taking part in the workshop.

In Thessaloniki I had answered the question as to whether my writing was serving the cause of national identity with "no." The only identity I was serving with my writing was my own. Perhaps. Actually, when composing a text, I only think about the writing. My answer came spontaneously. It was only later that I began to reflect on why I had said that, so please bear with me and allow me to explain.

I come from a small town in central Albania called Elbasan. With regard to my roots, I feel a strong sense of identity with that place. Unfortunately I spent very little time in Elbasan because, when I was three years old, my family moved to Tirana where I have lived ever since. This is where I feel at home. As such, my identity is also Tirana. And, of course, I am also Albanian. However, I do not believe that one's roots are a sufficient interpretation of one's identity. Identity goes much deeper. It penetrates an individual and surrounds him. We are talking about cultural roots that provide sustenance one's whole life long from rich sources that go far beyond one's origins. The identity of an individual is not carved in stone once and for all. It is constantly being formed, adapted, and enriched at different levels, all of which intertwine to create a "European identity," or to venture even further, that of a citizen of the world. All this is part of my identity, though I am not aware of this when I am writing.

As to the second question about the common identity of all Balkan writers, my reply, as far as I can remember, proved to be somewhat vague and ambivalent. It would have been interesting to present my thoughts to the participants at the gathering in Saranda. After all, we had come together to discuss issues of national languages and national minorities, though I was—as usual—not at all sure where my thoughts would lead me. The noted scholars, all with solid opinions and views, would no doubt have given me clear answers to my questions if I had had a chance to pose them. Alas, the solemn academic surroundings frightened me off. I felt like a first-year elementary school pupil seated before a pedantic teacher and was afraid of being misunderstood or of being suspected of "cosmopolitanism." In the meantime, an unexpected dispute arose between the Greek professor and his Albanian colleague. The latter had cautiously raised the issue of the nonrecognition of national minorities by our southern neighbor, Greece, and its refusal to provide education in their mother tongues—in particular for the hundreds of thousands of Albanian immigrants living and working in Greece. Professor S.K. replied in impeccable French and in an appropriately scholarly tone: the northern neighbor, Albania, has been called upon by the Charter of the Council of Europe to do more for the education of the Greeks—a minority in Albania—in their mother tongue.

The Albanians unfortunately suffer from a historical prejudice concerning the Greeks, and the Greeks no doubt feel the same about the Albanians. At all times and on all continents there have been people who, to put it mildly, have held negative views of one another, and this will certainly go on for some time. The peoples of the Balkans are often accused of an inclination to savagery. I do not really believe that the atrocities committed in the Balkans, including the bloody wars that resulted from the disintegration of Yugoslavia, were more brutal than atrocities committed by other peoples in other regions under similar circumstances. The well-known Bulgarian professor Maria Todorova, in her book *Imagining the Balkans,* quotes an American journalist as follows: "The notion of killing people . . . because of something that may have happened in 1495 is unthinkable in the Western world. Not in the Balkans."

I am not sure how true this assertion is. At any rate, it brings us inevitably to a concept, the controversial nature of which has been noted by many research experts: memory. Individual and collective memory. The memory of a nation. Living memory, kept up by individuals and passed on orally. And what one could call "extinct memory," found in books, that plays a long-term role for literature and for historiography.

The reply of S.K. reminded me of the writer Nikos Kazantzakis, one of the greatest Greek writers of the twentieth century, whom I greatly admire. I first had contact with his books in the 1980s. His novels were a fascinating discovery, in particular *Freedom or Death* (*Captain Michalis*), the first of his books that I read. It was at that time that the dictatorship in Albania was at its worst. We lived in absolute isolation, a society hermetically sealed off from the rest of the world. We were told that we were surrounded by foes and that we were living in an oasis of bliss under siege. The novels of Kazantzakis first gave me insight into the nature and characteristics of the Greeks, in particular of the peasants in the countryside, and I found an astounding parallel to the Albanians with their extremely sensitive and explosive temperament. I could go on about this, but to be brief, after the workshop session, something else moved me to go over and talk to Professor S.K. about the role of history and literature in the memory of a nation.

We are introduced to the protagonist, Captain Michalis, at the very start of *Freedom or Death*. We are in 1889, on the eve of yet another Greek uprising in Crete against centuries of Ottoman rule. The author succeeds masterfully in conveying the atmosphere of the era. The first time I read his prose (and I couldn't put the book down), I remember encountering the phrase: "God is not an Albanian. . . . He is an Orthodox Christian and will give me back my rights someday." I was very surprised by these words, which Kazantzakis had put into the mouth of one of the characters.

Indeed, I felt insulted. My first thought was to put the book aside. Into the depths of my indoctrinated brain flashed the word "anti-Albanian," a term used quite often in the official propaganda of the time. But it was such a beautiful, masterfully written book that I obeyed an inner voice which told me to finish the novel despite the "anti-Albanian" phrase in it. I was curious, and there were more surprises to come. The Albanians had committed crimes against the Greeks, too. The book described terrible atrocities carried out by Albanian soldiers in the Ottoman army against the people of Crete. That explained to me why the Albanians were objects of hatred for the protagonist of the novel. Yet, this was all in such contrast to my identity, my education, to everything I had learned as a child, and later from books. It was carved into my skull that Albania and the Albanians were the victims par excellence of hundreds of years of injustice committed by others. They had been subjected to five centuries of Ottoman rule and had then fallen prey to their rapacious neighbors, the Greeks included. It was difficult for me to admit that there was another side to the coin. This other side of the coin was reflected in Greek memory, in the above-mentioned words uttered by Kazantzakis's protagonist.

This is what it is all about, the other side of the coin. Everyone in the Balkans tends to see only the side he wishes to see, the pleasant side. Or the side that he is shown.

Albania was the last Balkan country to achieve independence, doing so in 1912. The preceding fifty years, the second half of the nineteenth century, known as the Rilindja period of national revival, had been full of patriotic ideals and lofty nationalist feelings. The great figures of the age—the Rilindja thinkers, philosophers, great poets—some of whom served as high government officials in the Ottoman administration—glorified their homeland and the virtues of the Albanian race, and for quite understandable reasons, actually. Their Albania was a blessed land whose inhabitants, as descendants of the Illyrians, were proud of their ancient traditions and of the fact that, under the leadership of the legendary George Castriota, known as Skanderbeg, they withstood the advance of the Ottoman hordes for a quarter of a century. Because of their geographical position as a bridgehead between East and West, the Albanian people struggled and sacrificed for the West and for Christianity. Destiny was always cruel with them. I must note at this juncture that this view holds true throughout the Balkans. All of the Balkan countries regard themselves as bridgeheads between East and West. Their legendary heroes all defended the West, and they deserved a better fate than that accorded to them by history. It's the same song everywhere.

It must be realized here that the cult of the nation, which was understandable and justifiable in late nineteenth-century Albania, was perfected by the Communist regime that lasted almost half a century. This concept was taken to the extreme, as was ethnocentricity in Albanian historiography, as many scholars have noted. The machinery that was put into place proved to be extremely effective, and the regime managed to plant collective thinking and Party ideology into people's minds. Seen from this perspective, Albania was a typical nationalist-Communist dictatorship, if I may call it thus. On the one hand, it played with people's patriotic feelings and fanned the flames of xenophobia, making of any foreigner a potential foe. On the other hand, the level of self-adulation that was reached in the country was grotesque.

But now back to the other side of the coin. I read recently that there is a new field of research called *imagology* dealing with literary images of the Other. I was not aware of this discipline in the 1980s, but I myself had some very clear and definite views of "other" nations. The earliest views with which I was inculcated were some rather silly stereotypes about the Turks:

Zot i madhe e i vërtetë,
Çdo gjë e bëre vetë,
Kur bëre derr' dhe arinë,
Ç'deshe që bëre Turqinë?

Oh true God and Lord Almighty,
Who yourself the world did fashion,
When you'd formed the bears and swine,
Why did you need to make Turkey?

I hope I have quoted this stanza of a *Rilindja* poet correctly. I had to learn it by heart as a schoolchild. It has remained in the recesses of my brain, and further elements were added to this derogatory picture of Turkey over the years. The day-to-day political propaganda was not even a major factor. For a number of reasons that I cannot delve into here, the regime itself was not anti-Turkish, primarily because, in my view, Albania did not have a common border with Turkey. The negative image of Turkey was implanted in me primarily by traditional and contemporary literature and the arts—novels, plays, poetry, paintings, and film. Even today, I find it difficult to extract myself from it.

In the northern regions of Albania there were, and still are, strong feelings against Serbia and the Serbs. They are called *shqa* or *shkia,* a word which can have a ring of contempt to it. This negative view is a direct result of the border and the historical complications that arose on and around it. It was primarily connected with Kosovo, and with the fate of the Albanians of Kosovo. In literature, this anti-Serb image finds its foremost expression in the poetic works of Father Gjergj Fishta, one of the greatest traditional poets of Albania, who for reasons I do not wish to delve into here either, was strangely banned during the Communist regime. Yet his works were known. They were read and discreetly discussed at different levels of Albanian society. I would venture to state that any Albanian who has read Fishta, and in particular his greatest work, *The Highland Lute,* is not at ease when meeting Serbs, whom the Albanians traditionally viewed as nothing more than "rabid dogs to be exterminated." I met my first Serb in 1998. It took other encounters and years for me to get used to the idea that we were friends—of course, in a personal and not diplomatic usage of the word.

With the exception of the northern parts of Albania, the negative image of Serbia and the Serbs is relatively limited as far as I can see. During the Communist dictatorship we used to listen to and watch Italian radio and television stations at home, and we found subtle, covert ways and means of receiving them. But we also had access to Yugoslav radio and television, despite the frightening images that the words "Yugoslavia" and "Yugoslav" conveyed. On holidays at the beach I often heard fellow vacationers listening to Serbian music on their transistor radios, with the volume up. Nowadays, Serbian and Slavic music are nothing unusual, and contacts with Serbia, the Serbs, and our other Slavic neighbors are on the increase. Everything is relative. I cannot accept the theory that hatred is inbred in people. It is nonetheless true that it is imbibed at an early age, like breast milk, and is passed on from one generation to the next. The question arises as to how we can protect future generations from this hatred, to prevent them from seeing the other side as "rabid dogs to be exterminated." In this connection, let me return once again to Professor S.K.

During the first break in the proceedings of the workshop, I met him on the terrace overlooking the sea, and the waiter brought us coffee. The professor was intrigued when I mentioned that I was a writer and that one of my books had just been published in Greece. He told me about an anthology for children that he intended to publish with texts by writers from all of the Balkan countries, and he wanted me to recommend a couple of

Albanian authors. We both believed that such publications were of great significance because they helped peoples get to know one another better and to overcome historical misunderstandings—all the myths and legends contained in myriads of books and works of art from all ages. This led me to tell him something curious.

I related that in the first Albanian-language edition of Kazantzakis's *Freedom or Death,* the phrase "God is not an Albanian" was missing. Even today, I am unable to explain why the Communist rulers of the time expunged whole passages from the book. Did they want to spare the reader the embarrassment? Or did they not want people to get a glimpse of the other side of the coin?

Professor S.K. was startled, but not because an author like Kazantzakis had been the object of censorship. In a dictatorship, everything was banned that contradicted the politics of the regime or that did not fit into the ideological framework of such a closed society that conceived the world in terms of them and us. He could not remember the passage and even doubted that it existed, although he admitted that it had been many years since he had read the novel. I maintained my position and insisted that I had read the passage in question in the French edition, and he promised to investigate the matter as soon as he got back to Brussels. About a week later I actually received a phone call from him. He explained that he had compared the Greek original with the French translation for the passage "God is not an Albanian." It turned out that it was a translation error. The original version said: "God is not an *Arvanite.*" I had to laugh. The Arvanites are Greeks who speak Albanian because they are the descendents of the Albanians who had migrated in waves to Greece and who had settled there several centuries ago, like the Arbëresh in southern Italy. I did not have to explain this to the professor. He was obviously better informed about the Arvanites than I. It was no matter of great importance, but I found my reaction to the French edition and the censored Albanian edition a bit embarrassing. It was obviously not that easy to free oneself of the term "anti-Albanian" which had been so ubiquitous in official propaganda in those years.

But times change and so does everything else, as they say. Can one assert that people's thinking has changed along with the evolution of the political regime and its values? Not necessarily. Let us take a look, for example, at what the younger generation is now studying in history and which texts of traditional literature they are required to read in school. It is evident that curricula are in urgent need of revision—not to paint an unduly rosy picture of the reality of our relations with our neighbors—but to free our children from the spirit of hostility, hatred, and contempt.

Balkan societies, to a greater and lesser extent, are all still closed and are rocked in the cradles and in the romantic myths of their pasts. Anything that does not suit our side of the coin is unacceptable, hostile, and against the interests of our country. It is more than evident that it is difficult for two individuals from different ethnic groups to find a common denominator. Their minds are stuffed with the "heroic deeds" of their ancestors and of recent sufferings caused by others. If we posit that both sides are now consciously aware of the crimes committed by their own people, we can assume that they will reach a pragmatic conclusion: What benefit do we have in accepting our own guilt? The role of "victim" is much more comfortable. We are the victims, and they are the guilty ones. The psychology behind this is eminently human. It reflects the fact that the past is still very much present in the Balkans. Paradoxically, this psychology often assumes the role of the present in the name of the future, and it takes both the present and the future hostage.

The reactions of the two aforementioned individuals reflect collective convictions, although I would not say that they reflect the attitude of the nation as a whole. It is hard nowadays to find homogeneous nations with one single unified culture and language. Compact, homogeneous nations are a thing of the past. Most now encompass a multitude of ethnic groups, languages, and cultures. Many problems in the Balkans would be easier to solve if this fact were realized.

Allow me at this juncture to present an oversimplified argument. As long as Balkan history lurks among us, can these two individuals ever find a common denominator? If we assume that, under certain conditions, they are representatives of collective thinking, an agreement reached between them would mean an agreement between their two ethnic groups, and, going farther up the chain, agreement in the thinking of the two countries concerned. Keeping with my oversimplified argument, conciliation between two individuals and consequently between two ethnic groups would, however, require compromise on both sides. Each side must be willing to forget something. To forget the past, or at least part of it.

There is much talk nowadays about forgetting, about amnesia, and as one can imagine, there are widely differing views. Some recall the well-known statement of George Santayana, who said: "Those who do not remember the past are condemned to repeat it." Others think quite the opposite—that it is dangerous to linger in the past all the time because you are simply recycling the same views—whereas forgetting, that "subtle form of forgiveness," as a one-time ETA militant in Spain put it, is future-oriented.

The resulting question is: are we capable of freeing ourselves from the past if, from cradle to grave, we are only shown one side of the coin? The naive answer to this would be: if you want to make a reasonably informed decision, take a look at the other side! If we could do so, logic would perhaps reign. Memory and forgetting, past and present, could be brought into balance without the one taking the other hostage. But how can people learn to respect what they find on the other side of the coin, to accept things that are completely foreign to them, or about which they have a one-sided or completely distorted view?

There is not an easy solution. The only way forward is to explain the truth. We must set aside reciprocal fears and reservations. In this connection, I would like to refer to an event that took place not so long ago on the eighty-eighth anniversary of the armistice that ended the First World War and which was seen on television screens throughout Europe. Of the millions of soldiers who fought in the trenches of that great slaughter, only about fifty are still alive. During the celebrations, two survivors, a 107-year-old Englishman and a 105-year-old German, met in comradeship. Ninety years earlier they were enemies entrenched on the two sides of the front. They would not have imagined after all the bloodletting that they would one day meet and embrace as two old friends. On this occasion, a 106-year-old Frenchman was moved to declare on camera that the whole war had been completely senseless.

This, in my view, is the only lesson to be learned. Will we have to wait another hundred years in the Balkans to comprehend this simple truth?

Translated by Robert Elsie and Janice Mathie-Heck

Strolling by the River

Maruša Krese

We are not the biggest, we are not the most powerful,
but we can be the best . . .
—*Janez Janša, prime minister of Slovenia (2006)*

I moved to a city,
a long river flows through the city.
The river reminds me of my city.

Perhaps this river will burn,
perhaps it has burned away in my city.

How often has it really been in my lifetime that I have stood here, on this 1920s bridge in the center of Ljubljana, in the middle of the capital of "my country," and looked into the Ljubljanica, the river flowing toward the sea? But the river sometimes gets adventurous and seeps away somewhere, and halfway along its path to the sea it reappears under another name, seeps away once again, and flows under a third name into the sea . . .

And today, as always when I return to Ljubljana, I'm standing once again on this bridge in the center of the city. It's basically made up of three bridges built at the beginning of the twentieth century by the architect Jože Plečnik, the hero of the Slovenian people. Incidentally, Slovenian authorities and church leaders are pulling out all the stops at the moment to have the pope in Rome at least beatify him, if he cannot canonize him immediately.

Today. "Today" on this bridge almost always means "yesterday" on this bridge. A yesterday indescribably filled with memories. I've twisted and turned them around in recent years, my memories, in every conceivable way to get rid of them, but each time I come across a new story about "my country," "yesterday" once again grows powerful.

Yesterday: it means for example an incident in the seventies when I surreptitiously "borrowed" Marx and Engels's *Das Kapital* from my father, and my friends and I folded some pages into paper ships in the middle of the night and dispatched them from the bridge in the direction of the sea. Anxiety-filled nightmares persecuted me for years afterward because I was afraid my father might ask me about the book. He never did.

Yesterday: it means we used to sit on the bridge late at night planning a revolution (God knows which) and expect a new miracle to happen, and if no terrific transformations arrived as a result, then at least there'd be a little joint and a farewell to friends who were taking off for India. Many simply stayed in Istanbul, many in Kabul . . . Yesterday: time and again we'd demonstrate against something or other; we published a student newspaper, and before every edition was distributed we'd pray to God (although we were all eager atheists, but you never know) that it would be confiscated so we could quickly be promoted to national heroes. "Heroes" were of course an everlasting problem for the postwar generation. Our fate was that we were born too late, and so we were filled with envy toward our parents, who had the good luck to have defended their homeland in the Second World War. We were continually making the effort in all sorts of different ways to set even higher goals and become the new heroes. It was tough, since we had to be infinitely grateful to the old heroes at the same time because they had made our "prosperity" possible. Nonetheless and anyhow, we were forever conspiring to find new ways to outsmart them.

Much later, when I told my friends in Germany about our sixties, they were surprised and asked why we were fighting anyway, because after all, we did have communism and this "wonderful" self-administration; that's how I suddenly realized I didn't even know what the "significant thing" really was that we were demanding at the time on the streets of Ljubljana. I simply couldn't remember, until my sister took me to her boyfriend a couple of weeks ago, a former photographer and reporter who revealed his photographic treasures to us.

The time of the partisans, the time of Yugoslav brotherliness and unity, the sixties, Tito's funeral, the new Slovenian state and, and, and . . . Among all these photos I found one taken during the occupation of the Philosophical

Faculty in Ljubljana . . . A giant banner with a red star was mounted on the building: "For the Fight Against Communism, For Communism!" That, too, was yesterday . . .

How long ago that was—"For the Fight Against Communism, For Communism!" Should I laugh? Should I cry? Should I be furious?

> Memory deceives me.
> Memory likes to deceive.
> Memory likes to put it into old stories.

> We travel on the sea
> in tiny nutshells,
> memory replacing the wind.

I wend my way from the bridge to the marketplace, another design of Plečnik's, the Slovenian "giant." A visit to the Ljubljana market is worth it, especially on Saturdays. It, too, has its yesterday and today. You used to be able to stroll among literally mountains of peppers, tomatoes, and watermelons from Macedonia, Bosnia, Serbia, Dalmatia, and Kosovo; in the fall mountains of plums, figs, and grapes on the above-mentioned Saturdays would still tower up on the display tables. But the market stands of today have lost their particular appeal because they look like stands in any other European city or, more accurately, any other EU city. The only thing of interest there is a certain wine restaurant, mostly on the above-mentioned Saturdays, let's say going on noon. That's because elite Slovenian journalists and intellectuals get together there after shopping and have a glass, and if you're lucky you'll even find the former president of "my country," Milan Kučan, there. It's only at the marketplace that you see those journalists and intellectuals belonging to the "powerful" who have been able, according to the Slovenian prime minister (J.J. for short), to make the foreign press their "tool"—just as Slovenian journalists under communism had been the "tool" of their foreign colleagues. J.J. knows all too well how that sort of thing works—after all, he himself had been an exemplary exponent of the Communist Party in Yugoslav days and in fact a reasonable student of the military, who'd occasionally taught pre-military education in schools.

In a word, he is of the opinion that the foreign press is at the mercy of Slovenian manipulators and that it reports too much on the negative aspects of the beautiful country of Slovenia instead of all the good ones. J.J. has made futile attempts to accrue power over the media to himself; with a new radio and television law; replacing heads of publishing houses and newspapers; threats against various businesses if they advertise in the left-leaning media—but in all these efforts he forgot about the power of the wine restaurant in the Ljubljana marketplace.

Now on Saturdays in the marketplace you can find out a whole lot about what's new. That's probably why the circulation of the biggest Slovenian daily papers has dropped so much. A few good people were let go. The rest of the journalists turned to self-censorship and stayed away from the wine restaurant. If a written reprimand came from the European Commission on Human Rights in Strasbourg or the State Department in Washington, they spent hours trying to find somewhere in that document a positive message for Slovenia in spite of all its negative statements, rather than simply publishing it with all the points listed in it: the unregulated status of the Roma minority and minorities in general; a media scene under government control; the ombudsman's admonitions regarding human rights that the government ignored; the excessive use of police violence; the perfunctory processing of applications for asylum; violence against women; discrimination against Gypsies and homosexuals; discrimination against the "erased," the inhabitants of Slovenia from former Yugoslav republics who no longer had any rights as citizens of the state. If they didn't trust their own whitewashing, the usual disclaimer followed: "This has been written by people with no knowledge of the situation in Slovenia." At the same time, they completely lost sight of the fact that there was a marketplace where anybody could easily discover the truth. Maybe that's the reason the new municipal administration would like to put an underground garage below the market area and cripple the merry goings-on for a couple of years?

If you leave the restaurant and return to the bridge, you go past the fish market. A fish market—today? And automatically your memory recalls the quarrel between Croatian and Slovenian neighbors. The quarrel among fishermen over qualitatively high-grade and low-grade fish recalls the maritime border between Croatia and Slovenia; access to international waters that the state next door denies to "our people"; the border with Istria and the eternal "it's mine" and "that's yours"; politicians having innumerable meetings and then a signing and shouts of jubilation because finally an agreement had been reached—but it turns out that both sides have (mis)understood the agreement each in its own way and the Slovenian government advises its citizens under no circumstances to spend their summer

on the Croatian coast ... But what are you supposed to do when there's
so little left of the *Slovenian* sea ... And the Italians, who accuse Yugoslav
partisans of murdering off countless of their citizens ... And the Croatian
president is indignant, and the Italian president tries to act as an interme-
diary to say that it wasn't the Croats who were meant but other Yugoslavs,
and these other Yugoslavs, the Slovenians, keep silent. So what? Japanese
and Norwegian fish are for sale in the fish market, and the Slovenian foreign minister, who continually threatens not to support our neighbor's
intention to join the EU, takes his vacation on the Slovenian coast.

Immediately next to the bridge, the three bridges, and near the Franciscan
church, stands the monument to the great Slovenian poet France Prešeren.
We learned his poems by heart in school and listened to his songs, his
ill-fated love, and his poem "Zdravljica" (Drinking Song) was chosen as the
national anthem of the new state. "Let us lift our glasses!" The rock band
Laibach—German for Ljubljana—is touring the whole world right now
and singing "*Hej Slovenija . . . for the spirit of our fathers, for the glory of our
sons, for the power of the Specter . . . for the glory of our sons . . .*" Homeland,
fatherland, people, mother tongue, earth, yours, mine. At the foot of the
great poet's monument—that's where you can sit down with young people, among tourists, the homeless, newspaper vendors ... You sit and watch
mothers with strollers, carefree youth who don't even know what Yugoslavia was, and if they do, they think it's something funny, dark, and thank
God it fell apart in the dim distant past. I watch passersby at the foot of
the great poet's monument and reflect on memories I'm trying to forget,
about the impoverished language of today, I reflect ... I reflect too much
... Sometimes it seems as if I've been set back a whole century; that's how it
actually appears to me every time I'm in the city.

I hear more talk in the city about the new church law that I really don't
understand all that well; I only know people were shocked because the Catholic Church is growing more powerful and the major share of their assets
was already restored to them after 1991, at least one-third of Slovenia itself.

Every now and then there's a gentle attempt made to prevent women from
having an abortion, but that's when even men are on the women's side. I
remember a moderator at a women's conference in Brussels who asked me
the question journalists from the old EU states always ask me anyway: "Are
you happy to be in the EU? Are things definitely better for you now?" How
am I to explain that my children and me, who live in the West, are so often

seized by longing for Ljubljana? I took them to kindergarten in Ljubljana in the morning and to school and went to work; I picked them up in the afternoon, and then our time was our own, only for us . . . How am I supposed to explain to those journalists that it never would have entered my head at the time that I was having a harder time of it because I came into the world as a woman? Things didn't change until I went to America: then I almost turned into a new Clara Zetkin. How am I to explain to them that we've lost what we had and will have to fight for it all over again? Fight? The Slovenian birthrate is said to be declining rapidly, which is why a clear majority wants to send women back to the kitchen, to the cradle. Let's hope it'll not come to witch hunts again.

I hear in the city about a mysterious government commission that is supposed to supervise the Slovenian Secret Service, and the whole country is puzzling over who's going to be pilloried next. Maybe the president of the state, who recently liked to make all sorts of trouble for the government, probably having forgotten that he himself had been in the government not so long ago. He cares about healthy lives and intellectual enlightenment, for world peace, and he lays his hands in blessing on the citizens. He pays a visit to the UN secretary-general in New York but then keeps the topics of conversation to himself.

I hear talk in the city about the new mayor of Ljubljana, who comes from Serbia and is one of the wealthiest Slovenes; about the millions the government has cut that Ljubljana was supposed to receive; and about the new mayor, who's now in a sweat because he knows that he won't be able to keep close to keeping his promise to the voters. First he cut money for alternative and social groups and media, thereby unintentionally doing the government a favor by so elegantly ridding it of all those troublemakers.

In this city I don't really know anymore whether I should laugh or cry. Sometimes I can manage to observe things from a distance, and then I can laugh—the way I used to laugh in the eighties when Slovenian writers suddenly began with all their might to look for a king and to describe the heavy Iron Curtain we lived behind. I've been afraid ever since to laugh about anything of the kind because I know it can all suddenly change into brutal truth.

I hear in the city about the new ombudsman—she's the new defender of human rights—who holds it against her predecessor that he sent reports of

Slovenian social injustices beyond our borders. She said she certainly would not do a thing like that! Because we Slovenes can work everything out so beautifully among ourselves! And the former human rights ombudsman, whom I still know from the bridge back then in the sixties, left the battlefield completely exhausted and ill. He didn't want to run again because he felt like a dying man in the wilderness. The government accused him of lack of loyalty and indiscretions, and he informed the public about the government's modus operandi. The Roma and the "erased" looked upon him as one of their own. When sentries were posted in villages almost everywhere in Slovenia because a Roma family was going around the countryside and nobody wanted to take them in, the ombudsman reported that the police duly noted who came in contact with the family: which politicians, which journalists, which social workers. And the public prosecutor's office protested that the police had not done anything illegal, because all this was done solely to protect the Roma family. Until the erased went off to Brussels to ask for help . . .

I hear talk in the city of whatever's happening. The current regime . . . the former regime . . . the party on the left . . . the party on the right . . . the Secret Service, the police, the ombudsman, the mosque, the city without a stadium . . . What am I really concerned about—the Left? . . . the Right? . . . Because every time I return to the city many people who were still leftist until recently have become rightist. The reverse seems to be less frequent . . . And every time I return to the city and go to buy a newspaper, I get slapped on the wrist because I don't know that this paper is being boycotted at the moment . . . And every time I return to the city, I'm hauled over the coals because I don't know who our friends are at the moment . . . the Croats or the Serbs . . . I know we were on good terms with the Kosovo Albanians earlier . . . And every time I return, it's with a heavy heart . . .

I've spent the last few years in Graz and Berlin. Let's say that I'm a writer and a journalist, and my little problem is that I still write for the most part in my mother tongue. A mother tongue that is understood by precisely two million people around the world, including my three children. And the mere fact that I write in Slovenian tells me that I've never truly left the Balkans, that I've never truly left Ljubljana, that it was only when I thought I'd really left that I began to think about my Balkan roots—not the Slovenian ones, because we Slovenes constantly try to deny the Balkans, to deny kindred souls and old friendships to the southeast of us.

* * *

Or let's take the statement of the Slovenian head of the government, J.J., who received a prize for it last year: "We are not the biggest, we are not the most powerful, but we can be the best." But we're trying all the time to show the populations of our brother republics that we are the best. And if they ultimately decide to point a finger at a very real abuse, we quickly recover and make the excuse that that was in former times.

When I return to the city I'm soon scared by my own emotionalism, by my own language. Not so long ago I met a young journalist from Sarajevo in the city. I knew him from the war. He was an editor with Radio Zid in Sarajevo, organized rock concerts in the middle of a furious war, and tried to deliver to the citizens of the occupied city the latest news from all over the world. He kept up the morale of a whole group of young people in Sarajevo so that they wouldn't give up and try at any cost to flee the city. He had come to the city because Slovenian TV had made a film about a Sarajevo tunnel that was supposedly better thought through than the tunnel under the Berlin Wall. He had to wait a long time in front of the Slovenian embassy in Sarajevo until he finally got a three-day visa for Slovenia with the help of a letter of guarantee. "Ljubljana is a true Mecca," he said, and I blushed. Now he's editor in chief of a large broadcasting station with state radio. "I would so like to send my young journalists out into the world. They know nothing besides their wounded city. But we fought for an urbane Bosnia, didn't we? And what have we got now?" An urban center, young people, EU visas that are impossible to come by. This is the United Europe that is celebrated time and again.

Young people in Macedonia make a pilgrimage en masse to Orthodox monasteries and turn to God; young people in Serbia and Montenegro are happy now because they've been cleared of genocide in Bosnia by the International Court of Justice in The Hague, and the Rolling Stones have announced they're giving concerts in Budva and Belgrade this summer. Young Slovenes travel to the former brotherly republics the way we used to travel to Calcutta and Kabul. What's in store for the Balkans? Don't even ask!

A friend phones from Belgrade who had sent her son to London during the worst time of all, where he of course couldn't stand it and had come back home. "He'll squander everything. That blockhead," she says. But she can understand him. "Shouldn't we both just stop talking about tanks, courts, war, criminals and browse through Jane Austen or Keats instead? What are you reading these days?" What have I been reading since the horror in the

Balkans began? Seven hundred pages of a diary from Siberia, diaries from Belgrade and Sarajevo . . . Sometimes poems by Emily Dickinson . . . When I went to Sarajevo during the war I stopped reading her and didn't even go to the movies anymore. Everything turned so pale, so transparent, so distant from real life. From their lives and in many a moment even from mine. "What's new in literature? In Germany, in England . . ." A yearning for life could be sensed at the other end of the line, the old curiosity that's dried up in me over the past few years. It's so embarrassing.

It was exactly that embarrassing when I met a friend from Sarajevo at the foot of the monument near the bridge there, beneath the weeping willows by the river. "I just knew you'd want to meet here underneath the weeping willows," and she wickedly recited a poem by our great Slovenian poet: "*O, Vrba, draga vas domača* (O, Vrba, beloved native village . . .)." I blushed. I never did know it by heart. "How nice you people have it here!" she sighed. We're having a coffee that absolutely must be Illy coffee. "I'd like most of all to stay here, you all look so contented. Young people sitting by the river in the sun and planning their lives. You'd have to come back to Sarajevo to understand what I'm talking about." I look at her. Her tired eyes. "The sun's shining," I say. "Probably in Sarajevo, too, at least for today."

We slowly leave the river. We walk past the monument, the Franciscan Church, parliament. I still remember when the building was under construction because my school was exactly opposite it. "I remember pictures on TV," my friend says, "when Slovenes bid farewell to Tito. And I remember the first Slovenian president, Kučan, proclaiming the new Slovenian state in a speech. We were so afraid in Sarajevo. But we never would have thought we'd also end up like this." And I automatically think of Sarajevo television and the comedies it broadcast in the eighties: the people of Sarajevo are eating grass and wake up one day to find a wall in the middle of their city. In the real world, somewhere up in Northern Europe, people in Berlin are tearing down a wall. We'll switch roles, I thought back then. "You know, people in many homes in Ljubljana still have photos or busts of Tito in their attic," I say, remembering how pictures of Tito were hung up in houses in Sarajevo for almost the whole length of the war. It was precisely those who suffered most who stayed loyal to him the longest. "We've got to hurry," I say. "A wind's been blowing through the door of parliament recently that seems to me to be a breath of neo-Stalinism." She laughs and says, "Just be careful that nobody hears you . . ."

* * *

A few more steps and we stop at the Tomb of the National Heroes of the Second World War. Before the tomb: a candle and three red carnations. Whenever I walk past here I check to see if it's still standing. Because these heroes haven't been heroes for a long time now . . . We Slovenes are rather ashamed of them because we believe that's what's proper in today's Europe. We try with might and main to find heroes among the Slovenian fascists, and innumerable books have been published in the last fifteen years about the War of Liberation that lasted ten days—about the ten-day war that stands for the onset of horror in the Balkans. We're constantly rooting around in the earth on the Austrian and Italian borders, collecting and counting bones, and it gradually looks to me that there are more excavated skeletons of partisan victims than there ever were Slovenes at the time.

I'm standing in front of the Heroes' Tomb, and I see the picture of the head of the government Janez Janša . . . "We are not the biggest, we are not the most powerful, but we can be the best . . ."

And the singer in the rock band Laibach is on a European stage somewhere singing a made-up anthem: "*We stand alone in history, facing East in sacrifice. . . .*"

Translated by Gerald Chapple

Odrod

Charles Simic

As the curtain goes up, I'm sitting naked on the potty in my grandfather's backyard in a little village in Serbia. The year is 1940. I look happy. It's a nice summer day full of sunlight, although Hitler has already occupied most of Europe. I have no idea, of course, that he and Stalin are hatching an elaborate plot to make me an American poet. I love the neighbor's dog whose name is Toza. I run after him carrying my potty in my hand, wanting to pull his tail, but he won't let me.

What would I not give today to have a photograph of Toza! In his wise and sad eyes of a country mutt full of burrs and fleas, if we had known how to read them, we would have found the story of mine and my parents' lives.

I had a great-uncle of whom nothing is known. I don't even know his name, if I ever did. He came to America in the 1920s and never wrote home. Got rich, my relatives said. How do you know that? I asked. Nobody knew how they knew. They had heard rumors. Then the people who heard the rumors died. Today there's no one left to ask. My great-uncle was like one of those ants who, coming upon a line of marching ants, turns and goes in the opposite direction for reasons of his own.

Ants being ants, this is not supposed to happen, but it sometimes does, and no one knows why.

This mythical great-uncle interests me because I resemble him a bit. I, too, came to America and, for long stretches of time, neither remembered where I came from nor had any contact with my compatriots. I never understood the big deal they make about being born in one place rather than another when there are so many nice places in the world to call home. As it is, I was born in Belgrade in 1938 and spent fifteen eventful years there before leaving forever. I never missed it. When I try to tell that to my American friends, they don't believe me. They suspect me of concealing my homesickness because I cannot bear the pain. Allegedly, my nightmarish wartime memories have made me repress how much dear old Belgrade meant to me. My wartime memories may have been terrifying, but I had a happy childhood despite droning planes, deafening explosions, and people hung from lampposts. I mean, it's not like I knew better and dreamed of a life of quiet strolls with my parents along tree-lined boulevards or playing with other children in the park. No. I was three years old when the first bombs fell and old enough to be miserable when the war ended and I had to go to school.

The first person who told me about the evil in the world was my grandmother. She died in 1948, but I recall her vividly because she took care of me and my brother while my mother went to work. The poor woman had more sense than most people. She listened to Mussolini, Hitler, Stalin, and other lunatics on the radio and since she knew several languages, she understood the imbecilities they were saying. What upset her even more than their vile words were their cheering followers. I didn't realize it then, but she taught me a lesson that has stuck. Beware of the so-called great leaders and collective euphorias they excite. Many years later I wrote this poem about her:

Empires

My grandmother prophesied the end
Of your empires, O Fools!
She was ironing. The radio was on.
The earth trembled beneath our feet.

One of their heroes was giving a speech.
"Monster," she called him.
There were cheers and gun salutes for the monster.
"I could kill him with my bare hands,"
She announced to me.

There was no need to. They were all
Going to the devil any day now.
"Don't go blabbering about this to anyone,"
She warned me.
And pulled my ear to make sure I understood.

When people speak of the dark years after the war, they usually have in mind political oppression and hunger, but what I see are poorly lit streets with black windows and doorways as dark as the inside of a coffin. If the lone lightbulb one used to read by in bed late into the night died suddenly, it was not likely to be replaced soon. Every year, we had less and less light in our house and not much heat in winter. In the evening, we sat in our overcoats listening to the rumblings of each other's empty stomachs. When guests came, they didn't even bother to remove their hats and gloves. We would huddle close whispering about arrests, a neighbor being shot, another one disappearing. I wasn't supposed to hear any of this, in case I forgot myself in school and got everyone at home in trouble.

This is the first time I heard people say that we Serbs are numskulls. There was no disagreement. Who else among the nations in Europe was stupid enough to have a civil war while the Nazis were occupying them? We had the Communists, the Royalists, and at least a couple of factions of domestic fascists. Some collaborated with Germans and Italians and some did not, but they all fought each other and executed their political opponents. I didn't understand much of it at the time, but I recall the exasperation and anger of the grownups.

Of course, the mood was most likely different in other homes where they welcomed the Communists. We were, after all, members of a mummified, impoverished middle-class family that would have preferred that everything had remained the same. My mother and grandmother hated wars, distrusted national demagogues, and wanted the kind of government that left everybody alone.

In other words, they were the kind of people, as we were lectured in school, destined to be thrown on the garbage dump of history.

Occasionally, one of our visitors would start defending the Serbs. Our history is one of honor, heroic sacrifice, and endless suffering in defense of Europe against the Ottoman Empire for which we never got any thanks. We are gullible innocents who always think better of our neighbors than they deserve. We sided with England and America when the rest of Europe was already occupied by the Nazis and it was suicidal to go against them.

Yes, my grandmother would say, we did that because we are conceited fools with exaggerated notions of our historical importance. A rabble of thieving and dimwitted yokels who were happiest under the Turks when they had no freedom, no education, and no ambition, except to roast a suckling pig on some holiday.

"Mrs. Matijevic, how can you talk like that?" our visitors would object. My grandmother would just shrug her shoulders. Her husband was a military hero in World War I, a much-decorated colonel who had lost his enthusiasm for war. I recall being shocked when I first heard him say that Serbs should not have kicked out the government that signed the non-aggression pact with Hitler in 1941. Look what the war had brought us, he would say.

I wonder what my unknown great-uncle in America thought about all that? I bet he had his own ideas on the subject as he sat in some outhouse in Kansas or Texas reading in last month's papers how on March 27, 1941, the heroic Serbs walked the streets of Belgrade shouting "better death than a pact" while Hitler threw a fit. I reckon he must have tried to explain to his wife now and then about Serbs.

If she was an Apache, or a member of some other Native American tribe, she may have understood more quickly. Serbs are a large, quarrelsome tribe, he would have said, never as happy as when they are cutting each other's throats. A Serb from Bosnia has as much in common with a Serb from Belgrade as a Hopi Indian does with a Comanche. All together, they often act as if they have less sense than God gave a duck.

On second thought, he probably never brought up the subject. The Balkans, with its many nationalities and three different religions, is too complicated a place for anyone to explain, or begin to make sense of, especially since each ethnic group writes its history only remembering the wrongs done to them while conveniently passing over all the nasty things they've done to their neighbors over the centuries.

When I came to the United States in 1954, I discovered that the conversation among the immigrant Serbs my parents saw now and then was identical to the one I had heard in Belgrade. The cry was still, how did we who are so brave, so honorable, so innocent, end up like this? Because of traitors, of course. Serbs stabbing each other in the back. A nation of double-crossers, turncoats, Judases, snakes in the grass. Even worse were our big allies. England, America, and France screwed us royally. Didn't Churchill say to Eden at Yalta that he didn't give a fuck what happened to Yugoslavia after Communists take over?

Much of this was true. A few sleazy political deals by world leaders did contribute to our fate. We, displaced persons, were a living proof that the world is a cruel place if you happen to find yourself on the wrong side of history. Still, I didn't care for all that obsessive talk about betrayals and internal enemies. It reminded me too much of how the Communists back home talked.

"It's exhausting to be a Serb," my father would say after an evening like that. He was a cheerful pessimist. He loved life, but had no faith in the idea that the human condition was ameliorable. He had Chetnik sympathies at the beginning of the war, but no more. Nationalist claptrap left him cold. He was like his father, who used to shock family and friends by ridiculing Serbian national heroes. Both he and my father went to church and had genuine religious feelings, but they could not resist making fun of priests.

"There is nothing sacred for them," my mother would say when she got angry with the Simic family. Of course, she really wasn't any better. It's just that she preferred that appearances be kept. Her philosophy was, let the world think we believe in all that nonsense, and we'll keep our real views to ourselves.

After my parents separated in 1956, I left home. I attended university at night and worked during the day, first in Chicago and then in New York City. If someone asked me about my accent, I would say that I was born in Yugoslavia, and that would be the end of it. I saw my father frequently, but though he liked to reminisce about his youth in the old country he had an equal and even greater interest in America, and so did I.

It was only when we went to visit his brother Boris that the eternal subject of Serbian national destiny came up. Boris was a successful trucking company executive who lived in one of the posh Westchester suburbs, where he had a house, a wife, and three German shepherds. He loved to organize large dinner parties to which he'd invite his many Serbian friends, serve them fabulous food and wine, and then argue with them about politics till the next day.

Boris was a lefty in Yugoslavia, an admirer of the partisans, but as he grew older he became more and more conservative, suspecting even Nixon of having liberal tendencies. He had a quality of mind that I have often found in Serbian men. He could be intellectually brilliant one moment and unbelievably stupid the next. When someone pointed this out to him, he got mad. Never in my life had I heard so many original and idiotic things come out of the same mouth. He was never happier than when arguing. Even if one agreed with everything he said and admitted that black was white, he would find reasons to fight you. He needed opponents, endless drama with eruptions of anger, absurd accusations, and near fistfights. Boris, everyone who knew him said, would have made Mahatma Gandhi reach for a stick. Compromise for him was a sign of weakness rather than of good sense. He was not a bad man, just a hothead when it came to politics. He died before Milošević came to power, and I have wondered ever since what he would have made of him and his wars.

* * *

Listening to Boris and his pals endlessly rehash our national history, I assumed this was just immigrant talk, old water under the bridge. Like many others, I was under the impression that Yugoslavia was a thriving country not likely to fall apart even after Tito's death. I made two brief trips to Belgrade, one in 1972 and another in 1982, had heard about ethnic incidents, but continued to believe even when the rhetoric got more and more heated in the late 1980's, after the emergence of the first nationalist leaders, that reason would prevail in the end. I had no problem with cultural nationalism, but the kind which demands unquestioning solidarity with prejudices, self-deceptions, and paranoias of the collective, I loathed. I couldn't stand it in America, and even less in Serbia.

The few friends and relatives I had in Belgrade were telling me about the rise of a new leader, a national savior called Slobodan Milošević they all seemed to approve of. I started reading Belgrade papers and weeklies and having a huge monthly telephone bill trying to understand what was taking place. After more than forty years in America, I became a Serb again, except, as many would say, a bad Serb.

"We don't want to live with them anymore," friends would tell me. They wanted a complete separation from Croats and Bosnians and at the same time a Serbia that would include all the areas where Serbs have lived for centuries. When I pointed out that this could not be done without bloodshed, they got very upset with me since they were decent people who didn't approve of violence. They simply would not accept that the leaders and the policies they were so thrilled about were bound to lead to slaughter.

"How can you separate yourselves when you are all mixed together?" I would ask and not get a straight answer. I could recall the ethnic mixture we had in our neighborhood in Belgrade and could not imagine that someone would actually attempt to do something so wicked. Plus, I liked the mix. I spent most of my life translating poetry from every region of Yugoslavia, had some idea what their cultures were like, so I could not see any advantage of anyone living in a ghetto with just their own kind.

Of course, I was naive, I didn't realize the immense prestige inhumanity and brutality have among the nationalists. I also didn't grasp to what degree they are impervious to reason. To point out the inevitable consequences of their actions didn't make the slightest impression on them, since they refused to believe in cause and effect.

The infuriating aspect of every nationalism is that it doesn't understand that it is a mirror image of some other nationalism, and that most of its pronouncements have been heard in other places and in other times. Smug in their ethnocentricity, certain of their own superiority, indifferent to the cultural, religious, and political concerns of their neighbors, all they needed in 1990 was a leader to lead them into disaster.

How did I see what many others didn't? Or as the Serbs would say, what made me an *odrod* (renegade)?

The years of the Vietnam War focused my mind. It took me a while to appreciate the full extent of prevarication and sheer madness in our media and our political opinion and to see what our frothing patriots with their calls for indiscriminate slaughter were getting us into. The war deepened for me what was already a lifelong suspicion of all causes that turn a blind eye to the slaughter of the innocent.

"Go back to Russia," I recall someone shouting to the antiwar demonstrators in New York. So, it's like that, I recall thinking then. You opt for the sanctity of the individual and your fellow citizens immediately want to string you up. Even today our conservatives argue that we lost the war in Vietnam because the protesters undercut the military who were forced to fight with one hand tied behind their back. In other words, if we had gone ahead and killed four million Vietnamese instead of two million, we would have won that war.

Milošević struck me from the beginning as bad news. I said as much in an interview with a Serbian paper. This provoked a reaction. I was called a traitor in the pay of Serbia's enemies, and many other things. This only spurred me on.

After Vukovar, one didn't have to be Nostradamus to prophesy how badly it would all end for the Serbs. I wrote numerous pieces in Serbian and German newspapers arguing with the nationalists. Many others did the same in Serbia, and far more forcefully and eloquently than I did. We were in the minority. As is usually the case everywhere, a craven, corrupt intellectual class was unwilling to sound the alarm that war crimes were being committed, accustomed as they were under communism to being servants to power.

The belief in the independence of intellectuals, as so much of the twentieth century proves, is nothing but a fairy tale. The most repellent crimes in the former Yugoslavia had the enthusiastic support of people whose education and past accomplishments would lead one to believe that they would know better. Even poets of large talent and reputation found something to praise in the destruction of cities. If they wept, it was only for their own kind. Not once did they bother to stop and imagine what the cost of these wars their leaders had instigated was for everybody else.

*   *   *

Many of my compatriots were upset with me. Serbs always imagine elaborate conspiracies. For them every event is a sham behind which some hidden interest operates. The idea that my views were my own, the product of my sleepless nights and torments of my conscience, was unthinkable. There were innuendos about my family, hints that for years there were suspicions about us, that we were foreigners who had managed for centuries to pass themselves off as Serbs.

My favorite one was that the CIA had paid me huge amounts of money to write poems against Serbia, so that I now lived a life of leisure in a mansion in New Hampshire attended by numerous black servants.

Or even better, how I went to see Clinton to ask him to bomb Belgrade. He was just about to lower his pants for Monica Lewinsky when I barged into the Oval Office shouting, "Don't forget Majke Jevrosime Street!" To get rid of me, he called General Wesley Clark on the phone and gave him the order. And that, according to some, is the true story of why Belgrade was bombed.

Incapable of either statecraft or a formulation of legitimate national interest, all Milošević and his followers were good at was fanning hatred and setting neighbor against neighbor. We now know that all the supposedly spontaneous, patriotic military outfits that went to defend Serbs in Croatia and Bosnia were organized, armed, and controlled by his secret services.

There is nothing more disheartening than to watch, year after year, cities and villages destroyed, and people die or be sent into exile, knowing that their suffering did not have to happen. Once newspapers and weekly magazines became available on the Internet, I'd rise early every morning to read them and inevitably fall into darkest despair by eight o'clock.

Serbs often say in their defense that they were not the only ones committing war crimes. Of course not. If everyone else was an angel, there would not have been several hundred thousand refugees in Serbia today. Nonetheless, it is the murderers in one's own family that one has the moral obligation to deal with first.

This, as I discovered, is not how a patriot was supposed to feel. The role of the intellectual is to make excuses for the killers of women and children. As for journalists and political commentators, their function was to spread lies and then prove that these lies were truth. What instantly became clear to me is that I was being asked by my own people to become an accomplice in a crime by pretending to understand and forgive acts which I know are unforgivable.

It's not just Serbs who make such demands, of course. It is not much better in America today, but that, too, is not an excuse. The unwillingness to confront the past has made Serbia into a backpedaling society, unable to look at the present, much less deal with difficult contemporary problems. It's like a family that sits around the dinner table each evening pretending that Granny had not stabbed the mailman with scissors and Dad had not tried to rape one of his little girls in the bathroom just this afternoon.

The worst thing is to be right about one's own kind. For that you are never forgiven. Better to be wrong a hundred times! They'll explain it later by saying that you loved your people so much. Among the nationalists, we are more likely to be admired if we had been photographed slashing the throat of a child than marching against some war they had fought and lost.

When I went back to Belgrade in 1972, after an absence of almost twenty years, I discovered that the window above the entrance of the apartment building where I had kicked a ball through after the war was still broken. In 1982, it was still not repaired. Last fall, when I returned, I discovered it had been fixed after the NATO bombing which hit the TV studio close by and broke lots of windows in the neighborhood.

The reason it was not repaired earlier is that all the tenants in the building had quarreled and were not on speaking terms. My late aunt did not acknowledge the existence of some of her neighbors for forty years, so it was unthinkable that she would knock on their door for the sake of a window or many other things that needed to be done. That, to my mind, is pretty much the story of Serbs and Serbia—or so I intend to tell my great-uncle whom I still hope to run into one of these days.

He'll be more than a hundred years old, sitting in a rocking chair of a nursing home in rural Alabama, deaf and nearly blind, wearing a straw hat and a string tie over a Hawaiian shirt, but still looking like a Serb despite all the guises he devised in his long life not to look like one. From time to time, he mutters some words in that strange language which his nurses take to be just an old man's private gibberish. "All you ever need is a roof, a bowl of bean soup, and some pussy."

A True Story

Biljana Srbljanović

THIS IS A TRUE STORY. AT ANY RATE, THE MAN IN QUESTION HERE REALLY existed. He was tall and not particularly handsome and had black hair. Many people considered his profession important: he was a physicist. Or, rather, he was a biologist. A microbiologist. I would have preferred him to be, say, a fireman. Firemen are definitely interesting people who can tell many stories about putting out fires. But who still takes an interest nowadays in an altogether ordinary, lanky, black-haired and—to be honest—truly ugly fireman? Who would have been interested enough in an ugly fireman to pay for his economy class flight (sometimes even business class, when a weekend lay between departure and arrival, and once, even—to be sure, only because the moderately priced tickets had been sold out—first class with a then still flourishing Swissair, complete with a breakfast of croissants and a fresh omelet made with real eggs)—who, I ask, would have paid for the travel and accommodation (generally a night plus breakfast in a Best Western) of so unimportant a man if that man had been an ordinary fireman? One does that only for physicists or microbiologists, who travel a good deal in order to tell the people paying their travel expenses about important things.

This is also a story about travel.

The episode begins at the Munich airport, Section D; the goal was Section A. As everyone knows, the Munich airport was, even before it was renovated, one of the classiest European airports. It was built for the most part on a single level, and hundreds of meters lie between the gates; the staff has a perhaps not altogether undeserved reputation for failing to accommodate late passengers. That is why travelers run in Munich. As they do, they drag their luggage behind them like poodles, mainly little suitcases on wheels that, in their hurry to get somewhere, pile up on each other, topple over, get caught in legs, and tear up the stockings of their female owners and other pedestrians who are likewise running so fast that, at first, they do not even notice the collision.

The man in question here (we have agreed that he was a microbiologist, have we not?) ran, sweating and utterly distraught, from one end of the Munich airport to the other. He was looking for "A." He had come from a city outside the European Union in a Lufthansa airliner that had just touched down; he had waited long and impatiently in the line for people holding passports of an inferior sort; he had watched as the Western businessmen had just held their passports up to the border police and been promptly waved through, followed by the travelers whom his compatriots were only too happy to deride, but who were well on their way to becoming the newest members of the extended European family, although they were among the most backward representatives of the former Eastern bloc. Our hero stood in line and contemplated the backs of Romanians, Bulgarians, and Poles who were, to be sure, subjected to checks, yet were hardly delayed by them. He looked at their backs; he looked at the clock and saw that the time left him before his connecting flight was dwindling; he looked at an official in a gray uniform who was meticulously examining the numbers and letters in the passports of all these travelers in the long outsiders' line.

"To New York for a conference," was his prompt response to the expected question about his destination, when his turn finally came. "My plane's taking off in ten minutes," he said, in an effort to accelerate the procedure of scrupulously checking all the numbers and letters in his passport and, in particular, prevent the flat thumbnail from scratching its way over the hologram, which had not, after all, been designed for such treatment. The official didn't answer him. "An East German. They're the worst," was what he heard instead, though it was said very softly, behind his back. When he turned around, a disgusting Russian was standing in front of him and smiling. He was holding his daughter by the hand, a girl not yet ten in an exclusively Gucci outfit. The microbiologist of course had no idea that the top (300 euros), the widely flared pants (600 euros), the pointy gold shoes (350 euros) and the handbag (900 euros) were Gucci. *I'm* telling you that. *I* know that because I keep tabs on fashion. And prices. With an indescribable chain reaction of scorn for the man who had addressed him, he, in his turn, did not answer the Russian. He simply turned his gaze back on the policeman at the precise moment when the policeman scratched the middle of his biometrical visa with two fingernails. "What are you doing? You're ruining the hologram!" The microbiologist was becoming visibly nervous. "I'm running an authenticity check on your travel documents. Please stop interfering."

"You're not checking, you're scratching. Please! You're ruining my visa," the man said in despair. The policeman had been waiting for just such an outburst. Without looking at the despairing man, he simply pushed aside the passport that he had just been scratching around in and, with a wave of his hand, callously ordered him to step to one side.

Those were also his words: "Step to one side."

"I'm going to miss my flight!" Our hero was nearly in tears, but the policeman ignored him with a practiced and, I must admit, irritatingly self-satisfied expression. Once he had turned around, the microbiologist was utterly helpless. The Russian with the expensively dressed daughter had already pushed his two passports through the humiliatingly small opening at the counter. Our desperate hero watched and wondered where he was supposed to sleep that night. He was sure to miss his flight to New York; his low-cost ticket came with every possible restriction, including one that ruled out changing the dates of his flight; he didn't have a visa for Germany or any other party to the Schengen Treaty; the first plane that could bring him back home wasn't scheduled to take off until the following morning; and, all in all, he was in deep trouble. "*Nyuyork otshen krasivo osenyu.*" The Russian turned to him again and insisted, for some unfathomable reason, on communicating in these extraordinary circumstances. Our traveler was now at a total loss, understanding only that he had a stranger in front of him who was telling him how beautiful New York was in the fall, an impression the Russian had garnered while watching *Sex and the City* on TV. (Our man also didn't know the name of the series or what it was about. I'm telling you that; I have recordings of every last episode.) He did know one thing, however: he had a disgusting Russian in front of him—because, first, the man was speaking Russian; and, second, all Russians were disgusting; and, to boot, this particular Russian was not having any passport problems. "The weather's lovely and you can take pleasant, relaxing walks through the city," the creep said. Then he asked: "Have you ever been there?" Our man shook his head almost automatically, without really wanting to; the girl turned on her heel; and the Russian sighed. "I haven't, either. They don't give us visas."

Who ever said that travelers weren't brothers?

When the official had at last completed his unjustified inspection of the passport and almost indignantly handed it back to the microbiologist, it was just six minutes to takeoff: one could hear, as it were, the sharp crack of the starting shot. Our hero began running like crazy. (We ought gradually to get around to deciding on a name for him; the constant repetition of "man," "microbiologist" and—even sillier—"our hero" is tiring and, besides, what if all that were wrong? What if the man were not a real man

and possibly not even a microbiologist? What if he should turn out not
to be a hero? I don't mean to insinuate anything when I say that; simply,
if it happened to be true, this business could quickly get out of hand. A
name, then. Let's call him Vladimir—Vladimir, because I don't know a single striking Vladimir. Not a single Vladimir of my acquaintance enlivens
this name with striking traits that might divert my attention from the basic
character of the man I'm writing about here. If there does exist a Vladimir,
then it may be precisely the one I'm writing about, although I must admit
that he's been made up from top to toe. On the other hand, you know, after
all, that our—are we agreed, then?—Vladimir certainly existed, that there
can be no doubting his authenticity and that this is a true story.)

While we were settling on a name, about two and a half minutes went by
(not counting the time for reflection to which I, as a writer, am entitled),
and Vladimir used this time to race from Section D to Section A. Boarding
was nearly over and Vladimir would unquestionably have missed his flight
to New York if a man and a woman had not confused the airline company
staff. The staff members were monotonously repeating, "Have you checked
your baggage at the check-in counter?"

"Have you checked your bags at the check-in counter?"

"Have you checked your bags at the check-in counter?"

The man and his wife had checked their bags at the check-in counter;
that was also indicated on their ticket stub. The airline staff had discom-
bobulated the computer and were rather impolitely trying to solve the
problem in German, English, and French. Neither the man nor his wife,
who was wearing Turkish trousers, a man's long jacket, and a gaily colored headscarf, had a command of any of those languages. They did not
even understand which languages were involved, since these Lufthansa
employees' dreadful intonation made all the words sound the same, while
the native or artificially acquired deformation did not exactly help matters.
Vladimir arrived on the scene just when a homosexual employee was getting all worked up over his computer. (I infer that this employee was gay
from his hair, which had been dyed "Dusty Blond" after being bleached—
with a view to reproducing the shade of color printed on the box as closely
as possible—but also from his condescending attitude toward the man in
his frayed, peasant-style suit and his wife in her headscarf. That, in turn,
is not necessarily just the sign of a fashionably emancipated steward, but
may also be a point in favor of the airline company's policy. The ring on his
right hand nevertheless proves that the cliché, perhaps just because it *is* a
cliché, is right on the mark.) To his own surprise, Dusty Blond cleared up
the problem with the computer, found, in his database, the names of the

contentious passengers and the number of suitcases they had checked in and let them proceed, with a sigh of relief, on their way to New York.

In the airplane, in the narrow economy class aisle, Vladimir couldn't make his way past the man and the woman in Turkish trousers. We now need the information that the individuals in question were old, although there is no saying just how old, since, in rural areas, life leaves harsh traces on the sensitive skin of people's faces and hands. Over seventy, Vladimir guessed, wondering where the two of them were headed and why they were traveling alone. What had also been torturing Vladimir the whole day long was the simple question as to why he *himself* was traveling, despite the fact that contact with other people was certain to stir up the most unpleasant feelings in him—contact with all people, but especially people he didn't know, people in uniforms and also people who served food or drink (this was the reason that, his whole life long, he had avoided restaurants or frequented only self-service restaurants). Near the very top of the list of his inner abysses stood his fear of using public toilets, especially in airplanes and trains; it was immediately followed by his disgust at the quantities and kinds of bacteria that people exchanged in such confined spaces. Besides, Vladimir was quite simply very tall; he had his problems with seats in the cheaper classes, inasmuch as they are designed for people of average size. But if I had said right out loud that he considered the division into first and second class to be, as such, the main injustice in the modern world, no doubt everyone in the airplane would have laughed at me.

"Really," Vladimir thought in surprise, "why do I travel at all?"

Meanwhile, the old woman's headscarf had almost slipped off her head, revealing her gray, unkempt hair as she tried to stow her overflowing bag in the overflowing baggage compartment above her seat. Because of both its weight and its size, the bag should never have been allowed into the cabin as hand baggage (the condescending employee probably had not done his job properly during boarding; he had not noticed the bag at all). The woman shoved and squeezed the bag, the bag obeyed the laws of physics, and the nervous stewardess behind Vladimir lost patience and almost shouted at the two people that they should sit down. The plane was already late on their account, she said.

"Where am I supposed to put it?" the old woman, so confused that she was on the verge of shock, asked her husband. He had already taken his seat and was acting as if he did not know her out of shame, discomfiture, and an inborn instinct for self-preservation. "Where am I supposed to put it?" the old woman, looking around her, repeated in the language that was

Vladimir's mother tongue as well. "Stick it under the seat!"—Vladimir couldn't hold back the words. At the same instant, "Boarding completed!" came over the loudspeaker. He glanced at his boarding pass and abruptly plopped himself down in the empty seat next to the grateful old woman; he wanted to make sure that the stewardess would not box his ears because takeoff was being still further delayed on his account. (Yes, I'm quite well aware that a stewardess would hardly box a passenger's ears, even if he arrived too late or held up takeoff in some other way, yet I would nevertheless like to remind the reader that deviations from the probable are indeed possible as soon as the usual laws are no longer in force in an aircraft and classes are abolished by the opening of the curtains. I would remind the reader only that the flight personnel of certain companies are provided with plastic handcuffs for the purpose of disciplining rampaging passengers. I would remind the reader of British Airways, in whose planes the stewardesses sometimes issue the passengers orders, or Aeroflot, where it can sometimes happen that a stewardess dies of old age in mid-flight. Why, then, don't you believe me when I tell you that this plump blondie—the very picture of a hale and hearty young miss from Germany—came close to taking a shot at Vladimir?)

The airplane taxied down the runway and Vladimir took a look around. Rather desperately, he tried to find an empty seat or, to be more exact, two empty seats side-by-side, so as to put as much distance as possible between himself and others. An empty seat next to a fat young man wearing glasses promised no significant improvement; nor did another seat beside a woman bedecked with gold, whose perfume you could still smell at the door to the toilet, where it blended with other pungent odors of barely human origin.

For Vladimir was looking for a seat far from other people.

Don't misunderstand me: the problem wasn't these particular people, but all people. Vladimir couldn't bear people. To be more exact, he couldn't bear their odors. True enough, nobody can, especially the unpleasant ones. Yet Vladimir had another problem as well. Early in his childhood, it had been discovered that he had an unusual anomaly: he had oversized tear ducts in both eyes. Even as a little slip of a child, Vladimir could, if he closed his mouth, held his nose, and forcefully expelled the air from his lungs, blow a dandelion puffball, for example, right through his tear ducts. In elementary school days, he could wipe the dust from a TV screen with his eyes, although that was a difficult undertaking because of the static, one with which he would fascinate his handful of playmates only on the very rare days when he was in a particularly good mood, usually just before weekends, when the dust lay thick on the screen before

Saturday housecleaning. This unusual capability emphatically had its negative aspects. First, because Vladimir's playmates considered it disgusting and thought he was a repulsive creep for having it. Second, because where air flows out, air also flows in. Vladimir, that is, breathed with nose and mouth and eyes, with the result that his system was never protected against odors. Whereas his classmates, for example, just closed their mouths and held their noses when a run-over cat was lying on the side of the road, Vladimir also had to screw his eyes tightly shut, so that he soon had a reputation as a wuss who could not bear even the sight of an ordinary dead animal. Later, once he had gotten used to putrefaction, cheap food, and bad, albeit natural, smells, he proved unable to accustom himself to effluvia from human bodies. Contact of any kind plunged him into minor fits of agony: after smelling someone just once, he already knew too much about his interlocutor. For Vladimir was particularly sensitive when it came to the smell of hair. Over the years, he learned to tell with a single breath for how many days the owner of the hair in question, who generally used hair spray, had not washed his, or—still more often—her hair. He detected the mildest cases of seborrhea, a disorder affecting the production of the sebaceous glands. He sniffed someone's hair in passing and knew exactly what he or she had eaten the night before. He had refined this talent to such a point that it would have gained him an international reputation if it had not been so useless. Were the human understanding better able to free itself from the fetters of custom, were the human understanding not so improbably predictable, Vladimir could have made a brilliant career with the police, as, for example, a profiler, as the profession is called in American detective stories. While the forensics lab was working to decode the murderer's DNA, Vladimir could have described, setting out from the smell of a single hair found under one of the victim's fingernails, the murderer's personality, lifestyle, and diet, as well as the neighborhood in which he lived. As his bad luck would have it, however, Vladimir lived in an environment in which people killed each other in the middle of the street, in the middle of the day, without superfluous body contact, out of crystal-clear motives, in front of droves of eyewitnesses, and without so much as bending their little fingers. Vladimir had consequently been unable to put his talent at humanity's disposition, for its betterment. Quite the contrary: he had lived far from the human race for thirty-six years, dreadfully lonely.

Now, as the airplane left the runway and found itself in that perilous stage between solid ground and stable flight, and as the old woman opened a package of something edible and offered it in friendly fashion to her neighbor, Vladimir held his breath and made a decision to switch seats, come what might. He would wait until the "Fasten your seat belts!" sign was turned off and then ask the stewardess to give him another seat. Fifteen minutes and one "Can I sit somewhere else?" later, Vladimir was sitting next to a bald German, with an empty seat between them, a few rows behind the old people, whom he had not even bidden good-bye. He looked around him in the airplane and was grateful for the Munich layover, since, thanks to it, there were a good many Germans among the passengers. The Germans, as one knows from experience, are the people with the highest proportion of bald men in Europe. German men lose their hair at an early age; that's why they crop it so short, as short as a two-day or three-day beard, if we ignore the mustachioed Tarzan-types whose hair does not smell because it is too well aerated by the wind that takes care of the hair under their noses at the same time.

The scene that Vladimir had truculently staged with the stewardess nevertheless continued to bother him somewhere in the back of his mind. "Can I sit somewhere else?" he had asked the chubby blonde (who had been intent on settling accounts with him physically just a few minutes earlier); but he had not offered her an explanation of any sort in response to her questioning gaze, confining himself, instead, to throwing a look at the people sitting next to him. The woman with the headscarf said nothing and probably wished she could melt into the fabric on her seat, into the stripes and polka dots and, as far as her head went, into the little white cloth on the headrest, simply so as not to have to disturb anyone else anymore. He had looked at her and her husband, who had, in return, shot a grateful glance his way because Vladimir had helped her, whereas he himself had betrayed her a few moments earlier by ignoring her. The stewardess had also looked at the people, uttered a curt "Follow me!" and ushered him toward the billiard ball in row twenty-five, where he had squeezed past the man and an empty seat and sat down by the window. The little racist conspiracy of the "civilized" versus the "uncivilized" had gained him peace and quiet for the next eight hours in the air, and he felt like a rat. But what was he supposed to do? Should he have given the stewardess an account of his congenital physical anomaly as detailed as the one I just gave you, and added that his tear ducts, today of all days, were being especially heavily taxed when he inhaled, due probably to his excitement over the first intercontinental flight he had ever been on? Even if the little blonde had believed him, rather than deciding to box him on the ears after all, would the other passengers, like all the other people he had met to date, not have considered him a repulsive creep to the end of the flight, one who, to top things off, also had a physical problem?

Thus a minuscule conspiracy contrary to the principles of humanity and equality, and contrary to the basic rules of decency as well, secured Vladimir the right to sit nine rows away from the old couple, with their food and their reluctance to wash their hair. He had not so much as said good-bye to them, so deeply had he been ashamed of himself.

"I like window seats" was all the explanation he offered the billiard ball by way of an excuse for the fact that he had switched seats. The German nodded at him, indifferent; he didn't give a hoot about Vladimir's likes and dislikes. He kept a firm grip on his boarding pass, imprinted with a 25B that corresponded to the seat he was sitting in, resolved to let nothing and nobody, whatever the circumstances, drive him from it. "Impolite, but well bathed," Vladimir thought to himself, and was even glad, since the man's impoliteness was a small, well-deserved cosmic punishment for his own beastly behavior, so that his conscience was gradually assuaged. What was more, this German was surely not interested in starting up a conversation which, had he been, would have exposed Vladimir to the danger of confronting the man's possibly bad breath. Thus he had the prospect of calm ahead of him: the stranger's lips were closed, his own eyes were accordingly open, and Vladimir thought to himself that he could, all things considered, watch the film.

A few hours later, in the wake of the meal that came with the flight, which had included, among other things, imitation seafood and unhygienically fermented French cheese that he had of course not touched (fortunately, his neighbor had not, either), Vladimir fell asleep about halfway through a hysterical American movie with an aging comedian in the leading role.

He slept for a full four hours, without dreaming, as if he had merited this blessing.

When he woke up and glanced at his watch, it was dark in the cabin, although, here and there, lights were burning over the heads of passengers who were not as fortunate as Vladimir, did not have his oddly serene conscience, and so could not sleep as peacefully as he had. Many of them were killing time with the boring, heavily thumbed magazines in the pockets on the backs of the seats in front of them. A little less than two hours of flight time to go, he calculated, and set the hands of his not-quite-accurate wristwatch six hours back. Then he noticed that he couldn't hold it any longer and got up to go to the toilet. He tried to clamber over the legs of the German dozing next to him without waking him up, but he did not manage to; the German's eyes flew open at the first move Vladimir made. The man was, however, too well-bred to betray his true feelings and uttered not a word. Vladimir excused himself and went off to answer the call of nature.

The aisle between the seats that led to the toilet of course ran past the row in which, in case you've forgotten, the two old people were sitting. It occurred to Vladimir that he could not possibly walk by them unless he kept staring uninterruptedly at a crucially important point at eye level somewhere off in the distance without, come what might, looking in their direction. He accordingly took a most extraordinary interest in the airshow map on which the current flight altitude, distance to their destination, and outside temperature were displayed. (Unfortunately, I cannot relay that information here, for Vladimir, although he stared at the numbers and lines on the screen, registered no information at all; he was far too intent on overlooking the man and woman whom he had very painfully left only six hours earlier.)

As he came back out of the toilet, in which, with a single breath, he had clearly perceived that the man who had urinated there just before him regularly took Centrum Pharmaceuticals multivitamin pills, as well as Fucus Weight-Loss Algae, Vladimir was surprised to see that the lights in the cabin were burning bright. The time allotted for rest was over; now he would be much harder pressed to ignore the old people. What is more, he was held up in the vicinity of their row and had to make room for the passage of the same full-bodied stewardess, who was now handing the passengers little cards that they were supposed to fill out before entering the United States. In the harsh light cast by pangs of conscience, the blonde at last appeared in all her true glory: she was soft as dough and had a subcutaneous acne problem.

When Vladimir was finally able to start making his way back to his seat again, something compelled him, despite all, to cast a glance at his former neighbors. They were both sitting quietly and almost sadly in their seats, clutching the little entry cards printed in English and German. Manifestly, neither of them had the foggiest notion as to what the cards said and what they were supposed to do with them.

Conveniently—allow me to stress this detail—the old people did not see Vladimir at all; thus he could have walked past them unperceived, reclaimed his seat, and forgotten that they needed help. He nevertheless came to a halt. On his own initiative, without waiting for anyone to ask him to (the woman had not looked at him imploringly, nor had the man looked at him thankfully), he came to a halt. Do you understand how important it is for me to portray Vladimir as a man with a conscience?

"Can I help you?" he asked the man. The woman just shrugged her shoulders. Then he sat down next to them, took the little cards out of their hands without a word, drew a ball-point pen from the vest pocket of his sport coat and started copying the information in their passports. The passports displayed the same state seal that Vladimir's did. Here I must note that this whole story takes place before the tragic events of September 11, 2001, when (I write this for future generations) "America was attacked in a terrorist act." This is important, because Vladimir would have been hard put, by the laws of ordinary human logic, to bring himself to help a Muslim couple entering the United States if all this had occurred after September 11. For even if not all Muslims are Arabs and not all Arabs are automatically terrorists, this simple fact has not reached the ears of every last border official. As a person who travels a great deal (as you can probably imagine) and is, physically, of the "Middle Eastern type" (you may take my word for it), I am very well acquainted with the sort of special treatment that Muslims and especially Arabs, and also dark-skinned men and women in general, can experience at the hands of airport police. In a word: people don't believe us anymore. Had Vladimir filled out other people's entry cards under *those* circumstances, it would have been a heroic or, at least, a very rash act, one that would have taken our story in an altogether different direction. For Vladimir was of course no hero, but he was also not one to take rash action. In the weeks preceding September 11, in the historic moment in which the present story takes place, a human being could, with a little effort, remain human.

Vladimir accordingly filled out the card: Last Name, First Name, Other Names (think up a man's and a woman's name yourselves), Home Address (a village in the southern part of the state in whose capital Vladimir resided), Date of Birth (here Vladimir hesitated briefly upon noticing that the two people were ten years younger than he had supposed), Place of Birth, Address while in the United States and Reason for Entry (they were visiting their son somewhere in New Jersey).

While the old people were scribbling little X's where they were supposed to sign, something strange occurred to Vladimir. He'd already been sitting right next to them in the tight quarters of economy class seats for fifteen minutes, and he felt nothing. To put it more precisely, he smelled nothing, for he did feel compassion, pangs of conscience, and even unmotivated rage against these people—not necessarily in that order. In short, they simply didn't make their presence felt. They didn't stink. They didn't give off a fragrant scent, either, and that was also not altogether unimportant for Vladimir, because people's propensity to daub themselves with blended extracts of natural aromas often enough drove him to despair. This man and woman, however, did not smell at all.

Humiliated, furious, Vladimir got up and headed for his seat. The chubby stewardess, of all people, was standing in his way again. His partner in a conspiracy of contempt looked quizzically at him while ignoring the grateful couple sitting in their seats, utterly, blissfully ignorant of Vladimir's real state of mind. And because nothing cleverer occurred to him, Vladimir now hated, with all the strength in his soul, the rotten little stewardess, witness to, and instigator of, his inhumanity. As if she were to blame for everything, he abruptly and impolitely barked at this woman, who had not been initiated into his private drama, "Get out of the way!" and hurried back to his seat.

After a second climb over the prematurely bald German's legs, a half-completed entry document, and another ten minutes, Vladimir felt somebody's hand touching his. When he looked up, he saw the old woman, who quickly, but really very quickly, pressed something into his right hand (he was holding the pen in the other). The old woman had already regained her seat before Vladimir grasped that a woman's gold earring was glittering in his hand. He gazed in alarm at this reward (fourteen-carat gold, handmade, a local product, an authentic, albeit worthless design) for the elementary humanity that he had shown these people. He didn't have the strength to protest; he couldn't go over to the woman and try to make her understand that there had been no need, that one did not repay friendliness with gold in the modern world and that it had, moreover, been his civic duty to help them. When he noticed that he was about to burst into tears, it occurred to him that the old people were not compatriots of his but, on the contrary, representatives of the opposing camp in the war, the intractable, forever schismatic side. Vladimir simply let the whole matter drop.

He contemplated the earring in his hand, which he did not even like: he hated the smell of the metal. He was thinking about the unhygienic process that must have culminated in this gift when he felt the German's eyes on him.

"I helped them fill out the form," he said, with a barely perceptible smile.

"That's your business," said the German unsmilingly, as he turned the other way.

Before long, the "Fasten your seat belt!" signs were flickering over the passengers' heads. They were informed that the temperature was seventy degrees Fahrenheit and that it was 6:00 P.M. local time. The voice wished them a pleasant stay in New York and said, "Thank you for flying with Lufthansa."

A few days later, after a successful talk and equally successful conversations with gracious American hosts, Vladimir made the first unusual decision of his life. He felt ashamed every time he touched the gold earring in the pocket of the only suit that he'd brought with him, and he resolved to take a radical step. While he was strolling through East Village, he decided to have his left earlobe pierced and wear the earring in it forever.

Whether it was because of the fact that he didn't speak English as well as he wrote it, or because of the New York slang that the tattooed piercer in the store in St. Mark's Place used, his contempt for tourists, or simply vengeful fate, the earring found itself, a single click of the piercing-pistol later, in one of Vladimir's nostrils.

The unusual pain, the blood, and the prospect of a pussy infection—all that was a matter of seconds.

Vladimir was standing by himself in a street in a foreign country, with one more hole in his body through which people's terrible odors were boring their way into him.

Vladimir was standing by himself in the street of the city that still had the next war ahead of it; the hole hurt; his conscience was bothering him; he didn't want to go back to the country in which you had to hate people who repaid you for a little bit of help with gold; he didn't want to live this life, but he was also unable to put an end to it.

Vladimir wondered, as he stood on the street, where he'd been headed in the first place and whether he had arrived. He wondered whether he had the right to look for a place that was far from everything.

He touched the side of his nose. Blood was flowing from it.

He looked around and, suddenly, forgot where he was supposed to be going.

He stepped into the street and forgot the law of the one-way street.

The bus coming from behind him at a legal speed ignored the traffic signal, and Vladimir was run over.

Somebody screamed, somebody didn't bother to turn around, one man even laughed—I can swear to it—and Vladimir was dead.

He had been run over in a world that he hadn't succeeded in getting to know.

Translated by G. M. Goshgarian

That Spring Cannot Come

Saša Stanišić

1

He woke up today as well: the dog had barked. Differently than usual, the dog had barked furiously, as overly ecstatic dogs do when something unfamiliar comes along. Because of the dog, he got out of bed quickly today. From the fireplace, inflamed eyes fixed on him, on his turtle neck, his scrawny legs— the embers turned in his direction. Embers see disappearance in all things, the old man braced his back against his disappearance, did not bend down as he stepped through the door into the cold, to his howling animal.

Engulfed by what feeds me, I too will disappear, was the thought that had flared up in the embers, had tortured them ever since the first light of dawn had fallen on the wooden walls of the small room. Dawn had crept under the wooden table, had taken a seat on the wooden chairs, had illuminated the wooden shelves for the embers, and had pointed to the wooden sideboard, where on bitter photographic paper people laughed and did not laugh. The bed frame, too, was of wood. Cherry. Too big for the old man alone. There he had slept and not slept, and when he hadn't slept he had thrashed about, screamed out. Above the bed hung another man, nailed to his half-naked disappearance. The man disappeared into a cross carved of the same oak as he himself.

All that sweet wood, my origin, could stave off my disappearance, the ravenous embers thought hotly, and crackled one last time. Am I more fire or fir the embers wondered, I am in need of that of which I am.

Am! Am! Am! the dog barked sharply, after the embers could no longer hear him. The chain stretched between the house wall and the hound's neck. The dog wanted to tear the world apart. The world, however, remained as it was. Only the mountains barked back across the valley.

The old man crossed the yard, his disappearance on his back. Rust, he rasped first today, to the chain holding back the dog. The dog bared its teeth, a warning to the new arrivals, and the man knelt down to stroke his dog's inflamed gums. They waited close together, the old man and his young dog. The empty pigpen waited, there. There, a cracked feeding trough. There, the last patches of snow had melted. There, a pitchfork leaned against the soot-covered wall of a neighbor's house. Caved-in roof beams waited there. There, a dandelion tried to convince itself of spring. There, a windowsill had something to say to the wind, not a secret. There were no more secrets, for secrets more than one person is required.

It was the wind, only the wind. The wind had woken the dog, who had woken the man. The wind had climbed up out of the valley and was so enveloped in loneliness that the young dog had mistaken it for a soldier.

Shall we go into the wind? the dog now asked the old man.

Shhh, the old man stroked him.

It's spring, the old man said—to Jesus on the cross. Then after a while: how cold it is—he said last today. In the window, night and rain exchanged their silver. The rain caused the snow to disappear. Talked at the dandelion. Washed off the ruins. Filled the trough.

The old man went to bed today as well. He got undressed and stood there. Stood and stood there and shivered with the cold. Put his hand on his chest and listened to his heart with it. On the wall around the oak Jesus four drawings were hung: a tiny red dot; numerous people in numerous embraces; the numeral 1992; and an old man in suit and bow tie, with big, bewildered eyes.

The old man didn't build a fire today, the ashes waited in the hearth.

2

And once, biologists came to the village. The noise of their engines could be heard in the valley all afternoon, it was a tough path for the car and for the echo, unaccustomed as it was to hauling such a roar up the slopes. It was tough for the villagers as well: Muhamed complained of a stomachache, Sulejman felt the motor in his kidneys, and Petar shook his fist at the echo and had his temples massaged with dandelion salve.

But at some point even the biologists had shown consideration for their groaning vehicle, and put their trust, as does any reasonable human being, in their feet. The path to the village was long and steep and the biologists coughed from under their rucksacks, which were hung with various pieces of equipment that the children from the village called what-is-that and and-what-is-that.

Good day, we're looking for the little humanfish, announced the biologists, two women, red-cheeked, two men, white-haired. Several of the villagers had gathered to greet the new arrivals, as was the custom, with ham and water and a mix of skepticism and curiosity. It was decided that this time the women would take over the skepticism. Little Malina handed one of the biologists a dandelion, at which he—after an uncertain glance at Petar's yellow temples—rubbed it over his own, at which the villagers stared, their eyes big, at which Petar offered the biologist an aspirin, at which the biologist, puzzled, thanked him, at which evening arrived and with darkness, the biologists' decision to spend the night in the village.

And tomorrow someone will guide you, Petar said, to your dragon young.

Dragon young? the biologists asked in surprise.

Yes, yes, the village answered, and thrust its guests into a celebration that went on late into the night, filled with songs and legends.

The old man knew all of the songs and all of the legends, including the ones about the dragon young. He promised to deliver the biologists to knowledge of the dragon young in the high mountain. And the biologists followed him—as he sang the songs and related the legends—uphill, downhill, through valleys, and over the sparse mountain plateaus for days. Everything that I sing and say to you, you can and will forget, the old man said, but there's one thing you shall always remember—how the high mountain acquired a heart and we, a legend about ourselves:

In times very long past, when the land knew nothing of people and people knew nothing of the land, four young brooks bet on which of them would reach the heart of the highest mountain in the region the fastest— and thus the underground lake, the sweetness and greenness of which the animals and trees had so much to tell. Skillfully and stalwartly, from the four corners of the earth, the four brooks cut into the mountain, bearing gold they wished to present to the lake as a gift. After years and years and years of talking to themselves and of silence, the brooks found—in a chamber deep beneath the mountain—one another. From four sides they plunged down the sheer walls into—after years of loneliness—one another's arms. They filled the empty chamber and left it together as one river. Their embrace, however, remained forever, and they, too, remained siblings, inseparable, in a sweet, green lake fed with gold.

Drawn to the roomy caves and to the gold, dragons soon took up residence in the high mountain and—centuries later—humans also sought the same glittering good fortune. Like the four brooks, there were also four tribes of humans, who created the heart of a country on this land. They became tribes only later, however; in the beginning they were merely hunters. In the old epics, the encounters between man and dragon were commemorated in song—as victories of man over dragon. Later, the encounters between man and man were commemorated in song—in which, to this day, there were only defeats for man.

The few remaining dragon young did not age once the last old dragon in the lake heart of the mountain had died—was murdered, because the dragon was what man was not. The dragon young hid in the underground rivers, persevered. At first they wanted to remain small the better to hide themselves from humans, but in the interim they had gotten so old they no longer remembered how to grow.

This and much more was related by the old man on the stony paths and on those paths that weren't paths. Four brooks were forded, the old man took water from each and carried it in a canteen to the next—until they once again reached the first brook. The biologists complained, we're going in circles, but the old man pointed to a little plant on the bank of the brook, and the biologists immediately sank to their knees before it, oblivious to the world, and as pleased as children with a chick they could hold gently in their hands and keep warm. They photographed the little plant and themselves beside it, and in the end plucked it and placed it in a transparent plastic bag together with its roots and a bit of earth.

The high mountain today has a proper name, the old man said on the seventh day of the journey, and once, cartographers came to our village and revealed it to us. But unfortunately we forgot it again. The high mountain is still home to the dragon young, and only he who knows the mountain well also knows the way to the dragon young. To the little humanfish, the old man laughed, and told them that the dragon young had adapted their skin to that of humans, believing that skin was the most important thing to humans and would protect them from annihilation.

The old man told, told, told things to the biologists, who in the beginning still laughed, then asked increasingly often where they were, geographically, and when they would reach the caves with the little humanfish. *Proteus anguinus,* one woman biologist said, politely holding up in front of the old man's face a drawing of a kind of yellow lizard without eyelids.

One can learn only from the truly courageous, the old man said and pushed the drawing aside, and geographically, that over there is Serbia, he said, pointing to a bush. Then they climbed for a long time up through a dense evergreen forest, and, on the morning of the tenth day of the hike, which had led them over creviced passes and along mountain lakes, all of which had "Silver" in their names, the little humanfish expedition scaled a steep precipice and from its peak could see far over the plains into the distance, where raindrops fell together with sunbeams. Directly beneath them, however, carved smoothly into the side of the mountain as if so intended from time immemorial, was the village, in which little Malina already was waiting with a smile, holding dandelions for the biologists in her lovely hand.

3

He woke up today as well: the thunder had screamed as if afraid of what its own lightning had revealed. The lightning had revealed the village. It can't bear up against the village, the old man said first today, and sat up in bed. The ashes fixed on him from the hearth: his stubble, his crown of white hair. Ashes see the extinction of all things—the old man, however, could forget nothing, the human screams, the inferno, the shots fired in the night, all remained inextinguishable.

The old man crept out into the rain. The clouds had shut out the dawn. His goat had gotten loose and was wandering about the yard.

Why do you always do this? the old man asked the goat, his last words today. No matter how he tied up the goat or where he confined her, she always worked her way free. Usually she lay down near the young dog, who had long since given up rebuking her. This goat no longer feared anyone, not the old man, not the young dog, and certainly not the thunder that sounded more frightened than this goat could ever be.

The old man gave the goat some bread. The goat ate the dry bread from his wet hand. The goat had eaten ash bark from his hand. Soon there would be nettles again, the goat wanted to say, to comfort the old man with spring.

It had thundered and the dog had growled.

The storm with the cowardly thunder stayed in the village all day and wanted to stay the night there, too. The old man brought the goat and the dog into the house, the dog lay down in front of the hearth, the goat ran around. The old man had reduced her stall to kindling. He could no longer stand the fact that the goat would force her head through the bars, even though he always fed her out of his hand.

Before going to bed the old man mixed rye flour together with warm water, stirred in a little goat's milk, later added salt, and placed the bowl, covered with a dishtowel, on the hearth.

The goat watched the lightning through the window with compassion. What did the thunder so fear that caused it to feel its way to the earth so quietly? Ruins and rot? Shamefaced stillness and sorrow? The taste and smell of a village in which for years there had been no spring?

Only once the old man had fallen asleep did the thunder let loose with a roar. It thrashed about as if transformed—in the way that mad people dance. The goat moved away from the window as far as her leash would allow.

It was the old man the thunder feared.

4

And once, surveyors and cartographers came to the village. They schlepped all kinds of measuring devices with them, polite people who wore khakis and asked few but clever questions. Before eating they washed their hands, and doffed their hats, if they had hats and were men, as the tall girls of the village passed by. Fall played its cards for the cartographers, they sat bent over their plans in the still, sunny air, sketched timberlines, registered elevation gains, taught little Malina the word "topography" with great care.

The surveyors clambered up every one of the craggy mountains that surrounded the village on three sides, they waded with neither fear nor guide through the four brooks, marked the places where the brooks disappeared into the high mountain, lost their way hunting for mushrooms in the forest, and nevertheless returned in good humor with rucksacks full and with lines for the timber. But they're all poisonous, little Malina told them, and, laughing, gave them to her mother to cook so that a feast could be dished up for everyone. It will come to nothing if you do it.

During the day the cartographers called out numbers to each other, and evenings they lay in the meadows, eating grapes and cheese, drinking juices the villagers brought to them. Everything from here? they asked and wanted to pay and didn't have to and said thank you with eyes closed.

They spoke softly, boasted of landscapes they had already committed to paper, discovered that the village had a different name than they did for almost everything in the region, and that the three peaks were the village children's godchildren—each in turn took the name of a newborn. The child was baptized on the western peak, circumcised on the eastern, and to the middle peak—the hardest one to climb—parents carried those offspring who could have been baptized as well as circumcised. But neither the one nor the other occurred, and the peak then was called Kristijan-Jusuf or Lejla-Marija.

In the second week, the surveyors and the cartographers helped the villagers with the hay. They praised the smell of all things, outside of the outhouses, and still doffed their hats, should one of the pretty girls lower her eyes in embarrassment in their presence or in their distance, which, despite all of their gadgets, they were unable to measure.

5

He woke up today as well: the other villagers had related their life stories. The lives had infiltrated the old man's dream: children were born, grew up and made friends, cherry trees took root in the earth, mouths laughed and kissed and ate and were silent. Neighbors climbed up onto unfinished roofs and hammered rhythms into the wood as they sang, raised new houses into the air. The old man was awakened by so much life, opened his eyes and closed them, opened and closed. Louder! the old man said first today, for he could barely understand his neighbors' whispering—the fire crackled in the hearth, the rain tripped over the roof, and the wind whistled to drown out the lonesomeness in all things.

I can't hear you, the man said last today, and it was a plea. He didn't want to miss any stories.

In the hearth the flames drew each other's attention to the man, to his bloodshot eyes, his pendulous earlobes. Flames see fire in all things, and memory had flared up in the old man. The voices of the others ignited and stoked it, sparks of memory streaked his eyes red. The sparks of blood mixed with the tears, the bloodtears with the rain, the bloodtearsrain with the earth—at the edge of the forest, at the edge of the village, on the cross of wood, on the columns of stone. It had thundered and the dog had growled and the goat had pawed the earth with its hooves.

The dough rose on the second day. The house smelled sour. The old man stirred a bit of flour and water into the batter.

The old man went to bed today as well. The bloodtearsrainearth stuck to his pillow, for he had listened with his ear to what his neighbors had to tell, had waited all day for their questions and their wishes. The cross was lopsided, the stone uncut, the dead had prophesied that it would be impossible for spring ever to come to the village or forgiveness to the land.

Logs waited in the hearth, but the old man didn't build a fire today.

6

And once, elections came to the village. Marko Petrović, a strapping fellow who had moved to the city many years before, brought elections with him from the city. The elections went like this: brown shoebox with a slit cut in the top, pieces of paper with the many parties—the three letters of one of them were on Marko's T-shirt—and some colored crayons that Marko gave to the children so they could copy the three letters and give them to their parents.

Before the assembled villagers Marko proclaimed that communism had been a thief, but the thief had been hanged, and now better times would finally come!

We're doing good as it is, and one shouldn't want to have it better than good. The land is fertile, the children are learning well and growing up with red cheeks, Marko's father, Radovan Petrović, said softly to his son, as if wanting to prevent him from making a bargain that could not possibly end to his advantage.

But Marko kissed his father on the forehead and took those who could not read by the hand and pointed to the piece of paper where they should make an *X*, so that Serbian land could remain Serbian land, or even expand.

Not everyone was allowed to vote. Are you registered? Marko asked Sulejman, Muhamed, and the other Muslims, and they just shrugged. And yet the shoebox remained almost empty, a mere eight votes were inside. So Marko invited—at first politely, then insistently, then promising to uncover a major conspiracy—the remaining forty-one Serbs to come to the house of his father. A speech! firing himself up once most of them had taken a seat, climbing up onto the table, and then climbing right back down again to remove his shoes. Shame on you, we eat there! his mother scolded him. So Marko stood on the table barefoot and gave a speech, a speech about the others. The others believe in Allah. The others think only of their own advantage. The others are up to something. The others are born ambitious and die avaricious.

They listened to Marko. The women coughed, the men nodded. Marko spoke rapidly and to the point, as only someone from the city could do. The children colored their hands with the new crayons and laughed sometimes, at something Marko had said or at something else entirely.

Marko closed his speech with: Is that clear?

Everyone looked at each other. Now we understand everything! they cried and opened the windows to air out the stuffy room. Finally they had grasped the gravity of the situation and asked Marko to leave them to themselves so that they could deliberate and vote for Marko's T-shirt.

That evening Marko, satisfied, descended into the valley with the shoe-box. They had returned the crayons to him, this is not something for our children, the villagers said, waving them away, and that, at the very least, should have made Marko suspicious. For in the village, great value was placed on art, education, and muscles. The child who could draw well was presented with a soccer ball, the child who was especially fast or strong received a pocket calculator, and those who could do numbers best in their heads were given watercolors and good paper.

Back in the city, Marko emptied the shoebox in front of the other campaign workers. The votes spilled out onto the table, and at the sight of them all conversation in the airless room ceased. On all of the ballots, houses and dogs and goats and flowers and mushrooms and snowflakes and sun rays and people could be seen, dancing brightly across the pieces of paper that had been colored by the village children. Laughing faces there, where an X belonged.

On one of the pictures Marko recognized himself: Marko speaking, his hand balled into a fist.

7

He woke up today as well: the cold had snuggled up next to him and lain its head on his chest. I don't need the seasons, the old man said first today, but bread, bread. He pinched the dough and smelled it. The dough still wasn't ready.

Again today the dead simply—perfectly and accurately—took protocol: responsibility for the crime, irreconcilability with that piece of shit called Fate, then names, then ages, then work left uncompleted.

In the hearth the logs were amazed by the man. By his hoarse laughter that suddenly filled the house, by the agility with which he shouldered a large sack and easily carried it outside. Wood sees growth in all things, but once chopped and awaiting disappearance, it can only be amazed.

Bent under the sack and his own disappearance, the old man crossed the courtyard. He climbed over the door lying on the floor, into Sulejman's house. He set the sack down in Sulejman's kitchen. He found a shoe behind the gutted chest of drawers. He placed Sulejman's shoe in the sack. With Muhamed's shirt and Radovan's pipe, and so forth. With the barrette of little Malina.

Bent under the sack and his disappearance, in Hasan's house the old man found a green pullover with a hole in the sleeve.

Bent under the sack and his disappearance, growing daily, the old man cautiously entered the ruins of Petar's house. From beneath the debris he dug out a hat, mashed flat. He shooed away his dog, who wanted to search with him as dogs are wont to do. Don't you see the beams, the old man explained to the young dog angrily, his last words today.

The old man had visited his neighbors every Monday for many months now. He found each of them in some piece of clothing that hadn't been devoured by fire or buried under the rubble or plundered. He tried to remember on which occasion this neighbor had worn this glove and that neighbor had on this skirt. He found less and less, in some of the houses nothing more at all, and so he stopped visiting those houses. He avoided them like something one is ashamed of. Once, he found the four drawings that now surrounded the oak Jesus.

Late that evening the old man drank a cup of coffee. On the chair across from him sat the bulging sack. The man and the sack remembered.

The old man went to bed today as well. But the coffee kept him from sleep. He got up several times, and each time he put on different clothes and warmed his hands at the hearth. The wood was amazed at the dusty hat the man wore, at the sweater with the hole in the sleeve, at the pipe without tobacco. At midnight the man went out into the yard and untied the goat, as he did every night.

When a sack was full, the old man put a piece of his own clothing on top, then made coffee for himself and his neighbors and, following a mostly sleepless night, tied up the sack.

8

And once, order-givers, corralers, separators, liner-uppers, fire-setters came to the village. Issued orders. Corraled. Separated: Ours/Others. Lined up fifty-four. Looked in cupboards. Took. Drank milk. Poured gasoline on cows, on stalls. Horses whinnied. The old man was away in the mountains with his young dog. The young dog screamed at the columns of smoke, the old man screamed as well and ran back, ran through the morning, ran and ran, he ran across four brooks, as if flying.

And once to the village came the out-of-sleep-wrenchers, the pummelers, slaughterers, revenge-takers. Deep in the night they wrenched the surviving forty-nine out of their sleep with blows, separated them from their nightmares with hunting knives, took revenge for those who had been lined up and set on fire. The old man was away with his young dog, setting traps in the forest. They had been surprised by a storm and had taken shelter in a cave. The wind uprooted trees, thunder lashed out as if it had learned to hate, entire rivers rained down on the four brooks, since the beginning of all legends the old man had never heard or invented anything like it. He warmed the young dog with his body. The dog whimpered. In the morning the sun was shining. The old man returned to the village. He called. Looked around. Called louder. Screamed. The young dog was still whimpering. It wasn't the storm the young dog was whimpering about. A goat limped out of the ruins, its right back leg was broken.

9

The old man got up today as well, he hadn't slept, he tied up the sack of clothes, buried it on the mound of earth. The dog lay down at his feet, the goat stood there. The old man looked out at the valley, where there was nothing and no one other than his gaze.

The old man baked the bread. The old man ate warm bread. The old man went to bed again today as well.

10

And once, forensic archaeology came to the village, and forensic medicine. They removed the top layer of soil. It was a matter of a primary burial site. Forensic archaeology and forensic medicine worked manually with shovels and spades from the top to the very bottom, from find to find. The victim is wearing a green-and-red checked shirt. Forensic archaeology and forensic medicine wore white dust masks. The hands of the victim are tied behind his back with wire. The language of forensic medicine filtered flawlessly through the mask and the data taken into the head of the recording devices were factually correct. The skull of the victim reveals a hole in the left temple. The hands of forensic archaeology in white gloves rest on the old man's back flawlessly and factually correctly. Is there anyone here but you? forensic medicine asked and led the goat away from the orange-colored ribbons for photographic documentation at the edge of the village.

11

The old man woke up today as well. He put on his boots. He strapped his hunting knife to his belt. He packed a little bread, a little cheese. The smoke stared at him from the hearth. Smoke sees change in all things. This smoke saw no change, it hardly saw anything at all after the old man poured water on the embers. That's enough now, he said first today, to the smoke, and the smoke, for the time being, had to concentrate on itself.

The goat was with the young dog, comforting it. Nothing and no one, the dog wanted to say, but no one is ever rested. What are we waiting for still?

Whoever reaches me first gets to come to the traps with me, the old man said last today, but the goat and the dog merely raised their heads.

Thick fog was lying over the valley and forest and the four brooks. Only the village and its three godpeaks—Safiya, Ivan-Mehmet, Malina—and the snow-covered tip of the high mountain on the other side of the valley were visible in the grayness. The man fed the animals, gave them water and more feed than usual. They didn't eat, hesitated to enter the fog with the man, the young dog even though the man took him off his chain. They watched him go, he disappeared into the fog with his disappearance.

Late that afternoon the young dog began to bark. The fog had eaten its way up the face of the mountain and swallowed the first ruins of the houses at the edge of the village, had swallowed the grave and the voices of the dead. The fog itself spoke with a voice that brooked no spring. Whimpering, the young dog followed the goat into the house. Jesus was waiting on the wall. The bread was waiting on the table. The goat clambered up onto a chair, licked the crust of the bread. In the hearth ashes saw extinction in all things. The dog closed the door with its muzzle.

12

And once, a man came to the village who claimed he knew the answer to no question. He wore a suit and bow tie and little Malina asked him, Why do ants have such a tiny waist?

I don't know, the man answered and sat down in the grass.

Does the heart of a louse beat faster than the heart of an ox? Malina asked again and sat down next to him.

I don't know, the man answered, rubbed grass between his fingers and smelled it.

And what is the word for all numbers? asked Malina's grandfather, Mirko, who could calculate every bill, every liaison, and every rain in his head.

I don't know, answered the man and stretched out in the grass.

What would our embraces paint if they could paint? Ivan-Mehmet asked, who was only seven but already painted the prettiest pictures in the village and, back when elections came to the village, had mixed a sun-yellow that was the envy of the sun itself.

I don't know, the man shook his head, which almost went unnoticed, he had sunk so deep into the grass.

Why do some people hate other people? Sulejman asked and ate a plum.

The man murmured something and shrugged his shoulders. He could no longer speak clearly. The grass had grown over his mouth.

What is the most important question in the world? the old man asked, and from the distant valley the wind carried up explosions in the crook of its arm. The grass, into which the man who knew the answer to no question had disappeared, waved in the wind, and never again in the village did people dance or kiss each other seven times or embrace twenty-two times, but four more pictures were painted.

One showed the heart of a louse.

One an embrace.

One the numeral 1992.

One the old man in suit and bow tie, with big, bewildered eyes.

Translated by Edna McCown

Borders in the Balkans

A Century in the Life of an Albanian Family

Luan Starova

THE LIFE OF MY FAMILY CONSISTED OF THE CROSSING OF BORDERS FOR AN entire century. More than any other, it was the border between Albania and Macedonia that affected us, all three generations of us. The border rose between Macedonia and Albania when the latter achieved independence in 1912. From the start, this border had quite a history and underwent many changes. During the Balkan Wars it was moved several times within a short period. Each advancing army pushed the borderline forward, but then another army pushed it back, returning the population in question once again to the country it had originally inhabited.

From what my grandfather, and later, what my father told me, our family had its greatest difficulties with the border in the Balkan Wars, in the First and Second World Wars, and during the Cominform. We were particularly affected by the invisible part of the border that ran through Lake Ohrid and upon its shores near the Albanian town of Pogradec. Throughout the wars, the border caused us to suffer. It was always the same story, always a looming threat.

The damned border was the object of our fear, but it was also the object of our hope. The family was virtually crushed and cowed by it. The pain that it caused us passed from one generation to the next. It never stopped and, because of the constant dread, it haunted even those who had never even thought of crossing it.

Everyone felt the burden of the nearby border. We all waited for it to disappear, but few of us ever believed we would see that day come. My grandfather once joked that the border would certainly follow our family to the grave, pursuing some to heaven and others to hell. It was our fate; there was no way around it.

The border continued to preoccupy our thoughts when some members of our family separated from the others and stole over to the other side in an old wooden rowboat one murky night. For my part, I was destined to play the role of a chronicler who hoped that he would be able to return one day when the border vanished or when it had at least lost its significance.

The border was carved into our memory from the moment it was created. When the old people told tales to the youngest members of the family, they would speak of the border as a many-headed dragon against whom no brave young man had dared to raise his saber to vanquish it so as to open the gate. The most frightening thing for us children was that the border dragon was somewhere deep in the lake where we couldn't see it.

Legend had it that whenever someone tried to cross the border, the lake would begin to seethe, and huge waves would rise to bar anyone from passing. Many boats and their unfortunate passengers ended up in the depths of the lake, in the jaws of the submarine dragon!

In my memory and in the recollection of the whole family, there are three tales that stretch over the border like sediment. Each of them tells a part of the truth. They are the tales of my grandfather, of my father, and of my mother, that I wish to tell you here.

The Tale of My Grandfather

Whenever my grandfather spoke of the border, he would always begin by saying that we, once upon a time, lived right on it. In his day at least, he could not remember there being any other peoples or families divided by a border. Grandfather held the view that we were the damned of the Balkans. The curse would only disappear when we got rid of the border that divided us. He implored his son not to leave the border region and not to cross it until the curse had been lifted. Otherwise, if he crossed it, the curse would be passed on to his children.

What our family knew about the border stemmed from ancient lore. It derived perhaps from the time the Eastern and Western Empires had divided Byzantium from Rome, when the first lines of division separated our Catholic and Orthodox ancestors. The Ottoman Empire brought about a new division when some people, faithful to their original beliefs, fled across the sea to other countries. They knew that they had caused an eternal gulf between themselves and those of the same origins who remained behind after the collapse of armed resistance, who converted in their majority to the new religion, and in this manner created new borders.

From the tales of my grandfather, I remember that my Albanian family was early to be confronted with the phenomenon of emigration. This emigration was divided into two parts. Some fled to foreign lands centuries ago during the first great exodus, and others settled, with their new faith, on the banks of Lake Ohrid, not far from the monastery of Saint Naum. This monastery was under the protection of our family until, with time, the prescripts of the new faith had spread. It was thought that the saint would heal their common wounds.

My grandfather spent over half of his life as a subject of the Sublime Porte and could not bring himself to recognize the new borders that were introduced during the Balkan Wars. The peoples of the Ottoman Empire were very mixed, so drawing borders would have made no sense. It was the wars of the next century that drew borders through fields, houses, people, and souls.

Time progressed, bringing uncertainty with it to the Balkans, as usual. What was special about my family members was that, by balancing their two original identities, they managed to create a new one and preserve it amidst the new immigrants from the Middle East and the native Christians, with whom they maintained good relations. The dividing lines within the family that were not of a geographical nature lingered within us for a long time before they were healed and overcome. They were not entirely forgotten amongst us, and were passed on from generation to generation.

It was only in the early years of the twentieth century when the Ottoman Empire began to crumble that my grandfather became painfully aware of the inner and outer borders. He predicted that the new century would also be one of borders. But because of all the borders around him, and around his family, his people, and the peoples of the Balkans, he was not able to see very far.

The Balkan Wars bestowed upon him a borderline right in front of the house, hindering his access to the *konak* where he received friends and passing travelers. It was intended to pass right through Grandmother's flower garden where, every spring, she would sow seeds sent to her by relatives who had settled in Istanbul. But the border was powerless to impede the spreading fragrance of her lilacs.

The border touched our family home's very threshold, a white block of marble that someone had brought from the nearby Roman road, the Via Egnatia. My ancestors had once guarded a section of that important means of Mediterranean communication and commerce. All of a sudden, the borderline made us eternal emigrants. A line drawn on a topographic map used by the military changed the fate of people and ethnic groups in the Balkans forever.

Part of the family remained on the other side of the border, that is, on the opposite shore of the lake, almost within shouting distance. Two shores of exile. Other relatives traversed the farther borders and immigrated to Istanbul where they had family waiting for them, or crossed the ocean to seek their fortune in the New World. My grandfather, for his part, decided to stay put with his wife, two sons, and three daughters, and wait for the border to fall. A whole century passed. The only thing the border could not do was to separate us from the beautiful sunsets on the lake.

Grandfather remained at the lake, right where the borders crisscrossed, hoping to get his family out of the vicious circle and to find an exit from the Balkan labyrinth.

Grandfather tried to fathom what the reasoning was behind borders, but he was unable to. They had been imposed by other people from other countries. Until that time, he had only heard of property borders that were fixed when land was inherited and divided among the heirs. These, too, caused problems in families—dissatisfaction, and even anger and hatred. The families eventually came to terms with the boundary stones more or less, but they were powerless to act against the new borders imposed from abroad.

Grandfather was even less able to explain the border to his grandchildren than he was to his children. All of a sudden, we were not allowed to visit the nearby monastery anymore and observe the birds wherever we wanted. We had difficulty understanding that the people on the other side of the border, who probably had the same ancestors as we did, were now suddenly our enemies. Brothers were being conscripted into different armies and would end up shooting one another.

He was unable to predict what evil the future borders would bring. They would be watched by armed guards. Relatives would be afraid of one another as never before. Bad times were on the march!

Grandfather loved to talk about the First World War, when the country was divided between the armies of the Triple Entente and the troops of the Triple Alliance. Soldiers from all over the world—from Africa, Asia, and Australia—white and black, yellow and red, had appeared at the lakeside, and began setting forth a boundary on our side under occupation—on our land and our part of the lake. The best story was the one he told to his children and grandchildren about Austro-Hungarian troops forcing the people of occupied Pogradec to mark the borderline with ropes.

As the eldest male in the community, Grandfather served as mayor at the time. Like everyone else he was terrified when orders arrived which commanded that all ropes were to be brought to the town hall. His immediate reaction was that people, God forbid, were going to be hanged. What could the authorities possibly want with all the ropes? Everyone breathed a sigh of relief when they found out that the ropes were simply to be used for marking the border.

Vicious tongues immediately spread rumors that the ropes were being used to strangle the land. At any rate, the ropes were all tied together and, under the supervision of the International Border Commission, were attached to stakes that had recently been dug into the ground. The stakes planted by day were of course shifted in the first night by families whose property, gardens, and vineyards had been divided.

The next day, the members of the commission, accompanied by heavily armed soldiers, appeared once again and returned the stakes and ropes to their original positions. That is, until the following night. When the commissioners realized that the stakes and ropes would not do the trick, they found other means of marking the border and, from that time on, no one could cross without fearing for his life.

Soon thereafter, the Austrians were defeated by the French, and the freshly whitewashed border stones were declared invalid. New ones would be needed.

Grandfather held the view that one could not avoid one's destiny by moving away from the border. Even borders could not change one's destiny. The only thing one could do, he believed, was to fight against the border. He resolved to take up the duel, Grandfather against the border, and he devoted his whole life to the struggle.

Before the old borders were restored at the end of the Great War, Grandfather attempted to dissuade his brothers and sisters from moving to Istanbul. He left the new borders as a legacy to his children. Before he passed on, he ordered them never to desert the border, their place of birth on the lake.

The family divided and many moved away. New times dawned and with them came new wars. The next world war confronted my father with the most difficult decision of his life. He was forced to betray the legacy of my grandfather.

The Tale of My Father

Grandfather had spent his whole life fighting with the borders as much as he could. The borders survived him. His legacy, passed on to his children, was that they should not cross the border or leave their country without important reasons. What those important reasons might be was difficult to define!

Grandfather had lived through the Ottoman Empire, the Balkan Wars, and part of the First World War. Father experienced the Second World War, fascism, and communism. The old border and the new border. Both of them—my grandfather and my father—definitely had border problems.

Grandfather must have turned over in his grave when Father decided one night to take his family over the border to the other side of the lake. He was an opponent of fascism in the little town on the lake where he lived and thus reckoned that he would soon be arrested, interned, and sent off to fight in the Italian trenches. So he decided to steal out on a boat and cross the lake at night.

He had just enough time to say farewell to his mother and sisters. He invited his brother to go with him, but the latter refused. Having once graduated in London, he insisted that he hadn't done anyone any harm and had no reason to flee. Later, because of his knowledge of English, he found himself on a list of names and fell victim to a purge conducted by the Stalinist dictator in Albania. But that is another tale . . .

Father was in the front of the boat. Mother held the two youngest children in her arms, and the older children including myself sat around her. Also on board were several books that Father had saved. Among them were three volumes that he could not do without—the Koran, the Bible, and the Talmud.

We were a whole family on board, struggling to reach the other side. It was a journey between life and death. If we did not manage to get over the border, we would die. If we reached the other side, we would survive. To be or not to be!

A close friend of my father had pledged to carry us over to the other shore. It was not the first time that he had undertaken the dangerous journey. He rowed cautiously, out of fear that the boat might sink before we reached the border in the middle of the lake. It was the farthest this particular rowboat had ever been from the shore.

Father held the rudder in his grasp, commander not only of the boat but of our lives. Mother began to murmur quietly. She was praying. We knew of the prayers she recited at critical moments, but had never paid any particular attention to them. We could not bring ourselves to believe in her God. If God existed, we would not be forced to leave our homeland forever. Mother's prayers were simple. She implored God to allow her children to be carried safely over to the other side of the lake.

A strong wind rose. The waves grew choppier, small at first and then larger. Because of them, Father lost his direction. Was there still a border in all those waves?

Mother's prayers became louder and louder. The older children now joined in her incantations, regretting that they had not learned to pray properly. Only God, they were all convinced, could save us and get us over the border. By the time we reached the other side and could finally see the shore, we were all convinced of his existence.

The Tale of My Mother

In half a century I had gotten used to the Albanian-Yugoslav, that is, the Albanian-Macedonian border. Thirty years had passed since we crossed over by boat and became eternal emigrants. We had suffered more from the border than most other people.

Only telegrams about deaths reached to the other side, in both directions. We had been wont for decades to visit the monastery of Saint Naum on a cliff overlooking the lake, right on the border. With our old binoculars we now looked over the invisible borderline in the water to see the other side. Father came to terms with his fate better than Mother did. He gave up hope that an end would come to his exile.

The die had been cast. Mother was seventy years old when she finally received a red Albanian visa, and nothing could dissuade her from her wish to cross the border and visit the place of her birth.

Father, a tall and steadfast man with an energetic glance, had become thin since the day of our flight, weighed down as he was by the passing years. He had grown old before his time, and the harsh traits in his face had softened. He was the only one who was not able to accompany Mother to the border, and it caused him great pain. They embraced and said good-bye at the doorway. Mother was in tears. The rest of us, all of her sons and daughters, set off along the lakeside in a convoy of cars to take her to the border.

It was a place where two worlds met, where two ideologies collided. Hope and despair. Mother stood on the Rubicon. In front of her was a small strip of no-man's-land. Under the watchful eyes of the border guards, she set off on foot, passing heavily armed soldiers and guards from the two countries on her way.

Pacing calmly and slowly with a suitcase in each hand, she reached the line. The crossing of which she had dreamed so long lasted for only a few minutes. We watched her tiny silhouette vanish. Another age awaited her on the other side.

Mother's Albanian visa was valid for two months but she could have gotten an extension and stayed longer, at least if she had been careful and conducted herself properly. To return before the visa ran out was unusual.

Such things were unheard of in the old country, quite unimaginable. Mother was the historic exception. She asked for permission to return fifteen days before her visa expired.

The same people who had brought her to the border were there to pick her up. Of course she would be surrounded by a barrage of questions. What had made her decide to return in advance?

Father was happy in his own way to hear that she was coming back, but he was uneasy about the fact that she was returning in advance. He probably knew why, but did not say anything. The rest of us were simply delighted to have her back, to be reunited.

We were so moved when we glimpsed her slight figure, pacing in our direction with her two suitcases. Our heroine was finally among us again. The wrinkles in her face seemed to be somewhat deeper but nothing in her expression betrayed her, although her smile was a bit artificial.

She endeavored to hide her sorrow behind a facade of tranquillity, the shield of her solitude. We did not ask her how the trip had been, neither on the way home, nor when we arrived, and we didn't have to ask her of course why she had come back in advance.

Days and months passed since Mother's return from Albania. She grew increasingly gloomy and withdrawn, and it was obvious that something was weighing upon her.

Father saw through Mother's secret even though he did not know everything. There were two versions of her trip to Albania—the one she told us about in great detail, and another that was wrapped in the depths of her silence.

She stated that she had been received with great hospitality. They had taken her to see all of her relatives, and she had finally met her brother after thirty years of separation. She had also said a tearful farewell at the graveside of another brother who had died many years ago.

She had been treated in a kindly manner. Her reception was well organized, as if ordered from above, by some unknown force. She soon grew tired of the facade, the almost aggressive gestures of friendship shown toward her.

Fifteen days before the visa was to expire, she asked for permission to return home. It was a major problem. They were quite taken aback by her request, because no problems had arisen. They entreated her to stay, but she insisted and they eventually gave in and arranged for her departure.

Mother was then back at the border, crossing first the military line, and then the police line. She hastened toward the large gate that someone had once described as the gates of hell. There she stood. It was like a mammoth, as high as four or five people on top of one another, and just as wide, and it was surrounded by razor-sharp barbed wire and innumerable spikes. In the middle was a rusty hasp that looked as if someone had attempted to lock out the advance of time itself.

This was it, the greatest barrier of Balkan savagery and senselessness. She turned around and had a last look at her relatives who were standing under a huge and intimidating portrait of Stalin, before the guards opened the gate for her. The bearer of the weighty key to the gates of hell was waiting at his sentry post, an attractive-looking young man with a rifle over his shoulder and the key, as large as a pistol, in his hand.

Travelers were a rare occurrence at the time and on that day Mother was the only person who wished to be let through. The border guards had no doubt been informed about her premature departure and had taken all requisite measures to observe her final steps on Albanian soil.

It was not the first time in her life that Mother was confronted with a border guard. She thought of the times when she had protected her children from Italian, Greek, German, and other troops. Now she was standing in front of a soldier from her own people. He could have been her son. What a situation!

Damned times, damned borders. But she had patience.

"Good morning, old woman," said the soldier in a friendly voice.

"May God protect you, my son," she replied.

"Listen, old woman, we have no God here, we have the Party."

"You know, young man, when you are as old as I am, it is difficult to rid yourself of old habits and beliefs."

"We have beliefs, too. We believe in the Party. Both young and old."

Mother gave no further reply. She did not want to find herself trapped at the last moment. She took her passport out of her bag and handed it to the soldier before he asked for it.

It was evident that the soldier would have liked to continue the conversation. He probably had instructions to do so, too. But Mother was resolved to cross the border as rapidly as possible.

The soldier lay down the heavy key and began to finger her passport. He leafed through it from start to finish, studied some pages two or three times, and returned to the first page, as if he were looking for something suspicious. His was the task of bringing Mother's official stay in the land of her birth to its proper end. His role in this Balkan border farce, staged specially for an old woman, was temporal but not unimportant.

Mother fretted as she waited. What else could they do to her? First was the fear of the border itself that was reputedly the worst in the Balkans, and now fear of the soldier. Holding her open passport in his hands, he asked her in a brusque official tone: "How old are you?"

"Isn't it in my passport?"

"Yes, but it's illegible."

"How many years do you think, son?"

"You must tell me."

"You want to know how many years of suffering I have gone through?"

The soldier was taken by surprise and gave her a reprimanding glance. The conversation had deviated from the official course it was to take pursuant to the instructions given to him by his superiors, and he was nervous. Unsure of what to do, he replied: "All right, as you wish, old woman. How many years have they been?"

"I am seventy, my son. But with all the suffering I have endured, they feel like one hundred. A whole century, do you understand?"

"I see, old woman. But what I don't understand is why you are leaving your homeland ahead of time and are returning to that country where you have suffered so much."

"Oh lad, I have suffered on both sides, and all because of the border. I have suffered from this border all my life."

The soldier gave no reply. He took the heavy key and inserted it into the huge lock; but before turning it, he asked her in a low voice: "Tell me, old woman, where is your homeland? On this side or on the other?"

"Son, my homeland is where my children live."

The soldier was silent. Without saying another word, he turned the key in the lock. The gate creaked open for all to hear.

As she was just about to pass through the gate, the soldier asked my mother one last question.

"Which are your people, old woman?"

"The people I live with, son."

Mother thus went forth, overcoming the Great Wall of the Balkans. She had learned that there was no way back from exile and that Father was right. The crossing weighed upon her and would be with her until the end of her days.

Epilogue

The end of the century approached.

The end of a century and the history of the border, of the Great Wall of the Balkans. The wall between Albania and Macedonia fell when Stalinism was abolished in Albania, when the statues of Stalin and Enver Hoxha were toppled by young rebels and dragged through the streets.

The border lost its one-time significance, and we could now cross it freely in both directions. The gates of hell were no longer there.

On a recent journey back from the town of my birth, Pogradec, the son of my uncle (the one who had fallen victim to a Stalinist purge) stopped the car right on the borderline and showed me a piece of metal in the asphalt.

"That is all that remains of the gates of hell! This is where the Wall was," stated my cousin.

It was a strange feeling for both of us. He was still uneasy because of what his father had suffered, and I was deep in thought about what my mother had endured when she passed through what had once been the Balkan gates of hell.

Translated by Robert Elsie and Janice Mathie-Heck

The Stranger I Know

László Végel

1

It was back in 1956. My father and I set off on our bikes to pedal to Újvidék, a town about thirty kilometers away.* On a little square somewhere off to the side of the town center my father suddenly braked to a stop. His face turned rigid as he looked at a sign with a swastika. I stood next to him, not knowing what was going on. What we were looking at reminded me of the films that we had to watch in elementary school and then write essays about.

Even today I can remember quite clearly the occasionally appearing swastikas in those films, the angry faces, the balled-up fists, and then what followed—euphoria after a victory. The partisans would achieve one victory after another, and like all children, I ended my essay with the confident sentence, Good has conquered Evil.

Bewildered, I looked at the stunned expression on my father's face. I didn't know what his agitation meant, because in my childish understanding there was always the conviction that the partisans would win out in any case. He calmed down only when he learned that filmmakers were making a film on the square about partisans. This event had clearly awakened in him his feeling of his Being the Other, remembering the white armband that he had worn in 1944. The scene from the film playing out on a real square in a real city had affected him with all the power of real life; for me, on the other hand, it was only a film showing reality, a film in which Good would necessarily triumph over Evil.

Via a little detour, we finally reached the old building in which the school set up during the Austro-Hungarian monarchy was located. My father had

* Then officially known as Novi Sad, Yugoslavia. The author was born into a Hungarian family living in Yugoslavia. —Trans.

bicycled with me to Újvidék to participate in the ceremonies at the beginning of the new school year and to listen to the speeches of greeting. In the previous year, when I registered for school, the nameplate on the entry door still had on it *Pál Papp Hungarian Language School*. At the beginning of classes in the fall, however, the sign had been changed for a new one with the inscription *Moše Pijade Mixed Language School*. Both of us acted as if nothing had happened, and the other parents of my future classmates who were present and the teachers reacted the same way.

Why did this topic even come up? Pál Papp had been a Communist and an anti-fascist who had been executed by the Hungarian authorities after the takeover of power by Miklós Horthy and the Hungarian Army, while Moše Pijade was then a Yugoslav anti-fascist and a trusted confidante of Tito. He was a leading personality of the Communist power structure. So both of them were Communists and anti-fascists, just like everyone around me. At all the many official celebrations we zealously sang a song about how the proletariat would soon rule in America and England and how the truth would triumph.

We were all Communists, even those who did not have a Party membership card. This wasn't merely politics; it was an authentic emotion of our lives. The world was like a film in which the good guys and the bad guys stood against each other and in which everything that was different was suspicious. The shadow of being stigmatized fell on any form of Being the Other.

Looking at the new nameplate on the school, I instinctively thought of Being the Other. I initially had the impression that perhaps they had changed the sign with the name Pál Papp because he had been Hungarian, but I quickly tried to drive off this depressing thought so that I would not become suspicious of myself.

Plain folks took refuge in their belief in the future, a legitimate belief at the time; we thought that living circumstances would get better every day. If you did not get involved in the clashes of public life, you could feel free in your private life. The kindly profile of Tito became ever clearer. In such a condition of happy ignorance, Being the Other was pushed out of mind and was to be forgotten like the past. Parents and teachers, relatives and friends, the older generation, all who had been a part of this past, shielded themselves in an anxious silence. They wanted to forget the bitter memories of the war when people on both sides had been murdered just for the fact of Being the Other.

The new Socialist system held Being the Other strictly within bounds. Josip Broz Tito began his rule as a dictator to continue on as a Franz Joseph of the Balkans, but in his breast there beat a Bolshevik heart. Shortly after the end of the war, springtime breezes began to blow in this part of the Balkans. The Other—the foreigner in another country—was pacified by the Communist utopia, but suspicion still fell on whoever was seen as Being the Other—the alien being inside one's country.

The *Other* and the *Being the Other* are on no account one and the same. A person could have a clear opinion of the *Other,* someone different; one knows exactly if one is dealing with an enemy or a friend. You know whom you are dealing with. *Being the Other,* on the other hand, is mysterious and full of secrets. This person inspires anxiety, and he makes himself suspicious quite quickly, for—as Rimbaud put it—you are always someone else, and never the one that you claim to be. You can turn out like Adelbert von Chamisso's hero Peter Schlemihl, the man without a shadow, but you don't have to worry about continuing to be such a man. Still, you could grow to have several shadows that differ from one another, and after a while you don't know which one is the real one. You try to find out which is the true one. Finally you get tired, and it remains unclear which is the true shadow, because the shadows only indicate that the Ego has multiplied into many egos. None of the shadows is authentic. Perhaps none of them is the true Ego.

The fear of Being the Other instinctively leads us to imitate one another so that we are not distinguished from one another. I too ran away because that was the only way that my experience told me that I could be equal to the others.

Nonetheless, I understood in the shadow play that power over Being the Other is a form of repression. This became completely clear to me as I leafed through a book on the history of the city of Újvidék. (Life had been changed in such a way that there was no difference any more between "true" and "false." But the books remained.) The swampy southern regions of the Pannonian Plain had remained empty after liberation from the Turks. The court in Vienna had attempted to make the region habitable by systematic settlement; after all, they needed citizens who could pay taxes. Then in the eighteenth century the movement of peoples began. From the south came the Slavs; from the north, the Hungarians; from the West, the Germans. With them came Jews, but also Romanians, Slovaks, Russians, and many other national groups, who found a home there in the hope of a better life. Due to its favorable geographic position on the banks of the Danube, Újvidék very soon became an important commercial center and rapidly blossomed. The Serbian, Jewish, German, and Hungarian merchants and artisans on the spot realized that they could purchase the title "free imperial city," and so they took loans and traveled to Vienna to purchase this title in 1748.

For a payment of 80,000 forints, the Empress Maria Theresa satisfied the merchants' wishes, but then she asked about the name of their city. It still did not have a name, answered the representatives, and they asked their patroness to be their "godmother." The ruler willingly took on this task and gave the city the Latin name *Neoplanta*—but only under the condition that every group that settled there would transfer that name into their native language. So from Neoplanta with its 4,620 Serbian, German, and Hungarian inhabitants, the place became Novi Sad, Neusatz, Újvidék. And so it remained until the end of the First World War, when the whole region was attached to the newly created Kingdom of Yugoslavia after the collapse of the Austro-Hungarian monarchy. Thereafter the city was known only as Novi Sad.

After 1918—in the short and, in the eyes of many, the brutal twentieth century—the epoch of nation-states broke out. The small, suppressed nations had their dreams come true, in which the European centaurs, meaning the national minorities, eventually turned into hybrids.

As I was flipping through the book on the history of Újvidék, the nameplate of my school once again occurred to me. What had become of Being the Other, I asked myself, what had happened to the centaurs? Where had the Germans disappeared to? Why didn't we hear anything more about the Jews? Why did the individual groups no longer call the cities by the name in their own language, which had become one of the encouraging metaphors for Being the Other in Europe? And finally: is Being the Other some kind of sin?

Just about four decades later, at the beginning of the 1990s, the overwhelming majority of those who had once been such inspired Titoists had now become militant anti-Titoists. Moše Pijade's tablet had been removed from the wall of the school—on account of his enmity toward Serbs, as the belligerent anti-Titoists explained. That's why he—and Tito as well—was not worthy of having a school bear his name. Besides that, Moše Pijade was a Jew, they noted with a wave of their hand. But nobody should think that they were antisemites—no, don't imagine that!—they cautiously justified themselves. (One should note—these same Serbs in 1992 razed Croatian Vukovar to the ground in the name of patriotism.) Pál Papp should have expected no better fate. He too had been a Communist, something that was as bad as being a Jew. He too would be unworthy of having his name bestowed upon a school in Újvidék, so claimed the once-Communist Hungary, which from one day to the next was beginning to glorify Horthy.*

---

* Admiral Miklós Horthy, regent of Hungary, 1920–1944. —Trans.

In East Central Europe and southeast Europe, one after another new biographies appeared, in which nationalism was just as strong as communism had once been. Democracy began with a change in consciousness of the masses, which involved a denigration of Being the Other. Expressions popped up on the walls of houses such as "Death to the Hungarians!" and "Go home!" Quite often swastikas disfigured the walls. The animosity toward the Roma and the disparaging distinction among ethnic groups became a daily phenomenon, and people spoke only contemptuously about Croats, Muslims, and Slovenes. These events prompted me to consider once again the story of the school nameplate and why my father had been so stunned when he saw the sign with the swastika.

Jew, Hungarian, Serb—this or that name was not the occasion for any concern. So long as the labels could be clearly distinguished from one another, everything is in order; but only so long as the Other does not exist among *them,* but among *us,* and even a bit *in us.* When it is not only strange, but is "the stranger I know." The person whose name appeared on the sign on the wall of the school was both a Jew and a Serb; the other was both a Jew and a Hungarian. One could exchange one for the other, for their shadows had made their true Ego unrecognizable.

The drama of Being the Other exists precisely in the fact that the protagonist can no longer be unambiguously defined. The Other, meanwhile, can be named generally only as "strange"; he can be both friend and enemy. The Europe of today can be proud of its accomplishment in having made friends out of many enemies and in having brought closer many others. We wish to act peacefully with each other and to respect our differences. The signs for the satisfaction of the Other seem promising. Everyone is coming together on a common European playing field in their own name—the Germans, the French, the Romanians, the Hungarians, the Bulgarians, the Czechs. The Other has received an ambiguous but clearly defined name and boundary, and the intermediate areas are gradually disappearing.

Outer peace has thus come over the horizon, but what is the outlook for inner peace? I am still upset about what will become of the unnamed Being the Other,* who is both trusted and strange, and who presents a more complex phenomenon than the Other.† Being the Other has many shapes and stands for many Others all at once, thus having many shadows. In the globalizing world it is an easy matter to place an equal sign between the many Others, but this is a vain hope. They must recognize that they are

* The one at home. —Trans.
† The one abroad. —Trans.

increasingly less different from one another, something that triggers general anxiety in them. This is a matter of the typical trauma of the intellectuals, because it is the intellectuals above all who want to be different. This is however a labor of Sisyphus, since the differences have been smoothed out; consequently they have become of little importance and have become banal. To substitute for them, large international conferences regarding the Other have been set up for the intellectuals. However, there is really nothing to discuss, which is why the nation-state elites pretend to be Being the Other, where the Other has become a decorative embellishment and a gemstone of globalization. The nation-state elites have created in the Europe that is uniting a proper arena for the apologia of the Other as an end in itself. They are simply concerned to preserve the appearance of Being the Other so that no one shall come upon the idea that the national anti-globalization elites could hinder the existence of Being the Other in their own countries or could contribute to its suppression by being silent. The conscience of the Others could not be pure if it were to suppress Being the Other.

While in the salons of Europe of today the Other is greeted with sublime words, one remembers with bad conscience the Being the Other. What is to become of the inhabitants of the marginal areas of the European nation-states, who have so many shadows? What awaits the European hybrids, who live in several parallel worlds, none of which belong to them? What happens to those who speak at least two languages, neither of which are foreign to them, but neither of which are their own? They don't talk about the differences, about the Other, because they have their own problems. They do not want to be the Other—they are forced to be the Other; they are condemned to it. They not only represent the Other; they are also a part of that which they are different from. It is their bad luck that their Ego encompasses several Others. In them several foreign elements come into conflict. What is to become of the "stranger I know," who is not a real stranger, but is the Other marked with this stigma of the Being the Other?

In the Eastern Europe of the twentieth century, the numbers of the centaurs, meaning the national minorities, continue to diminish. While ethnic national maps of the Western European large cities are turning more and more into mosaics, the demographic trends are condemning the minorities in the nation-state areas in Eastern Europe to gradual extinction. Europe is increasingly sacrificing its centaurs, the European hybrids. Cases of ethnic cleansing are allowed, but only as long as these nation-state operations are carried out quietly. While in the European salons the Being the Other is praised, the centaurs in the areas around the edges are in their death throes. Like stepchildren, the national minorities receive no place in the salons of the ruling house, where the Being the Other might be praised.

In any case they wouldn't do that, for Being the Other is an apocryphal experience, whose voice bursts forth "from the depths of the earth" like a buried treasure, as though from a hideout or even a ghetto. This is the polyphonic discourse that even feeds the suspicion that the centaurs talk in an unintelligible language. This assumption is really quite justified, since they have several languages, and it is difficult to say which one is really theirs. The real answer lies in the language that they initially learn to speak, one that is always other than the language in which they are speaking at the current time. Such tension arises between what they say and what they mean that you ask yourself whether they have a mother tongue at all. Usually they are not at all understood by those who now and again sing their praises in order to get satisfaction from the imperative of being politically correct.

2

Being the Other does not lack *one* Other, because such being is a kind of alloy of various and divergent Others. Being the Other does not want to be the Other, but wants to be equal. The Other speaks the dominant language of the nation-state, but the language of Being the Other arises away from power, on the border to nowhere, in no-man's-land. The Other has a cultural aura that the Being the Other lacks. The Being the Other means pain and degradation, constant anxiety of one's own Being the Other—internal mimicry.

I discovered this phenomenon for the first time in my grandfather. He was the first "stranger I know" whom I met. During the great economic crisis of the 1920s—in order to avoid bank foreclosure on his two-room house and garden, which he had bought on credit—he went to France as a guest worker. At that time the Kingdom of Yugoslavia distributed land to the landless, but my grandfather did not receive any because in the eyes of the new rulers Hungarians were not worthy of such distribution. His Serbian neighbors agreed with this decision by the authorities. My father was familiar, but also foreign; and "familiar foreigners—the stranger I know" did not deserve any farmland. He temporarily traveled to France where he was "only" a stranger, but not a familiar one. In this far-off strange country, he was free from Being the Other; he was "only" the Other, without the stigma of Being the Other. He would no doubt have been inspired by the comment of Joseph Roth that he did well only in foreign surroundings.

But the second half of Roth's sentence should not be neglected, because only then can the entire picture be understood—he fared very poorly in his homeland. However, he would only find that out later, but at first he only knew that he did best while being away.

The guest worker, who had been driven abroad, became quite skilled while working in a market garden. This way of earning a living became his profession, and pleased him so well that he made the decision to pay off his bank debts and then to grow flowers in his garden at home. As a person who owned no farmland, he could support his family by growing flowers. He liked France, and besides the skill of growing flowers for market he learned many other things, not least that there were such things as trade unions.

After returning home, he began to grow flowers. He had brought along special seeds and bulbs. To his great surprise, he met only failure in bringing these new types of extraordinary flowers to market, since buyers simply were not interested in them. To his great regret, he could do nothing other than grow those that were in local demand. As a result of this change, he suffered hard times. He tried to survive by mimicry—he did not want to fight, merely to adjust. Still, he did not forget his passion for France, his special flowers, and with great care and for his own pleasure he continued to grow them. This was something that once again aroused the suspicions of his neighbors. Distrust of my grandfather also grew because quite often he would let drop a few words about the French trade unions just at the time when the trade union movement was gradually beginning to spread in the Kingdom of Yugoslavia. For him, the trade union movement had the same exotic value as his special types of flowers.

He was considered a suspicious element, for how could he, a Hungarian, dare to spread suspicious Communist ideas? The police even hounded him with the question as to why he, once he had begun to travel, had not made his way back to Hungary. Why didn't he sound off on communism there? Even these special prized plants, the extravagant French flowers, challenged the imagination of the simple-minded police. They wanted to know why he was raising foreign flowers that he did not have any use for. But they were bothering him in vain. They could not bring any serious charge or any evidence against him; he was only a "stranger I know," whom it was necessary to be on one's guard against.

After Horthy marched in, the Serbian police turned over their documents to the Hungarian police, who became quite busy studying the reports. Once again suspicion fell on Grandfather. After all, the Francophile grower of exotic flowers, the Hungarian sympathizing with the trade unions, could certainly be a Communist. In the eyes of Horthy's supporters, every Communist was dangerous, and the greatest danger came from a Hungarian Communist. Once again Grandfather became a "stranger I know," this time within the Hungarian world.

He was arrested and taken for examination to the Csillag jail in Szeged, where for months on end the guards mocked him by having him peel potatoes. He was not convicted of anything; he was just suspect. It might be all right for a Serb to be a Communist, they said, but it was unpardonable for a Hungarian to be one.

After almost one year in jail, Grandfather was released for lack of evidence. According to the verdict, he had received only as many months of imprisonment as he had peeled potatoes, and therefore he could not ask for any compensation after being released. At home, his many relatives and friends sympathized with the fate of my grandfather, the grower of exotic flowers, but he still dreamed of France. In the hidden corners of his garden he secretly continued to grow his flowers, and kept the memory of his own inner being, which he had to publicly denounce.

After a few months the battlefield remained without an enemy; the Germans and Hungarians had lost the war. Serbian partisans and Russian units marched into the little town. My grandfather remarked on this with satisfaction since he thought that the worst was now over. But the truth proved otherwise. One night partisans banged on his window. He went outside, but before he could say anything, he was thrown to the ground and trampled so hard that he could no longer stand up. His attackers cursed him and screamed at him at the top of their lungs that he was a Hungarian fascist. He had been a Communist, but now he was a fascist, without having changed his views in the slightest. That is the unpredictable fate of the centaurs. My grandmother dragged him into the house, nursed him, and took care of him as well as she could.

In the meantime my father had returned from his hiding place. He had never wanted to be involved in politics in the way that my grandfather had done, and therefore he had hidden himself at several out-of-the-way farms so that at the last moment the authorities could not hand him a draft order into Horthy's army. It is true that as the supporter of his family for some time he had been exempt from military service, but toward the end of the war the general staff of the Hungarian Army desperately needed reinforcements. All men, without exception, were drafted. The farms where my father survived the dangerous months belonged to Serbian peasants with large landholdings. They gave him refuge, and in return he worked without pay for them as a farmhand, taking care of the cattle, feeding the pigs, and milking the cows.

After the entry of the partisans, he returned to his family—but then one morning there was a bang at the window of his house. The unexpected guests told him that he would have to leave immediately, taking only a coat. He was shoved onto a truck with a few other Hungarians he knew, all of whom anxiously asked each other where they might be going. They ended up at a large peasant farm somewhere in the countryside, received white armbands, and were required to harvest corn as forced laborers. This meant very arduous labor from sunup to sundown.

Events, however, took an unexpected turn. Although there was no front line in the immediate vicinity, columns of military marched up and down the field improvising battle stations and preparing themselves for the last blow against the Germans and the Hungarians. The rickety wagons of the Russians were drawn by exhausted little horses. The "little fathers" whipped their nags to make them go faster, all the while screaming "Giddyap to Berlin!" Now and then a single truck would appear. During the corn harvest, my father noticed in the distance another military column approaching. Shortly thereafter the truck at the head of the column reached the cornfield. Armed soldiers jumped out, disarmed the partisan guards, and drove the forced laborers harvesting the corn from their rows.

The officer jumped onto the roof of the car, ordered up his interpreter, and gave a flaming speech, saying that there was no longer any fascism. The interpreter translated the speech of the Russian officer into Serbian. From then on there would be communism—the man made a significant pause, and looked meaningfully at the forced laborers with their white armbands—Comrade Stalin had conquered the seven-headed dragon, and from then on no one would have to wear an armband any longer. "Long live Comrade Stalin, long live the victorious Red Army, long live the Soviet Union! Death to fascism—Freedom to the people!" The Russian soldiers cheered on their officer, threw their weapons into the air, and vigorously applauded.

"Why aren't you applauding? Why aren't you celebrating?" the officer addressed the intimidated forced laborers. When he saw their terrified faces, he commanded that the Jews should rip off the armbands immediately. "Don't worry! From today on you are free!"—"They're not Jews, they're Hungarians," snarled one of the partisans. But the Russian officer didn't want to hear anything about it and lectured the man, "All those people wearing an armband, a yellow star, or any other kind of mark are Jews." The forced laborers looked at each other without any idea of what to do.

Then they looked at their guards, and did not dare actually to remove their armbands. Finally the officer slapped himself on the forehead and commanded his soldiers to get the armbands off the forced laborers. Lurching around, holding on to the prisoners, the Russian infantrymen tore the armbands off everyone. Then they embraced them and kissed them in the Orthodox fashion, three times on the cheeks. The motor started up, and the officer and his people drove away. The caravan of cars followed them, while the Russian soldiers laid into their horses, and as if they had won another battle, shouted triumphantly, "Giddyap to Berlin!"

A few of the forced laborers left behind suggested that they should put their armbands back on and continue working. After all, the partisans would sooner or later come back and take their revenge. Others were of the opinion that they should rather obey the Russians, since they were stronger. Finally the men agreed that the best thing to do would be to continue to harvest corn but without armbands. They gathered up the white armbands that were lying around and stuck them into their pockets. As the sun went down, they looked at each other indecisively, and then one after the other they quietly went back to their barracks.

My father certainly remembered those ominous white armbands when he stopped his bike in front of the sign with the swastika, since he often talked about the fact that he owed his life to the Russians for having taken him for a Jew. They were unable to distinguish between the two differentiating signs, the yellow star and the white armband.

3

What might have happened to them, to my father and my grandfather, if it had turned out differently, if the Russian officer had not taken them to be Jews, if the one Being the Other had not been transferred into the other Being the Other? My father came out of it relatively unscathed, but my grandfather on the other hand fared very poorly. Both of them had to acknowledge, though, that Being the Other is a dangerous situation with unforeseeable consequences, since the individual finds himself on the inside as well as on the outside.

They grasped the principle, even if they were not quite clear about it, that the two frightful cultures of our century, the Holocaust culture and the mass grave culture, were both inspired by fear of the Being the Other. Divergent interests, lust for power, and desire to conquer have occasioned wars, but on the other hand the Holocaust and the mass graves—aside from all the other reasons that one can name—were initiated by beliefs and convictions. The victim of the Holocaust and the mass graves is not the enemy, the simple enemy, not the Other across the border, but the "stranger I know," the Being the Other inside the country. Wars have always been unleashed by someone else with evil intentions who wishes to conquer and rule; genocide, crematoria, and mass graves have always arisen through the desire to exterminate the Being the Other.

Jews were not sent to the death camps by a foreign army or by a foreign power, but by their own fellow citizens, who saw in them both the familiar and the foreign. Behind the devilish plan lay other interests, plans, and intentions as well, but first of all it was through the fear of the Being the Other that this mass passion of such fundamental energy developed. The minorities were also driven into the mass graves by their fellow citizens, who saw in them both the familiar and the foreign.

As the result of my grandfather's garden and my father's armband, I learned to understand the anxiety that Being the Other brings with it. In elementary school I had classmates whose fathers had not fallen in the war, but who had "disappeared." Older people knew what this word meant, a word that was so mysterious for us children, but they concealed it with deep silence. Even in the closest family circle they did not let out their secret, for they feared being stigmatized. Many wives of men who had disappeared into the mass graves were themselves victims of rapes, and they brought children into the world who thought that their fathers had fallen at a foreign front during the war. These were children who could not imagine that in their ramblings in the countryside they often passed by the unmarked mass grave in which their presumed fathers lay at rest. The victim of the war often spoke out publicly, either complainingly or defensively, but the victim who was the Being the Other masked his or her secret in incomprehensible and repressed pain.

Most mothers did not admit to their children that their fathers were buried in nearby mass graves, but they stubbornly stuck with the remark, "Your father disappeared." If that child had a doubt or if the child learned the truth, the mothers would pretend that they had no idea. The number of the "guilty war orphans" robbed of their memory is anything but small. Between the fall of 1944 and the spring of 1945 in Vojvodina some 60,000 Germans and 20,000 Vojvodina Hungarians disappeared. Even today exact numbers are not available, because studies were forbidden for decades. The representatives of the perpetrators give a lower number, while the spokespersons for the victims give a higher number. It was a mass murder in which sloppiness ruled. Verdicts were usually without a standard court process; the story is merely reported that during the night someone banged on the window. Who of the murdered was innocent and who was guilty is something that can be related only by family chronicles.

Even today, in the areas surrounding the small towns and remote villages, open mass graves can be found in the unknown sections of fields and cemeteries. The more fortunate generations of the Tito era for decades had no notion that they were surrounded by mass graves. They wandered through this area of the Pannonian landscape just as once did Stendhal's hero in *The Charterhouse of Parma,* Fabrice del Dongo, the idealist incapable of having any luck, and who, full of great ideals, was plucking flowers for his loved one in a meadow. In the distance he heard the thunder of cannons, but he had no notion that he was standing right in the middle of the battlefield at Waterloo.

In 1945 a new historical past was born, and the old had to be forgotten. With deep horror I heard the story of the "cold days" in Újvidék, when Horthy's soldiers in a three-day raid killed some 1,300 Jewish and Serbian citizens and threw them into the Danube. This morbid scene of the mass grave culture awakened feelings of guilt in me, and I had to learn how to live with these feelings. In the streets of Újvidék a Star of David shines under the covering stucco of many a house, something that makes me remember my father's white armband.

My youth played out in the midst of anti-German and anti-Hungarian socialization. In films, in schoolbooks, in public, one always said that the Hungarians had been Hitler's last vassals. Now and again a teacher would sympathetically add that we had not been the guilty ones, just they. That is the only way that I can explain to myself the shock that 1956 was for me. After the crackdown on the Hungarian Revolution, Hungarian refugees popped up in the provisional reception camps in the Vojvodina.

For the first time since 1944 the older generation met Hungarians from Hungary, and for the younger generation it was the very first time for such a meeting. The centaurs were confronted with their other self and with their feelings of guilt. These were then those people that the schoolbooks talked about, so we thought to ourselves. We did not think very well of them, but we did not want to lay any guilt on them. The conversation within a close family circle was very difficult. They too were Hungarians, but their history was different from that of my parents. They had other memories, other cares. They spoke the same language, but they spoke from another world. For the Hungarians from Hungary, we embodied the "strangers I know— the familiar strangers." It is true that they all spoke the same language, but their stories dealt with different world experiences. They did not understand each other. And so the circle of centaur existence closed. Anyone who wanted to be freed of it would have had to change his language and identity or to change his territory. If a person were not ready for both of these, for his entire life he would miss something, and he would drag his shadow around with him, belonging neither to one world nor the other. He would not be able to make himself understood either here or there, and it would not have been at all surprising if the two worlds of his inner being did not understand each other.

As a writer who comes from no-man's-land, this has happened to me often, both on the Hungarian and the Serbian side. I knew the history of one and the other, and both lived within me. They, however, do not know my story or know only one of the two sides. The literature of the no-man's-land does not really belong to anyone, not to the Others. They are children of the nation-state, while I am a denizen of no-man's-land.

4

Given recent history, it is worthwhile embracing the Other in the world of East Central Europe and southeastern Europe with tolerance. The stranger is beautiful, it is claimed, but only as long as the stranger is far away and unknown. This unknown person is, however, no longer as exotic as had been the case in the nineteenth century, but we continue to act as if he or she were exotic. We are condemned to this, since we stumble over one another every day.

In order to put an end to this mess, the intellectual, cultural, and political life is organized like a multinational concern in which everything is connected with everything else. Even though it is now apparently the fashion to turn against globalization, it is important to maintain its rules. At international literary symposia, one person values one Other, and another person values another Other, even though the two are quite similar to one another—the same foods, the same fashions, the same technologies, the same literary currents, the same jargon for discourse. Dialogue about the Other serves the purpose of keeping one's distance from the Other. It is a matter of valuing the representatives of the nation-state centers, the authentic Others, and in this ceremony we get the "multicolored single-color state." In the end the Other is symbolized by the representatives of the nation-states, meaning that there exists only one single authentic form of cultural narrative, that of the nation-state. And so the supposedly cosmopolitan, European circle is closed.

As long as the proper distance is maintained, one can reckon on mutual understanding; that is why it is important to carry on the friendly relations that maintain this distance and mutual understanding. The epoch of barbarism is gone. One fine gentleman does not publicly disparage the Other, and the one-time proletarians of Central and southeastern Europe no longer try to become fine gentlemen themselves by such means.

The wars on the territory of the former Yugoslavia presented the last great convulsion of the barbaric Others. Despite all the barbarism, the wars have resulted in the obligatory Western doctrine dating from the beginning of the twentieth century, namely, the creation of nation-states in East Central Europe and southeastern Europe. The short twentieth century began with the creation of the Eastern European nation-states and ended in Yugoslavia with the same result. In this ethnically multicolored region, the nations have laid down their territories and their borders, and the muddle has passed to the representative Other.

Following the collapse of the national confederation, which had been put together like a mosaic from many ethnicities, no one wanted to remain as a national minority in one of the mixed population regions of Yugoslavia. No wonder! Even though the representatives of the nation-states, each speaking for his own state, announced with deep conviction that things were going quite well for the national minorities in their state and that the "minority question" had been resolved (which at least theoretically would mean that it was soluble in the first place), they all knew that under the current conditions in Europe this was a hypocritical lie. The collective memory in history showed them clearly that it was humiliating to be a minority and to find oneself in the terrifying situation of Being the Other.

They all wanted to be in the Other, but without the misery of the Being the Other. And so the war broke out in the main out of fear of the Being the Other, and caused the greatest destruction precisely in the areas of mixed population. We are outraged about this, but we are outraged in the same way as if there had been an unexpected natural catastrophe. We don't have the courage to classify the mass grave culture in its place in the larger European chronicle, which has been repeatedly blessed by the Western great powers by not having the perpetrators bear responsibility. At the most a few European criminals have been punished, since according to the traditional codex of Western jurisprudence there is no collective guilt, even though there are clearly collective victims.

A cautionary example of this is the Holocaust culture directed against Being the Other, which we cannot erase from our memories because of its gigantic extent. A second example, just as illustrative for this situation, comes from the mass grave culture that has been hushed up due to a bad conscience. The Holocaust is the final result of antisemitism; the mass graves are the result of the exclusion of minorities. The two are not identical, but there is a common denominator—the fear of Being the Other. Where there is antisemitism, sooner or later the exclusion of minorities will become a strong force. In both cases the victims are those who are burdened with the curse of Being the Other.

The "stranger I know—the familiar stranger" will no doubt remain in the future a half tolerated, half suspect individual, who carries around his many shadows. The members of the European nations smile correctly, appear friendly, and act as though this is all a marginal issue. In the meantime the number of "strangers I know," the orphan children of Europe, declines asymptotically. The narcissistic European Other has conquered—it has prevailed over Being the Other.

Translated by Lawrence Schofer

Bedel

Nenad Veličković

> If only I could find someone who would
> live in my stead. Like a *bedel*.
> —*Ivo Andrić*

To the Editor:

I assure you, you made a mistake in asking Nenad Veličković to write an essay for your readers who want to know about the Other and the break-up of Yugoslavia, discussing: *Why this strife and struggle, why conflict, why the neighbor as an adversary and not as a partner? What is the relation to the Other?*

Veličković is an utterly inappropriate choice, and should you stand by it you will get a twenty-page text that will simply take your readers for a ride.

Here is the proof: your readers want to know *Why this strife and struggle, why conflict, why the neighbor as an adversary and not as a partner? What is the relation to the Other?*, but look at what he (Veličković) is doing. They (your readers) have in mind images of emaciated people behind barbed wires, bullet-pocked buildings and torched houses, the horror-stricken eyes of the tortured and raped, unending columns of refugees, blood on the streets and mutilated bodies; meanwhile he is lying in bed, the covers pulled up over his head, his hand between his legs. If you know what I mean . . .

So you have contacted a brazen boor of a person with little education and a big ego, ambitious and money-grubbing, but, above all, intelligent and sharp, with a talent for both serving and disdaining his readers, for flattering and insulting, entertaining and baffling them.

Bedel: Arabic for "substitute." In Bosnia before 1914, a rich man could buy off his military service by hiring someone to serve in his place. —Trans.

Your readers are already feeling slightly uneasy. They are not used to this kind of provocation. Why the covers and the hand between the legs, when the subject proposed is important, the question clear, and the matter topical? Any average European professional intellectual, any expert from roundtables and panel discussions, would already have launched into a clear introduction, citing Levinas and Derrida and Lacan and Said and Todorova and Maalouf. But, he, that where-did-you-dig-him-up Veličković of yours, what does he start off with? Masturbation, if you'll pardon my French. Puhleez!

And why? Simply because it (masturbation) was what the doctor ordered as part of his preventive therapy for a potentially festering prostate inflamed fifteen years ago in the trenches around Sarajevo. (Where he spent three-and-a-half years of the war with the army of Bosnia and Herzegovina.)

Please note the perfidious talent at work here. Just when you thought that you would stop reading and thank his nibs for the text you won't publish, what did the sly dog do? He mentioned Sarajevo, and his involvement in the war, and you were immediately touched and are already prepared to forgive him his unseemly beginning. And I understand you: from an observer's point of view, and mostly television's, Sarajevo is synonymous with victimhood, a status that, understandably, has been transposed to its citizens, intellectuals, artists, and also writers. However, was this Veličković of yours really a victim? Or simply a plain old war profiteer, who would have remained anonymous and beyond the realm of any anthology had the flash of an explosion not shone its light on him and had the force of the detonation not hurled him into the arms of a compassionate Europe?

Sir,

I most humbly and mindfully ask you not to fall for the tricks of this complex-ridden literary outsider. Really, why would you let him make such a boldfaced, gratuitous mockery of the European intellectual? Instead of holding his chin between his thumb and middle finger, his index finger pressed against his cheek, and looking into the camera through his glinting glasses, what does he do? Rub his penis, pardon my French again. Is *that* the image of a Balkan writer and intellectual we want to give to the European public? Can *such* a person have anything worthwhile or intelligent to say to your readers on the subject? Had you asked me *Why this strife and struggle, why conflict, why the neighbor as an adversary and not as a partner? What is the relation to the Other?*, I would have immediately replied, without giving it a second thought: because this is the Balkans. And what are the

Balkans? The outskirts. The outskirts of Catholicism, the outskirts of Islam, the outskirts of Slavism, the outskirts of the Mediterranean, the outskirts of Turkey, the outskirts of communism, the outskirts of Europe. So, a space that (like any outskirts) is neglected, run-down, underdeveloped, exploited, discarded, humiliated—interesting and useful only as a garbage dump or potential building site. A space, then, that is outside the boundaries of the decent, law-abiding worlds that surround it. A paradoxical space, because it is on the outskirts and yet it is in the middle of several disinterested centers. The inhabitants of this space (Balkanites) are constantly trying to prove their political credentials and loyalty to the capitals of their (respective) centers by emphasizing their own ideological purity, always in contrast to the impurity of others. They are of interest to their centers not as some family bastard left at the city dump, but solely as a potential labor force on the building site that such a dump might one day become. And since fidelity and allegiance are not enough, and plain physical strength is of no value without corresponding land, these poor wretches strive to appropriate and register as much land as they can. Needless to say, at the expense of their neighbors—their equals in every respect—whom they try to deny, by force and through culture, an equal right to their common space.

Sir,

I am sure that your readers might like to know how force and culture serve each other, and how literature contributes to what you call *strife and struggle*. Let us start with an obvious, widely accessible fact, that is, with the number of hours allotted to the teaching of literature in the school curriculum. Why is it given two to three times more time than any other art? Why does it enjoy a privileged position in education? Because, I am so bold as to say, its medium is language, and language, unlike colors or tones, is not nationally neutral. Why did the Serbo-Croatian (Croato-Serbian) language fall apart and why, parallel with the armed fighting, did national elites purge their dictionaries and redefine their spelling and grammar? Because language can be a tool for recognition, a means for expressing belonging, and once that is what it becomes and already is, it no longer needs to express thought. Orthographical standards were changed with only one purpose in mind: to enable exclusively national languages to come into their own as quickly and as sweepingly as possible. Linguists whose patriotism outweighed their expertise radically did away with synonyms, they revived archaisms, cloned compound words, and raped grammar, all in the name of a people who, frightened and unsure of themselves, once again buckled down to learning how to speak and write properly.

In the Balkans of the nineties, language-washing came before brainwashing. A language relieved of the responsibility of conveying thought could be used to persuade people that it was more important to express belonging (to the collective) than opinions. A language forced to declare subservience to the nation and state makes it impossible a priori to voice any criticism. Language was used in the Yugoslav space to help divide people into *us* and *them.* And language continues to do so to this day, subtitling Serbian films in Zagreb, translating the *ekavian* dialect into *ijekavian* in Sarajevo, ignoring the speech of Bosniaks in Belgrade and problematizing the language's name (*Bosniak,* not Bosnian).

Language, I hope it is now clearer, is one of the reasons for literature's privileged position in education. But it is neither the only nor the most important one. Why, for instance, is it *compulsory* for students at Sarajevo University, future teachers of literature, to study three separate but equal subjects: the history of Bosniak literature, the history of Croatian literature, and the history of Serbian literature? (In the course of their studies, they have more classes in national literatures than in methodology, pedagogy, theory, world and children's literature put together!) Because, if you will permit me to answer, school curricula offer not works of literature that encourage independent, critical thought, but those that teem with ethnographic fossils testifying to the antiquity and constancy of the nation.

Five or six hours a week account for a fifth of the school curriculum not so that tomorrow's generations will stand up in defense of ethics or aesthetics, but so that they will defend their tribe and its country. Literature is one of the most powerful sources of this lethal radiation. It is insidious: once fiction has circumvented, unopposed, rationality and logic (we have declared both to be incompetent in matters of the imagination), it takes hold of the victim's brain (the critic's, the historian's, the student's, the reader's), where it unrelentingly and incurably transforms itself from a blatant lie into an absolute truth. Novels, debates, reviews, scholarly papers, even the poetry of the Yugoslav 1980s are rife with examples of such alchemy. Take, for instance, the following:

Two years before the war in Bosnia, the NIN Prize, the most prestigious Yugoslav award for literature, was given to Vojislav Lubarda's novel *The Ascension,* which depicts Bosnian Muslims as neighbors who cannot be future partners because they are dangerous, aggressive, and completely focused on destroying the Bosnian Serbs. One of the jury later stated that he had been asked by the Serbian Academy of Sciences to vote for this book, which the critics had hailed as "an important literary testimony," "erudite reading which gives a literary slant to a wealth of historical, geographic, ethnographic and psychological material," "stylistically and linguistically sumptuous," "Homeric," "epic," "modernistic," "polyphonic" . . .

Lubarda's *The Ascension* was preceded by Dobrica Ćosić (later president of the state) and Danko Popović, whose books spawned a wave of writing about the Croats, Bulgarians, Albanians, Muslims . . . as being *false* brothers, weaklings and cowards, who were just waiting for the right historical moment to stab the Serbs in the back and divvy up their land.*

The media, accused, and with good reason, of fanning the madness of those days, squawked from *literary* nests (as the above examples show!). Literature was and remains, if you will permit me to resort to an image from epic poetry, the *fairy blood sister* of nationalism; nobody is louder in glorifying ethnic belonging as a divine gift and privilege (forever threatened by its envious surroundings), drawing its strength and persuasion from its epic and mythological roots.

As an act of art that is relieved of the oath to speak the truth, the whole truth, and nothing but the truth, literature is neither legally nor formally responsible if judges and executioners repeat its false testimonies when pronouncing the death sentence. But it does carry a fundamental and moral responsibility; there is a connection between negative images of the Other in literature and mass expulsions, harrassment, and killings. Along with forming a negative image of the Other, it is literature's task to affirm in the mind of the individual the absolute values of the community to which he or she belongs by birth. On the eve of the collapse of Yugoslavia, these values were redefined as patriarchal; they implied the purity of the tribe on the territory possessed, and faith in a male god. Yugoslavism did not satisfy this ideal of purity: it was atheist, it affirmed mixed marriages, and it viewed land as a common good. Rashly and maliciously equated with communism (the infamous Other in Western eyes), it fell as collateral damage. Two million people who had declared themselves non-nationally as Yugoslavs were shoved under the red carpet laid out for the victors. The memory of their existence was erased with the same painstaking thoroughness as in the case of Vukovar, Mostar, and Sarajevo.

---

* There are examples on other sides and in other genres as well; by equating it with Greater Serbianism, Muhsin Rizvić's study of Andrić (*Bosnian Muslims in Andrić's World*) helped to brand Yugoslavism as an "otherness," which was supposedly the precondition for Bosniaks to revert to their patriarchal roots. The abuse of literature, a course taken on the eve of Yugoslavia's disintegration, continues to this day. Textbooks in Bosnia and Herzegovina are clearly nationally intoned; the choice of texts and their methodological treatment favor the cultural (national) identity of the majority nation in the administrative region. Once established, the rule that patriotism is a higher virtue than expertise explains and justifies why below par books by anonymous writers are being foisted on children, and why excerpts promote negative stereotypes of others. —N.V.

Your readers, Sir, surely remember pictures of these towns in flames and ruin, and perhaps that is really why you invited a Sarajevo writer to explain *Why this strife and struggle, why conflict, why the neighbor as an adversary and not as a partner? What is the relation to the Other?*

Sir,

I hope you are beginning to realize the moral and literary fallacies of your choice of writer, who still has the covers pulled up over his head, amusing himself with his hesitant erection. Does it not seem to you that by indulging in such behavior and silence he is making a mockery of our subject of discussion? Or, worse yet, that he has *metamorphosed* into a contemporary European intellectual and his literary *engagement*? It frightens me to contemplate how low this discussion would sink if he were now to decide to participate, and what pornographic images he would use to fill these pages.

So, permit me to continue. Unlike him, I do not consider a conversation about the Other to be outdated. The world is full of the Other. Islam is the Other. The poor are the Other. The south is the Other. Women are the Other. Animals are the Other. Nature is the Other. Everything is the Other. To approach everything as if it were an enemy rather than a partner is to live in hell. I believe that was what Sartre meant. I also believe that your question *Why this strife and struggle, why conflict, why the neighbor as an adversary and not as a partner? What is the relation to the Other?* is focused on the future, not on the past. That you are interested in peace, not war. Is peace possible here? I believe it is. I believe in the Partnership for Peace. I believe in democracy and economic reform. I believe in NATO. Unlike Veličković, whose heaving and sighing under the covers suggests that once the whole world joins NATO, it will feel relief and pleasure and a sense of peace. Like after masturbation!

Do you see how banal his very presence makes our monologue? Why don't you, as the editor, simply evict him from these pages? Why this soft spot for him? Because you need an insider's view, from a land scorched by hatred, from the very pits of the Balkan hell. But war was not hell for him! His neighbors were not his enemies. Omer ran over to his apartment so that he would be the one to open the door to a gang of street patriots and send them packing. Old Sadija shared his last remaining heart pills with our man's pregnant wife. Oto, looking like Asterix with a huge tombstone on his back, showed up between two shellings, toting a stove hammered together out of old tin, with a big red bow around its neck. Alma saved her last few liters of gas for the drive to the maternity hospital. When little

Marina was born in the summer of that first year of the war, the neighbors sang her name under the window. During the baby's first weeks at home, Tyronne came from the other end of town to bring an unopened roll of film which still preserves the story of war in thirty-six images. In one of them, Veličković, twenty pounds lighter and with fewer teeth than today, is staring into the lens with the smile of a happy man. If his words sometimes carry a note of nostalgia for those years of shelling, of going without electricity, food, water, and heating, then it is out of gratitude for a lesson learned: that a person's life is worth not what he hides and keeps from people, but what use it can be to them.

That is why, Sir, I do not think you will manage to draw Veličković into this story about the Other. He sees it as an intellectual invention, a trendy term, an alibi for keeping silent about the person, the individual, his solitude, insecurity, fear, discontent, in short, about what Marx calls the alienated.

Instead of answering your question, he will ask you whether your reader is less alienated for having been born in Europe than someone who was born in Sarajevo. Does he have nicer dreams because he sleeps in a better bed? Does he take pride in clean streets unsullied by spit and in nicely painted buildings with no pockmarks? Does he enjoy bigger discounts and lower interest rates? Do cheap flights and not having to go through the humiliation of waiting in line for a visa make him happy? Does it give his life more meaning when his Germany or France or Sweden wins the World Cup? Is his fear of illness and death any less? Is his joy at the birth of a child any greater? Is his day longer than twenty-four hours? How does he spend it? Does he get up in the morning happy, without aches and pains, without wrinkles, without the feeling that somewhere there must be a better, fairer world, a life where a person can be more than a slave to the drug of cheap money? Does he go to bed at night without wishing that there is a *bedel* somewhere who will get up in his stead? If there is an Other, then it is not a Muslim, Black, Serb, Palestinian, Roma, Jew, Russian, Chinese, Albanian, Kurd . . . It is what they have made out of the child in us: a being whose wide-open eyes no longer shine with curiosity but with fear.

Sir,

Was the purpose of your question *Why this strife and struggle, why conflict, why the neighbor as an adversary and not as a partner? What is the relation to the Other?* to learn what happens when the world is transformed from a miracle into a monster? If it is, then I admit that perhaps you were not so wrong to approach Veličković. He could actually answer your question if only he would interupt his therapy for a moment. (Although, between you and me, I doubt it is therapy that he is practicing. In fact, I've got my doubts about the diagnosis itself. It's not his prostate that is the problem. It's loneliness. And here's the proof: his cell phone pings with a new message. It is something that can wait. But all the same, Veličković reaches out from under the covers for his phone and reads it. Why, I ask you, unless those few words are maybe a better cure? For loneliness, not the prostate . . .)

You will have observed that Veličković does not share my optimism about NATO and the Partnership for Peace. One can understand him: he was optimistic about (and before that, served) the Yugoslav People's Army, only overnight to become the target of its tanks and howitzers. Disgust best describes his feelings about the military profession, officers, and weapons. All generals, whatever flag they serve under, have the same passion for sacrificing the small lives of others to nourish the magnificent lie that death in the course of action is the route to heaven.

Veličković does not have a good word to say about economic reforms either. Disgust is what he feels for those smooth-shaven, expensively dressed financial bandits, war profiteers, loan-shark journeymen, media tycoons, in short for that entire new liberal-democratic elite charged with joining the European Union.

Veličković is very skeptical about the EU, as well. He cannot but compare it with Yugoslavia. His cynicism, bolstered by experience, does not see why the Union's future would be any brighter than Yugoslavia's past. Look for yourself: Yugoslavia developed between East and West, Europe between the USA and Asia; the euro is not immune to inflation, neither was the Yugoslav dinar; criticism of the distribution of power and goods is loud in the EU just as it was loud in Yugoslavia; here we have a simmering rivalry amongst the strongest members and dissatisfaction amongst the poorest, and there it was the same; mutual relations are burdened by the weight of history which remembers wars, crimes, occupation, betrayal; the bureaucratic apparatus is growing like a carcinoma; internal borders are invisible but not eradicated; soccer fans make the same grimaces and have the same deadly instincts; the economy brings in the same nice revenue from the manufacture and export of arms . . . As for literature, in the French, Polish, Irish, and Bulgarian school curricula, as in the Yugoslav, it sits like a hen on the eggs of reborn national romanticism.

The only point on which Veličković agrees with me is when comparing the Balkans to a rundown suburb, whose sole value is as a marketplace that can be turned into a dumping ground for secondhand goods and bureaucrats or into a building site for yet another hyper-multiplex-mega-shopping-center, above which will fly the flag of fifty yellow stars orbiting around a void.

Inhabited by *bedels,* he would say.

Bedels like me, I would add.

Sir,

Let me try and explain to you and your readers my own particular role here. At the very outset I assured you that your question *Why this strife and struggle, why conflict, why the neighbor as an adversary and not as a partner? What is the relation to the Other?* was being put to a brazen boor of a person with little education and a big ego, ambitious and money-grubbing, but, above all, intelligent and sharp, with a talent for both serving and disdaining his readers, for flattering and insulting, entertaining and baffling them.

Did I lie to you? (Did he lie to you?) No. Why did he accept your invitation if from the start he thought (a) that this was a hackneyed topic, and (b) that he was invited as that Other, as a victim, in other words for mostly nonliterary reasons (vain!). However, since he was offered (a) what is, by our standards, a huge fee (money-grubber!), and (b) a place in a prestigious anthology (ambitious!), he accepted.

Did he show any great erudition? No, he did not; except for a few factual illustrations, he did not spew out reams of relevant details, statistical figures, findings, inescapable quotes . . . He gave not a single European example to corroborate his flippant theory about the invidiousness of literature.

Was he servile? Did he flatter and amuse? Yes, I did.

And did he also conceal his disdain? No, he didn't. (What else was that story under the covers about?) Was he also offensive? Yes, he was. (Isn't the metaphor of the intellectual-masturbator offensive?) Did he also baffle? Yes, he did. (Would I have to be explaining all this, if it were otherwise?)

Did you, in the end, get the answer to your question? Yes, you did.

Did he take part in it? No he did not. The *bedel* did.

So here we are at the heart of the postmodern condition. Everything is and is not, everything is true and is false, we killed and we didn't, we expelled and we didn't, we are responsible and we are not. But it's more that we didn't and are not than otherwise, because the line between reality and virtuality has been erased. Life is only life to the extent that it provides material for a script. After all, or, if you prefer, first of all, a script is a literary form, and its final shape is decided by somebody's volition. And since one's conscience, in spite of everything, cannot have a *bedel,* that volition hid under the covers, declaring itself dead. By accepting the death of the author, literature legitimized nonresponsibility; a dead author is the equivalent of an anonymous perpetrator.

However, the author obviously is not dead. He charges fees, accepts awards, gives lectures, and looks out at us from bookshop posters (chin between thumb and middle finger, index finger on cheek . . .), with an enigmatic, self-satisfied, Giaconda-like smile.

Meanwhile, beneath his covers he is firmly convinced that he is changing the world by turning it into words.

Sir,

I hope it is now clear why *I* had to respond to your question *Why this strife and struggle, why conflict, why the neighbor as an adversary and not as a partner? What is the relation to the Other?*, while Veličković kept amusing himself, except for that one moment when he received the message that illness had gotten the better of his friend's mother. Just that one moment!

What man would let go of the erection he had made such an effort to achieve (the same effort it took to squeeze 23,000 characters out of a few simple thoughts), and what writer, in an essay about self-gratification, would forgo the fireworks at the end?

That is more or less all that he, without a trace of false modesty, had to say about his attitude to the Other, and about his paltry attempt to change literature since he cannot change the world.

Translated by Christina P. Zorić

Allowing the Other

Dragan Velikić

THE OTHER IS A PROJECT LAUNCHED BY TWO GERMAN FOUNDATIONS; THE editor is Swedish and the audience German.* I see this book as a ship with an international crew and Berlin as its home port.

These facts will determine the perspectives of the southeast European writers whose essays appear here. On their coming voyage, they will use the map of their own experience to navigate the territorial waters that shape the notion of *the other*. But audiences that read these essays in translation are themselves *the other;* their worlds are the land beyond the horizon, from whose ports they have set sail.

Let us imagine that two Bulgarian foundations engage a Serbian writer, living, say, in Berlin, to gather together some fifteen Western European writers and ask them to pen something on the subject of *the other*. The very fact that they would be addressing a Bulgarian audience, and sailing on a ship whose home port was Sofia, would determine their navigational course. For Western European writers, thinking about *the other* would probably have less of that centrifugal component of the ship's home port than it would for a southeast European crew. I cannot think of a single instance of a German writer, for example, who has grown up in Bulgaria and decided to write in Bulgarian. But here we are within the orbit of cosmic movements. The sun, like nations, moves from the East.

The other is an illusion. Our own projection. It is always us and our *other*—the coral reef is formed out of prejudices, misconceptions, and stereotypes. For, when *others* are pepper and silk, in other words things that, at no risk to us, fit into our world and merely reinforce, enhance, and enlarge it, that is one thing, but when the *other* is *Allahu akbar,* then a line is immediately drawn as to when and to what extent one can hear *Allahu akbar.* Admittedly, there are always those who will be a threat to pepper and silk, and it

---

* The present book originally appeared in German under the title *Der andere nebenan.* —Trans.

221

is then that the notion of tolerance is raised. There is never total tolerance anywhere, because it would mean cohabiting with pedophilia, cannibalism, necrophilia, incest. . . That is all well and good. But it is not well and good when partial tolerance, partial acceptance of *the other,* is turned into a myth, and truncated tolerance is promoted as the ideal model of behavior. This only further undermines the possibility of being *other.*

Is the other everything that we are not? It is easier to create the other than it is to get to know and accept it as other, to let it be other. The possibility of otherness depends on our own capacity. Where there is no room for true otherness, there is no room for anything, save for prejudices and misconceptions whose purpose is to protect.

What is it that such an other—our other, protects? What is it that it threatens? Broadly speaking, it is so-called traditional values. It is worth noting, however, that the notion of traditional values has least to do with true values. Does the average German think of Goethe and Beethoven at the mention of German tradition, or does he think of beer and sausages with sauerkraut? And will *Mahabharata* ever threaten Goethe, or is it more likely to be the spread of Indian fast-food restaurants on the streets of Berlin that at some point starts to bother the average German? It is, of course, the clash of traditional values, not true values, that provides the explosive charge, because true values never clash. The homestead is what matters. It is our small, banal everyday life that is protected at the cost of another's. And the only thing that threatens it is somebody else's small, banal everyday life. Two samenesses battle each other for primacy.

The first step in this battle is to draw a clear line between *us* and *others.* The homesteads have to be fenced, so that every member of the community can see when his territory—our territory—is about to be attacked. The Pax Romana was able to last two hundred years because a strong wall was built along the border of the Roman Empire, guaranteeing that Rome would never cross that line in search of conquest. A boundary is rule number one, and its existence marks the beginning of a game that plays by the rules. Unclear, porous borders open up the murky field of doubt, do away with the rules of battle, and offer scope for personal initiative.

That is why civil wars are the most brutal, why there is more antagonism within a faction of the same movement than between different movements. The violent war in Yugoslavia was fought by peoples who speak the same language. Slovenia and Macedonia, the only two republics whose languages are different, separated with next to no bloodshed. Their identities being defined by a different language, they were always *the other,* even when Yugoslavia looked integrated and united. One always plays with others according to the established rules. It was the other four nations, divided into three religions, but connected by the same language, that engaged in the feast of blood. The principle of *small differences* confirmed its virulence once again. In most of the former Yugoslavia, it was not possible to build a wall, it was not possible to section off *others*. *Others* were intermixed, especially in Bosnia; they were constantly within sight, like a continuous threat and provocation.

What is important, then, is the border and how far *the other* will be allowed to go. Where there is no border, or it is not strong enough to guarantee security, the sensitivity toward others grows in proportion to the fear. Not to be afraid of others denotes a strong identity. A strong identity means, inter alia, not lowering the barrier at border crossings. As soon as there is fear of a threat, something is wrong with the identity. Because identity is not a structure, it is not carved in stone; it is a process which, like the universe, has no beginning and no end. Life is growth, and growth is exchange, the physiological activity of body and soul. Exchange is possible only with others. Others make us what we are. We ourselves are others to someone else.

Part of Josip Broz Tito's *practical mind* was to produce the other in his own mold. The outside space needed to be filled with content that was familiar, content that could be controlled and never allowed in, unless we so wished or it was in our interest. I remember Tito's time. Part of his wisdom was to have an opposition in his own mold; he created his own *other*, corrupted and legalized it, thereby dispensing with the possible emergence of a real other that might pose a threat to him. Tito's dissidents were renegades who did not doubt communism; their heresy was not that they doubted the end objective, it was that they doubted the road to achieving it. It is no accident that the standard-bearers of Yugoslavia's then opposition lived in luxurious state-owned apartments; they had their sinecures. During Tito's rule, many writers acquired the aureole of hard-core opponents; the regime flirted with banning their work, but in essence, they were no threat to anybody. They were extras; the regime allowed them to occupy the space that could potentially be filled by real others, whom the regime would be hard put to control. Real political opponents, those who did not believe in any road to communism, were marginalized once Tito's power was entrenched after World War II; they were not even worth arresting (save for a few exceptions), their aureoles as martyrs were not real.

This brings us back to the principle of *small differences*. For Tito spent time and energy only on the opposition of *small differences*. The truly *other* were unimportant, relegated to the margins of a system that was successful in controlling distances. Because those of like ilk, this opposition of "small differences," lent themselves to being turned into enemies by the broad masses. In the days of sweeping euphoria and indoctrination, the truly different were relegated to the realm of the phantasmagorical, like prehistoric monsters. And as such, they were unimportant. Rather like the Amish. Who bothers with the Amish? Nobody! Because they are so very different and, as such, of no interest.

It is politically dangerous to leave free scope to those who are other and to let them form spontaneously. This is something Milošević learned from Tito. But Milošević's time was different from Tito's; his was a time of tectonic upheaval, big words and change; a time of pluralism. Monolithic political conformity was shattered, and the countless movements, parties, currents, and groupings that emerged slowly became polarized. One Serbia was with Milošević, though this same nationalistic Serbia also gathered around part of the opposition. The other Serbia recognized itself in the person of Zoran Đinđić. In its desire to ensure that the *other* fits its own mold, from the outset Milošević's regime perfidiously and consistently demonized Zoran Đinđić, branding him a German spy, a henchman of the West who wanted to enslave the freedom-loving spirit of the Serbs. Đinđić was the real opposition to Milošević, the dangerous virus of individualism and the civil option in the populist and collectivist body of the Serbian people. He was the real *other* political option; to put it bluntly, even in *civilizational* terms, Đinđić was another story.

Tito's era of complete control in a nonglobal world belongs to the distant past. Moreover, Tito had an idea, a vision. He helped to launch the Third World. And he was himself a part of the world Communist story. To what degree that was a delusion is another matter. Milošević's only objective was to hold on to power. Devoid of sweeping ideas, his regime was forced to manufacture crises in order to keep going. That is why his world always kept a sharp eye on those who are other, they are suspect, a threat to the idyll of our sameness. It is important to say here that Milošević's policy was a pure hybrid of various irreconcilable elements; it was in no way a clear strategy. To stay in power, he built his policy out of a patchwork of utterly opposing parts; it can hardly stand as a model for anything, except chaos.

The other is our destiny, an inevitability. It is only in relation to the other that we can ascertain our own qualities. Whether we see the other as an enrichment or a threat, it is inescapable. Our uniqueness is determined and measured only in comparison with the other. Robinson Crusoe is meaningless without Friday, and the same can be said for Juliet without Romeo,

Winnetou without Old Shatterhand. The other is a potential road to one-self. Without the other there are no differences, and without differences nothing can be established.

Equally inevitable, however, are prejudices, and from them come the breakwaters of stereotyping that protect our port against the winds. For every stereotype is a reprieve from having to accept the other, a moment when we are no longer ready to absorb differentness into our spiritual being, when our identity ceases to accept nourishment and grow. The only question is: at what point does one have enough of the other and tolerance cease? For there is always a moment when the alarm is sounded, followed by the alert: pontoon bridges are erected and we eye the other through the sight of a gun. The point at which we give up polyphony for monophony is proportional to the degree of our open-mindedness. Put simply, to be open to the other leads to Hellenism, to be closed leads to fascism.

However, our attitude to *the other* is also largely determined by the exter-nal context. Namely, tolerance varies within a time period, within a society, even within one and the same human being, depending on the extent of the external threat. Wars, unrelenting disasters, and economic instabil-ity drastically, and quickly, lower the threshold of tolerance. The German madness of the 1930s grew out of the country's unprecedented, protracted economic collapse, coupled with the Germans' sense of peril and feeling of general injustice following the new state borders drawn at the end of World War I. The 1990s' Yugoslav war stemmed from years of uncertainty and a plummeting living standard in the wake of Tito's death, not to mention the collapse of a great ideology when the impotence of a phantom economy became tangible, an economy based as much on foreign loans as on large financial gifts from the West, gifts which the West used to reward Tito's Yugoslavia and secure for itself a buffer zone against the Eastern bloc.

Intolerance between the peoples of the former Yugoslavia was perhaps no worse than the antagonism that exists, for example, between the Flemish and the Walloons. Economic stability and a high living standard are actually the Augustan wall and guarantee of Belgium's Pax Romana. This is a truism that no one is happy to accept and that, unfortunately, can be proven only by experience. The *virus of Nazism* syntagma (Nazism being an irrational hatred of the *other*, taken to a paroxysmal degree), so often used in the case of Germany, attests to an inability to perceive the problem because a virus is something external, a foreign body which destroys the organism. What it means to say is that a people with a centuries-old cultural tradition, one of the undisputed leaders of the European spirit throughout the continent's entire latter-day history, suddenly, almost magically, fell ill. The paradox of this German position within the European family of nations has never really been fully resolved. The Germany of the 1930s is something *other* than the rest of Europe. The Germany of the 1930s is also something *other* than most of Germany in the 1980s, 1990s, and today. If it does exist, the voice that would say *the Germany of the thirties, that is us,* is drowned out by the countless voices that talk about the Germany of the thirties as *other.* If it does exist, the voice that would say, *Serbia, that is us,* is drowned out by the multitude of voices that support Serbia's position as being *other* in today's happy, stable Europe.

"Hell is other people!" Sartre said ironically, but the global village would easily, and without any irony, inscribe this as a neon graffiti on the sky of the European Union. And it would do so without dilemma. If nothing else, the mindless fighting and rioting of soccer fans across Europe, the brutal clashes between the police and demonstrators in France only a year ago, testify to that same festering virus, if I may resort to the euphemism myself. Whether it is a virus or not, it should certainly be examined more thoroughly, because the 1930s do not belong to some remote past. It is as clever to relegate the problem to the realm of history or someone else's backyard—that is, to the realm of *the other*—as it is for the ostrich to stick its head in the sand.

Historical upheavals aside, the direction taken by the individual process of opening up or closing in depends, too, on the circumstances in which our identity is shaped. The biotope in which we grew up wrote programs for recognizing and experiencing the other. The backdrop is very important, regardless of whether we belong to the ethnic majority or minority in the society in which we live. The experience of the minority teaches us tolerance, because that is the basis for regulating relations; it allows us to think about *the other* more subtly, since the perspective is different. Nothing is ours by *default,* there is no carte blanche for what we possess. Because of our dual membership, we participate in the realm of the *other,* and slowly gain the experience of being a double agent. For we have two sides to us, and our notion of loyalty is much more complex. There is no respite from the countless demands for us to find our own position and accept a simplified picture of the world.

I often think of Kafka. As his experience is profoundly instructive, let us examine it for a moment. Kafka lives in Prague, in what is today the Czech Republic. But Kafka does not write in Czech, he writes in German, one of the minority languages. Yet Kafka is not German, he is Jewish, a Jew who does not write in Hebrew, for whom Judaism offers no solution, who writes to his father: "Your Judaism has for me dribbled away." That, then, is Kafka's monstrous situation: rootless, homeless, deprived. A German among Czechs, a Jew among Germans, and vice versa, a German among Jews and a Czech among Germans. Kafka always belongs to the minority, the marginal, with no country and no home to call his own. Hasn't Kafka bequeathed us an experience about the need to shift, to glide, the need to reject any identity that would reduce us to just one shore? For, if we consist of several shores, then the other is an inexhaustible reservoir and our gravitation will not be jeopardized by its presence.

I am by origin a Serb, born in Belgrade, Serbia. I grew up in Croatia, in multiethnic Istria, in the town of Pula, which, since Roman times, has always stood on the edge. The mild Mediterranean climate softens the sharp edges among nations. I mean to say that Istria has always been multinational, and the principle of tolerance is strong there. Yet, my ears still ring with the ironic intonations exchanged between *us* and *them.* Here, too, there was a border separating two basic groups: the locals and what were called the *furešti.* The *furešti* were newcomers, outsiders. When I was a child, people from all the nations of what was then Yugoslavia came to settle in Istria, filling the demographic void left by the Italian population who had emigrated after World War II, or, to be exact, after 1947. Istria was part of Croatia, but even Croats from other parts of Croatia were branded *furešti,* even they came under the sweeping notion of *other.*

A Serbian poet once said that a nation feels strongest in the border region. On the fringe, far from the center, in the coves of the periphery, the minority's presence is a threat to the majority nation. It is here that the battle to preserve traditional values begins. Whether there will be an opening up—Hellenism—or a closing in—fascism, depends on historical, economic, and political circumstances.

In his book *In the Name of Identity,* the Lebanese writer Amin Maalouf, who lives in Paris and writes in French, points to these very same *others* who are formed, in every respect, in the border area. "They are frontier-dwellers by birth or through the changes and chances of life, or by deliberate choice, and they can influence events and affect their course one way or the other," says Maalouf. "Those who can accept their diversity fully will hand on the torch between communities and cultures, will be a kind of mortar joining together and strengthening the societies in which they live. On the other hand, those who cannot accept their own diversity may be among the most virulent of those prepared to kill for the sake of identity, attacking those who embody that part of themselves which they would like to see forgotten. History contains many examples of such self-hatred."

The prosperity that makes Western Europe the promised destination for its poor relations from the East, as well as for emigrants from Africa, is partly based on *forgetting* the centuries of antagonism that prevailed between the Germans and the French. Western Europe's derivation of "Hellenism" emerged after the disaster of World War II. The economy offered a common denominator for building the community of European nations.

I cannot accept the theory that the Balkan peoples have a particular mentality that places them in a subordinate position to Western Europe. To be blunt, we could say that Yugoslavia's violent break-up in the early 1990s occurred because of the failure to *forget* the antagonisms of the nations that lived together in the country for seven decades. Missing was that generation that had grown up without the experience of war and was capable of *forgetting* the enmities that had burdened the Yugoslav peoples.

For a writer, there is no more important experience than that of *otherness*. I would say that without that experience, without that feeling of being a kind of outcast, we do not have the restlessness that generates and is at the heart of the creative process. A true work of literature is an attempt to establish this *other*. Every individual is merely a collage of many others. And their number keeps growing. The writer steps out, all the while carrying within him two shores.

I can attest firsthand that during the Western media's worst demonization of the Serbs, a good Serb was a *contradictio in adiecto*. German translations of my novels were well received at the time, and my political writings were published regularly in Germany and Austria. Just as regularly, the short blurbs written about the author invariably had the following sentence: he grew up in Croatia. This was meant to tell the German reading audience that even though I was born a Serb in Belgrade, I am an intelligent, civilized man, I am something *other* than the Serbs depicted by the media. Though I did not doubt that this recurrent sentence was well meant—after all, the Croatian littoral is my literary home—it did make me slightly uneasy because I could sense the real reason for its presence: my example was not to undermine the Western stereotype of Serbs in the 1990s.

There always has to be an external story. A work of literature's actual worth is, in itself, not enough to arouse public interest. Danilo Kiš said long ago that the French are not interested in a love story about some Serb or Bulgarian, that is a subject reserved for the French. But the exotic or testimonies to the hell of socialism, now that might draw the attention of French readers.

There is a more recent example. In the late 1990s, a best-selling novelist in Serbia caught the eye of a big German publisher who commissioned a translation. But when her book was due to be published, he suddenly had a change of heart, on the grounds that the political context was no longer there. They were now looking for an Afghani writer. Serbia was no longer in fashion. Gone was the external story, the tugboat that was to tow the ship of literature.

And there is also my own experience. In December 1999, my novel *Dante's Square* was presented on the celebrated German ZDF television program *Das literarische Quartett* (*The Literary Quartet*). After the show, one of the quartet's members, who had spoken scathingly about my book, admitted that he had not read it. He had been irritated by all the praise heaped on it by another quartet member, who had dared to compare me with Robert Musil. The sheer impertinence of connecting a Serbian writer with a classic of German-language literature after the Serbs had expelled hundreds of thousands of Albanians from Kosovo! Now, had I written about the exodus of the Albanians, I would have undoubtedly had a gratifying external story and such stories arouse media interest in even minor works of literature, if only for a while. Because it is the role of East European writers to be and to remain *other*. How can a Serbian writer tell us about our world? Let him stick to the exotic, to folklore, we want a whiff of the Orient, the bustle of the Balkans, with more stories about human rights, then everything will be fine.

The Western reader needs something that will confirm his or her view of the *other*. The West opens up to the kind of Balkan literature that talks about the absence of democracy, that cries out for it, using the West as its yardstick. In other words, it opens up to the kind of literature for which the image of the West is its point of reference. Here the West can again revel in its own image and convince itself that it is absolutely desired, that it is on the right road. In this kind of literature, the West takes narcissistic pleasure in itself as the unattainable object of desire of others. The West is relatively closed, as far as I know, to the kind of literature, and it exists in the Balkans as well, whose subject matter and plot are not defined by political or ideological preconditions, the kind of literature that cannot be reduced to bearing witness to the harshness of life on Europe's periphery; it is relatively closed to what I would call *pure literature,* writing that looks inward, that reexamines the literary possibilities of language and discovers the limitless territory of the individual as such. The Western cultural space reserves such experimental aspirations for itself, it gives only itself the right to twists and turns in the practice of literature. The explanation is simple:

this is the only way that the West can ensure its own domination, that it can confirm the ideal image of itself as a place of sophisticated intellectual endeavor, and that it can continue to take narcissistic pleasure in itself.

For me, it is the writer's mission to resist the temptation of taking the easy way out, which so often only reaffirms misapprehensions and reinforces stereotypes; it is the writer's mission to trace the contours of one's own universe. This is more of a physiological process, and it has no preordained path to measure itself against. The moment we leave our own oasis for the unlimited territory of *the other,* furnished with diversities that are but samples of our own possibilities, we have opted for Hellenism, for the principle of synthesis, for creation as a way of life and of experiencing the world.

Translated by Christina P. Zorić

Planet Mila

Irena Vrkljan

WHEN I THINK OF HER NOW, SEVERAL YEARS LATER, STILL AND ALWAYS
present in my mind, I always think, too, of the poet Marina Tsvetaeva and
her last years of exile in Meudon, on the outskirts of Paris—I think of the
fate of women writers and artists living in foreign lands far away from
home, of the miserable lodgings, years of persecution, cold kitchens, poverty, and loneliness that turbulent times bring.

Exile is a fate that is being repeated over and over again in this century.

We used to sit in Mila's kitchen in Wedding, in Berlin, talking about all
manner of things, including Marina, the loss of home, their similar inept-
ness at keeping house—because for Marina, too, writing was the only thing
she was good at, she was always snatching time to write down a poem,
while cooking on the stove in that distant past, like in the kitchen here now,
was a watery soup with a few pieces of carrot in it—yes, probably there was
no real comparison—and yet. But Mila had stopped writing poetry.

We spent many an evening sitting at that bare table, smoking, staring
into the dark courtyard where an occasional light could be seen burning in
one of the windows. Mila did not know any of her neighbors.

Throughout those years, we could smell the faint odor of oil paint from
the hallway of the little apartment and hear the occasional stroke of a brush
against the canvas. Mila would say to me: "He's still painting, but I'm afraid
for him. As for me, I'm less and less able to lift his spirits."

Marina was extremely lonely in Meudon, she was without her husband, she
was tired, but when she finally returned to Russia with her son, she was too
tired to start a new life.

Mila's tiredness was for reasons both similar and different, and at the
time, in the nineties, going back home was out of the question.

"All those long columns of refugees, of people expelled," she whispered.
"I'll never be able to get them out of my mind, out of my heart, the pain

I feel is constant and everything now is just a cursed fate doomed to be repeated. Like your Marina, I have only one dress that I can wear when I go out at night"—she, too, wore her only dress on those few occasions when she recited her poems to émigré audiences in Paris. "But we don't go out much here. We hardly know a soul, so my dress simply hangs in the wardrobe, it's a miracle the moths haven't gotten to it the way they did with my late mother's jacket in the trunk in Belgrade."

Yes, she spoke more and more about death. The voices of anonymous tenants passing under the kitchen window on their way to the staircase of the building opposite wafted in from the narrow courtyard. There was the constant sound of doors slamming in the apartments above and below the cold room where we sat; the sound of words, shouts in an unfamiliar language, sometimes screams.

This foreign existence of hers, I thought, and these old lodgings, maybe forever?

"Tell me, how is it that we have lost even the past?"

I did not know how to answer Mila's question.

And I still don't know even today, sitting here in my room in this late autumn of 2006, so many years after that evening in Wedding. Even the passage of time has failed to heal the bitterness we felt then. Because not only have some landscapes, towns, people, refugee children from the *Südost-kultur* disappeared forever, so has she, along with that fire that would still sometimes light up her eyes. Along with her hope for a different life. Memory is fragmentary, and so remains my recollection of that conversation about the dress and the moths and the banging doors and the night and the shouting.

And so in my room this fall, I see only fragments, only a few remaining images, and they are like those small, serrated photographs where the faces have already yellowed with time, those difficult times of war.

She once said to me: "Anyone who can't forget is doomed to my kind of memory, to permanent insomnia."

My reassurances were not enough even then, I know that now. Like my stories about Marina.

In Meudon in May 1938, Marina rises early, does not wake up her son Mur, but rather sits down at the wooden kitchen table to write a letter to her friend Ariadna: "Nothing here has changed, with one difference—I have sold some of our things (for next to no money, of course, I am not business-minded). But to my great relief, the following are gone: my enormous bed, the wardrobe with its mirror, my big oak table, and a few other things. Now I'll be stripped completely *bare.*"

We sat and smoked some more; Mila listened. But she was not writing letters to anyone at the time, and there was nothing to sell. She had already been stripped completely bare.

Today, in my room, I scour my diary, with its spare jottings, constantly looking for traces of the times we spent together.

Mila and Marina, two women on their way out.

Inscribed on the white canvas of life, along with all the events, places, and partings that will, almost randomly, fill it by the end, will be the names of other travelers, names familiar and foreign.

And who is that other traveler, anyway? Somebody from the family, who can be as distant as a star, or somebody completely foreign, who is as close to us as the other half of our own body?

Different names are, therefore, to be found on that white canvas. Among them, in black ink, is the name Mila.

At the time, did I even know who she really was, and what did I learn in that short period of our friendship? What do we really know about somebody else?

At school, I never felt any difference among the children. I did not ask who somebody was, who their parents were, where they came from. My class was certainly full of children from different parts of the former Yugoslavia, but those were not our questions, once.

And so it remained, as the axis of life, as memory.

If there was one thing that did not interest me in school, it was those spoiled girls wearing makeup too young. All the others, including those who were not from Zagreb, made up my crowd. Later, after high school, many of them disappeared in unknown directions. They were no longer in Zagreb. I didn't run into them anymore.

When the time came that people started asking, who are you, where are you from, we got used to that too, and avoided, if possible, mentioning places, last names, especially here in Berlin, places often lost in the wake of the tragedy that was to follow, but that remained in one's memory like an old, long misplaced letter.

Mila was from Belgrade. She had left her hometown with her husband for the unknown. She told us that right away. She said it emphatically, almost defiantly. With maybe a trace of fear; the war was already on.

Before leaving Paris, Marina wrote: "Now nothing is hard anymore, now it is fate."

Mila's fate was defined by her and Ivan coming to Berlin.

And the Mila of before? Ivan must have missed her laughter, her strength. Her erstwhile burning passion for people, for art. He said: she was a fireball. Hanging on the hallway wall of their small apartment was an old, black-and-white photograph of Mila at her desk. A dark-haired young woman, smiling, with penetrating eyes.

That evening in Wedding, Mila said to me: "I am not a combatant, but now I have to live in the minefields of the wars in Croatia, in Bosnia. I have to live in the battlefields. They are now part of my biography. I can't do it anymore." For a long time she had been listening to the news every night, reading all the newspapers; she was devastated. She did not say that she was not writing poetry anymore, that she could not sleep at night. She did not say, "I can't help even Ivan anymore."

Who, then, is the other? Often, it is not a matter of geography, it can have to do with social differences, differences in biography, in opinions and feelings. The other is not tied to a landscape, no, that other is somebody whose hatred we do not understand, just as we still do not always understand somebody's urge to destroy everything they once held dear. It can be a husband who beats his wife and children, a rapist, crazed rampant soldiers. And it can happen anywhere in the world, in Congo, Croatia, Lebanon, Bosnia. We are inconsolably helpless in the face of violence, and speechless long after. We cannot understand it, get over it; we can no longer breathe.

And so for me, the first so-called "other" people were the young women who in 1960 came from all over the former Yugoslavia to work in Germany, in Berlin, where I met them. And from them I learned about a way of life that had been unknown to me, for the first time I saw small, sparsely furnished rooms in the dorm in Flottenstrasse, for the first time I heard the words: piecework, fear, foreignness. (Sometimes I think that the whole collapse of the southeast started with that exodus of the country's vital force, that great migration of people who were unprepared for what awaited them.)

Most of these women did not speak German, we interpreted for them, went with them to the doctor, looked for cheap apartments, talked. We set up small women's centers, read what they wrote, what they wanted, why they had come to the unknown city of Berlin. Later the *Südost-kultur Center* was founded, where a brave woman started taking care of them and where they could find help, advice, somebody who would listen to them.

The road taken by these women—where from, where to? For this was not just a road leading from different regions on the edge of Europe's southeast to this particular city. It was not just a road taking them from a familiar life into the unknown, onto huge factory floors, confronting new machines. It was also a road that crossed the invisible borders of time, peoples, customs, experiences. These women were thinking about the future, but what they experienced was constantly connected to their past.

This we learn only later, however, when we embark on such journeys with yesterday's baggage and hope in tomorrow.

And much later still, when the war started in the nineties, refugees and children began arriving in the center, frightened, pale, without even suitcases. And so help was organized for the traumatized, along with housing and assistance with the immigration police. We also organized a kind of school for the children, language lessons, talks. The children wrote about their own experiences, their dreams, I still keep their papers to this day.

Monday, a sad December day. Darkness all around me, I can't see a thing. Nobody could ever have imagined that everything could change in just one day. Like when you take a sheet of paper and light a match to it, and it disappears, along with the writing, turning to ashes.

I wish I could wake up from this bad dream, look forward to seeing the people I care about again. Forget hatred, war, and revenge, and live in love, love not war.

Ljiljana, 1991

That is how Mila arrived, too, carrying a small suitcase and wearing a small, tight winter coat. The war had already started when we met. But Mila was not a child like Ljiljana, she was sixty-five years old, very thin, with graying curly hair, dark eyes—and already frightened. Ivan was a bit older, a taciturn, pale man. I had known about him for a long time, once in Zagreb I had seen an exhibition of his mysterious, surrealist paintings. They left Belgrade immediately, in 1991.

And so Mila crashed into our lives like a meteorite, like a planet from the dark warring skies of those years, and, like a loud explosion, her arrival changed our lives.

Yes, nothing here was the same for me after that.

In the dazzling tail of her fall she brought with her Ivan, her husband, that balding, quiet man. Mila was a poet, whose ardent "Elegies" I had read once long ago.

But none of this did we mention that stormy Berlin evening. An icy wind was raging outside, rolling empty cans along the sidewalk, whipping into the air plastic cups, paper, all the litter of urban life.

What did our city look like that evening to Mila, who was seeing it for the first time, holding her old coat tightly across her chest, her cap pulled down over her head? I could see only her eyes—burning as if she had a fever.

The coming tragedy, including our own, was not yet in sight.

I had not yet even thought about Marina in exile.

That evening, Mila was simply that other star that had strayed into our constellation, slightly mysterious, as if she had stepped out of one of Ivan's paintings of solitary figures; she was, in any case, a new, unknown person.

Her bitterness, fatal, as Marina would say, together with our own, combined to create something unexpected and entirely new to us. Especially in those days, when hatred and distrust were as rampant as a disease. There was none of that that evening.

Only now do I realize that even then Mila intuitively sensed everything, she knew that nothing would ever be the same as before and that neither she nor he would ever find happiness again. There would be none of her ardor, her optimism would vanish, and with it her strength.

Her loss of identity, this alien soil suddenly under her feet, this windswept icy city of Berlin, I did not notice it right away.

For me she was and will always remain that still sometimes red-hot planet that, much later, slowly began to cool here.

Who could have known that evening that we would be her last stopping place?

That wonderful couple, horrified by all the hate speech, simply got up one morning, donned their coats, took two suitcases, and set off into the unknown, for Berlin, where Ivan knew a gallery owner who had been collecting his paintings for years. A modest, small gallery, with modest prices. Still, at least they had an address to start with.

The gallery owner had been a friend of ours for years, we often went to his gallery and that is how we met Mila and Ivan that stormy evening. They both spoke quite good German.

We sat and smoked. There were no little cakes on the kitchen table in Wedding now, and it was only when I would sometimes talk to Ivan about one of his new paintings, it was only then that I felt what a fighter this woman was, how alive, how much she loved him, and how important she was to his work. But as soon as she left the hallway, which served as his improvised studio, she would look tired, absent.

And many a favorite tome
Was left behind in my old home,
In my dreams, waiting there I find,
An unfinished childhood left behind.
This childhood I must reach out to,
This new home I must step up to
My heart I must put into,
How, when, can anybody say?
Lest not one but two hearts wilt away.
                              Enisa, 1992

Much later Mila told me, "That evening at the gallery I was afraid you wouldn't want to talk to us, because we're from Belgrade."

I looked at her in astonishment.

"I will never forget it," she went on. "You were so normal. You weren't distrustful at all." She was silent for a while and then said softly: "But me, I am full of distrust, wary, afraid of people."

"But Mila, how could you have imagined that we would even give a second thought to where you come from? There are so many people, so many children here now in a kind of exile, and you left your country. You went into a foreign world without any money—I know how hard that is at your age, this new life in another country, without family, without friends, in the coldness of a new city, of unfamiliar people. No, Mila, those were never our questions."

But Mila was not listening to me anymore. She was tormented by the war in the country; like a cursed garment, she sheathed herself in blame for everything that was happening, and the more time that elapsed, especially during the siege of Sarajevo, the more she grieved before our very eyes. She practically stopped eating. She could no longer endure all those sleepless nights, or the nightmares when sleep did come.

I discovered something unusual recently. Every so often, sometimes only every few months, an apartment appears in my dreams, it looks more like a shelter. It is inside an old family house, but the tenants don't know it is there. The road leading to it, I want to hide, passes through ruin after ruin, narrow little streets, tunnels. The fear wakes me up.
Tanja, 1993

* * *

That first evening at the gallery we phoned around, and that very same night the gallery owner found them this little apartment in the Wedding quarter, which they could rent with the advance from one of Ivan's paintings that the gallery owner had immediately bought to help tide them over during those initial days. At home we collected some dishes, towels, bed linen—lots of friends stepped in to help—and so they were able, at least temporarily and modestly, to set up house. Mila quickly arranged everything in the apartment, she worked nonstop and perhaps there were moments when she forgot about the war.

But no, the very next evening she said to me: "I thought that various little things were important to me, things that I had collected, old porcelain, my grandmother's glasses, paintings, rare books. Now I know that none of it matters to me anymore—all that matters is that people are people and that I'm no longer surrounded by that terrible fanaticism anymore. Wishful thinking, yes, I know. If we were younger we would have gone somewhere far, far away, even left Europe maybe, left all these nations, all this blindness. But, of course, that's impossible at our age. Ivan can't start his career as a painter all over again either—he was never really a marketable painter, and he's no longer so young as to believe in miracles, in fame. You need different skills for that, it's not enough just to paint."

"And poetry, writing?"

For the first time that evening Mila laughed: "Poetry, my dear, abandoned me a long time ago."

The apartment was cramped, two rooms. One had just two beds and a wardrobe, the other a table and chairs for guests, who used to visit in the early days, a couch, on which nobody ever spent the night, and a little table with dishes, plates, a bottle of wine.

The floorboards were bare, there were no rugs.

On the walls were Ivan's paintings, and a poster of his first exhibition.

As soon as they moved in, he set up his studio in the narrow hallway, with an easel, oil paints, and a bright lightbulb so that he could paint at night.

He immediately got down to work, but Mila was still not writing any poetry.

Sitting in their bleak kitchen, as we often did, we could smell the oil paints.

The apartment was in Berlin's working-class district, where foreigners lived alongside the occasional poor or jobless German. The building was run-down, gray, flaking plaster everywhere; the apartment was not especially nice but it was cheap, a fourth-floor walk-up. That did not bother Mila. She hated stepping into any elevator.

And I was able again to read to her some lines from Marina's letters to Ariadna in 1938, written from the Innova Hotel: "What an irony, isn't it: the Innova Hotel? Two ironies, actually: *innova* and hotel—and me there, me who loves old houses more than anything—because they have everything: views and ghosts and grass in the cracks (of the floor) and the moon in the cracks (of the roof) . . .

"This letter could have been written even a hundred years ago—in 1838—it is a hundred years old, old like our friendship.

"We're on the fifth floor, thank God there's no elevator, I'm (*insanely*) afraid of any elevator, but if it did exist I would have to take it . . . The fear would give me a heart attack—and so that's how we live and expect nothing . . ."

Along with the names on the white canvas of life, there were also some imaginary drops of blood.

Because the war years followed us, too, like a nightmare, like something I have not and never will be able to get over entirely.

How many of just the women I knew were huddling in cellars somewhere over there, in the strange night, listening to gunshots and grenades exploding outside?

Every telephone conversation with my sister, with friends in Zagreb, was like a knife stab. I felt their despair and their fear. We felt helpless in the face of the news, the newspaper articles here in Germany. We all slept badly, took pills. We, too, could not forget those images of destruction, the devastated landscapes.

I can still remember those wan children at the center, who wrote about everything, about what troubled them; I stood in front of them like a school-teacher, and at the end of the lesson collected their papers and read them.

I arrived in Berlin on September 30, 1991. I got to know Berlin well, practically the whole place. But when people asked me what I liked most about it, I found it hard to answer, because I liked almost everything. Still, there is something that I miss, that I basically miss here, and that is the freshness and quiet of mornings, and nights, something you can find only back home. I miss my neighbors, I've been here six months now and I've run into the neighbors in my building only a couple of times. Where I come from, as soon as you step out into the street to buy bread and milk, you run into your neighbors, you talk, invite them over for coffee, cake—but there's none of that here.
Slavica, 1991

* * *

Later, Mila and Ivan had fewer and fewer guests—there was probably less of a desire to talk about art, about everyday things, now that it was allegedly all over.

We were often alone with them and looked at Ivan's new paintings.

In one of his oval paintings, a slender woman in a long black robe is floating through space, through a landscape of rubble and Berlin houses. There is a round moon in the black sky, spilling white light onto the ruins, and red onto the urban houses. The woman in the middle of the painting seems to be flying, accompanied by strange birds, like angels.

The picture was mysterious, sorrowful, yet full of hope.

Angels accompanied the woman in black.

Later, as the number of guests dwindled, Ivan stopped cooking those fine dishes he had learned to make from his mother. She was no longer alive. Mila's parents were also deceased, but they often talked to us about them, and about their own childhood.

What was our childhood like during that war year of 1941? We did not know much about events in the country, our parents' generation did not discuss politics in front of the children.

Mila and her brother—she never spoke about him—grew up in a middle-class family, where, unlike Ivan's family at times, nobody ever went hungry. I always imagine a cheerful, lively little girl with ribbons in her hair, pretty dresses, patent leather shoes; I see a large garden, her running to the swing, playing with the dog, named Dixie.

The little girl rode her bicycle, sat in the boughs of the young apple tree, and somewhere in the house just kept on reading and reading.

"After I had read all the books on my father's shelves, I went to the nearby library—I cared about books more than anything else." Mila suddenly fell silent.

Ivan lived with his mother. His father had died very young of tuberculosis, and his mother, a seamstress, supported her son on her own. There were no books in the house.

"Even though we were poor, she was a wonderful cook," Ivan said. "She did not stint on meals, and I used to stand beside her at the stove and remembered her recipes."

That was all they said about it, nothing more. Except that they both went to the same high school and that by the age of seventeen they were already a couple.

When Mila started her studies of literature, Ivan was at the Art Academy and he painted constantly, until late at night. They saw each other every day, met for coffee in the college canteen, and talked about art.

Ivan illustrated Mila's first collection of poems. They were already married and lived in a nice apartment, bought for them by Mila's father.

Mila said, "I also fell in love with his paintings." Ivan said, "And I with her smile, her optimism."

What remained of that former life of theirs, now that they were émigrés?

They left behind everything, their apartment, studio, many of Ivan's paintings, books. I thought, that's how it is, as if a bomb had been dropped on their house, destroying everything. Here they lived as if they had been stripped bare, on their own, with no trace of their former biography, none of their work. "What I regret most are his paintings," Mila said, "especially one of them, called *The Dream*. A little girl in a yellow dress is sitting on the ground in an empty Belgrade square, surrounded by watches, each of them ticking to a different time. They weren't the melting watches of Dali. No, here the dials pointed like swords to different numbers, there was something menacing about them; maybe even way back then, all those years ago, they were already marking the times to come. Or somebody's death."

Ivan looked questioningly at Mila: "You never told me that that's what you see in the watch painting."

"Maybe my memory has failed me, maybe the picture wasn't that prophetically ominous after all."

Mila shut her eyes: "My father always used to take me to the theater. It was nice, I liked everything about it, the comfortable seats, the lights, the actors, the theater in general."

That is all they said about their previous lives.

Later, when they were alone, they didn't feel like talking either, about art, about their daily lives, or whatever plans they didn't have anyway. And they never again mentioned the picture with the watches.

It was around then that Ivan stopped cooking those fine dishes he had learned to make from his mother; there was usually a pot of soup on the stove, which we shared in the evening.

And so there were often three empty plates and two glasses of wine on the table in front of us where we sat and smoked. Ivan, who would cook the modest meal, would quickly leave us to paint in his hallway studio.

"His paintings are so gray now," Mila once said. "All the figures are blurred, as if in a fog; he's lost the ground from under his feet, and that one-time city of our childhood and youth which, at least for him, is now shrouded in falling cold, gray ashes. A world surrounded by barbarians can be nothing but cold and colorless. I know, it's not right that I'm so weak, that I give him no peace, that I cry too much. I'm completely useless the way I am now."

"Don't talk like that."

"But it's true. I'm stupidly killing myself because of something that is not, that cannot be my fault. And so I'm punishing the person I care most about."

"Write, try to go back to writing."

"The source of my inspiration has run dry," Mila responded, "and so has any hope that art can combat evil. No, there are no more verses in my head, or in my soul, if you like, that I would want to write, even my language has run dry, I'm surrounded by foreign words and all I can think of are the dead, the destroyed towns."

"Oh, I so wish for a peaceful bed in a white room—and oblivion."

We were not strong enough for the times, which moved into our bodies like a dangerous intruder. We were utterly unable to find answers to the questions that kept following us. For a while, and that was already after the war, the stars in the sky did not twinkle for us.

Once, when I opened the kitchen door abruptly, I saw Mila quickly swallow a pill, then she immediately turned around and said, "It's nothing, just something to help me sleep at night." I can still see her grave, pale face in the dark kitchen. And how nothing could cheer her up, not even the opening of Ivan's first exhibition at the gallery in Berlin, where all our friends came. The show was a great success. It got good reviews in the press, and Ivan sold several paintings. Now they had a bit more money, but Mila refused to buy anything for herself, no books to read or something to wear; at the opening she wore her one dress, an old pair of shoes, and in winter always that same tight, black little coat.

Graying hair, crow's feet around her eyes—suddenly it all reminded me of Marina in that last photograph of her in France.

Sitting in my room, I remember how one morning we went to the center. I wanted to see R., a refugee from Srebrenica; for some time I had been having strange conversations with her about her fears. This was at a time when she was truly traumatized and when she told me: "At night before going to bed, I close the balcony door to my room so that I can't walk out in my sleep and jump from the third floor." R. had been undergoing various kinds of therapy for a long time, and now she was finally getting better. She no longer had nightmares and was gradually coming back to life. The center had become the focal point of her stay here in Berlin, which was now permanent. She made wonderful pies, and whenever we came she would welcome us with Turkish coffee, the pies, and various cakes and baklavas.

R. had lost everything in Srebrenica. Her distant relatives, neighbors, house, and the only thing that she still possessed, her beloved cow. It was hit by some stray bullets and R. told me, "Imagine, my cow died crying, big tears spilled from her loyal eyes." All of R.'s stories were unusual, they were like ancient tales. And that's how she spoke about the siege of the city, about going hungry and fleeing, being expelled, to be exact. The bus was blue, but the sky wasn't. No, there is no sky above that little town anymore.

There was a huge walnut tree in R.'s courtyard and every evening she would pick some walnuts and divide them up among the children when they came, hungry, the following afternoon. The children knew that they would get a few each. And so the tree was slowly picked bare, until one evening all the walnuts were gone. When the children came and asked for the walnuts she told them, "I'm sorry, dears, but I have nothing left."

The children silently left the courtyard and its bare tree.

But one little boy soon came back and asked: "Auntie, give me that nothing then."

I told Mila about my own arrival in Berlin in 1967. But my journey was different from hers and the women working the machines. I had not come as a migrant. I had been granted a stipend to attend the Film Academy and after graduation I stayed on. I'd fallen in love. Unlike Mila, I had not come here because of a war, frightened and sad, and I already spoke German. I had learned it as a child.

But at first, I, too, found it hard in this big city, where I did not know a soul to begin with. The streets, the neighbors, people in the shops, they were all strange to me. I, too, had had to leave behind my studio apartment, my paintings and books, and in the early years I, too, was unable to write. Students at the Academy, that was that famous year of '68, talked only about politics, they did not care about any kind of art. But I had had enough of political debates, though I did not realize how spoiled I was.

I did not know the meaning of real fear for one's own livelihood. Here, I quickly learned about the power of money, and I know even today that in this society you are nothing if you have no money. As for poems from a small country, or films about artists, nobody was interested.

My husband and I, too, lived in a cheap attic apartment with a coal stove; we were often cold, but we wanted to write, and pay the price for the freedom we had.

I attended the Academy, made films, met women who had come here and in their helplessness were so different from me, we translated for them, my husband wrote.

I gazed into the distance, to my lost city and people, and waited nine years for the first sentence of my first prose, which I wrote here.

But every year we could go to Zagreb, where my little studio apartment was waiting for us—it, too, was slowly collecting dust; our ties with family and friends remained unbroken.

For a long time, for as long as the war was on, Mila could not, did not want to return home.

The fact that I, too, had had a hard time here at first, that I, too, had found everything unfamiliar and strange, was no comfort to Mila. I had been younger than she, I did not have to think of the dead.

And then, one day in a bookstore, I discovered Marina, her books. I started reading everything I could lay my hands on, and later I wrote about her; her poems and her fate follow me to this day.

And so I keep talking to Mila about her. And I try to give this tired woman the comfort I had found in Marina's poems and letters, but often it was not enough even for me; at the time, I could not find warmth in the cold heart of the north.

We had not suspected what was to come.

We had not suspected that we would find it so hard to articulate what was happening.

Mila stared into the night and was silent. She had never been that other kind.

And so, at least twice a week, we sat there in the kitchen in Wedding, we sat there like that for a year, two years, eight years. The war was over but it had left invisible scars on our bodies. I was surprised that even now Mila did not contact her brother or friends. She firmly rebuffed any attempt by Ivan to persuade her to write or phone.

It always brought out a streak of obstinacy in her. No, no, and no! The atmosphere in the kitchen would change, her eyes would flare up, and I hoped that she might get over her sorrow after all, that maybe she could live here, maybe even start writing again. Ivan hoped so, too.

Sometimes we would go for walks, along Lake Wannsee, in the Grunewald woods. After visiting the grave of Heinrich von Kleist, she always wanted to do that. We would sit by the lake and gaze at its calm waters, at the swans and the occasional heron. If only we had had at least the tranquillity of that bird standing there so still, waiting to catch a fish. On the way home, walking through the woods to the urban railway, our shoes would sometimes sink into the sand of the narrow pathways. I said, "The sea used to be here, this whole city lies on sand."

"Yes, the soil we're walking on is sandy," she replied. "That's why the paths are uneven, and the ground under our feet is slippery."

"What do you mean?"

"I don't have solid ground under my feet anymore, not even in my dreams."

In my last dream, war was raging here in Berlin, too. I was in a huge sports hall and didn't know where to run. Then I remembered my shelter and happily started climbing over the old, familiar ruins of my small town. But then I discovered that I couldn't find the shelter.

I hope I will find it again, though I have a feeling that I will never manage to get there. The ground is slippery, uneven, the ruins suddenly foreign. But people have told me that there is salvation in hope and I will keep on hoping till the end.

Tanja again

Walking with Mila through the woods, I remembered the girl Tanja and her dream.

Mila never talked to me about her dreams.

She never told us that she was seeing a doctor, never said anything about check-ups and diagnoses. Why did she keep silent?

But one day she suddenly decided, without us immediately understanding the reason or why she had resisted it for so long, that she did, after all, want to visit her younger brother in Belgrade.

"I want to see him, to hear what he thinks, what our friends think about everything, about what happened, what they will say to me, how they will receive me."

Ivan absolutely did not want to go; he said, "The trip will be too exhausting for you, and anyway, why? We've lost everything there." But Mila was insistent. She wanted to go home and to do so right away and by herself.

On the day of her departure she looked to me even thinner than before; her hair was now completely white. She never mentioned any illness to anyone. We were at the airport, the plane quickly soared into the sky, and with it Mila disappeared into the clouds. I said to myself: "May the angels in Ivan's paintings go with her."

She wrote only once, from the hospital.

One day Ivan's face was ashen. Without a word he handed us a small note bearing her already almost illegible handwriting: "Forgive me, dear hearts, but I don't want my bones, at least, to rot away in a foreign country." Ivan immediately departed for Belgrade.

Mila, our mysterious planet. We have lost her forever. She journeyed away, never to return.

After the funeral, Ivan quickly returned to Berlin. He continues to paint in the narrow hallway, eking out a living on his own, and whenever we see each other, we always talk about Mila and wonder why we couldn't have done more for her. He is now more taciturn than ever. We don't know how he will survive without her.

Sometimes I think that Mila was like that little girl Maša, who in 1992 wrote:

> *Times of fear and sorrow, if days of hunger they survive;*
> *Cold nights, long weeks. Who in others' suffering pleasure takes?*
> *What is it that a wisher of death makes?*
> *I love my town, its buildings white,*
> *My school, its green fir trees upright.*
> *I love my mother, my brother, my dad,*
> *That is why I am for world peace,*
> *That nowhere war be had.*

Yes, wars also destroy the lives of people who were not on the battlefield. They change the world, feelings. They are the indelible trace of hatred and affect the innocent as well, no matter how far away they may be. Mila, a poet, could not escape her memories, her sensitivity.

She remained rooted in the darkness of the past. And what remains for us? An empty chair, a forgotten pack of cigarettes on the kitchen table in Wedding, a black cap she once gave me, and the photograph on that wall of gray paintings in the hallway. What remain are loss and memories.

I embrace her silhouette before the dark windows of the night. She is now a distant planet in the skies above Berlin. It twinkles sometimes and then we hear her words: "Don't grieve, this is best for me." Marina would have said the same thing, once.

The kitchen in Wedding, where we used to sit, now stands cold and empty.
The faint odor of paint still wafts in from the hallway.
Whenever I look at the night sky, I feel like crying. Across the scrawled white canvas of life are traces of tears, the lost traces of our friendship. That is all that will remain of us: text and memory.

Translated by Christina P. Zorić

Man's Destiny

Vladimir Zarev

THE MAN SEEMED TO COME FROM NOWHERE. MISERABLE AND TATTERED, with no known background, he radiated that penetrating absence that seems suited for the barges that popped up behind the Calafat bend in the river,* majestically crossing the shipping channel, only to once again be lost in the ash-colored stream, leaving behind neither memories nor any other trace—nothing more than the assumption that the world is infinite and beyond comprehension, nothing more than nostalgic desire for something far away and unachievable.

To put it more precisely, he came to the city with a wandering circus. Its linen cupola dominated the center of Vidin just at the spot where the market square, with its artisan tables and noise from the taverns, came to an end and where the green of the city park began, pushed into insignificance by the majestic shadow of the officers' casino. On Sunday a brass band gave some movement to the stiff ensemble. Sandy avenues led from there down to the river, whose eternal stream had reduced people to their own lifetimes.

The faded ropes of the circus tent stretched over the square as large as an Orthodox church, but transient like all amusements. On the outside it was crowned with a colorful pendant and marked by human gawking; on the inside it was decorated with garlands and filled with the odor of sawdust on the floor of the ring.

The presentation was intoxicating. There were real Chinese jugglers, whose eyes had become slits because of the strain of constantly staring straight ahead. A huge hulk of a man with the mustache of a Russian soldier bent iron bars, broke chains, and was ready to wrestle with anybody so fearless as to foolishly volunteer to go at it with him. You could see the fattest lady in the world and a fetus in a large glass bottle. There were trapeze artists and other acrobats. A trained bear. A horse that could count. A talking parrot. A sword and fire swallower.

* Calafat, Romania, across the Danube from Vidin, Bulgaria. —Trans.

Our man, however, stood near the entrance and in the boiling heat he sold tickets, little slips of paper written out by hand, which he tore off from a thick block. You could pay with money, but also with five eggs, a live chicken, a glass of honey, or a freshly caught sterlet. This democratic form of entry filled the children with enthusiasm; the man with the folded ruffle collar, which concealed his yellowing shirt, got them all confused.

In the circus program itself he came out as a clown. His number was long and boring. With his giant shoes, he wobbled into the ring and stumbled, but he didn't get anyone to laugh. They only felt sorry for him when he pulled on the suspenders of his mighty pantaloons and began to play all imaginable instruments—a violin, an accordion, an ocarina, a trumpet, a guitar, and a barrel organ. But above all he played on a flute, which gleamed as though it had been cast from a golden October.

Nobody applauded. His chalk-besmeared face made people sad. His bizarre hat recalled suffering. His battered trousers made people uncomfortable, since when they looked at him they thought of their own poverty . . . Sleepy Kosta hit the nail on the head when a week later he made the comment that the man had not preferred to stay in Vidin, with its medieval city cemetery and the Danube flowing by. Instead, the circus had decided to move on without him. There could be no talk of the man having returned to the city of his birth to spend the rest of his miserable life there—no, it was more like the fact that the circus had rolled up its tents and left town with its fire-eaters and fat lady and had simply left the man behind like a useless object. And truly, he had only remained because he had racked his brain in vain over where he could go. He stayed overnight at Ilia Valtchev's caravansery on the edge of the city, and among the snores of the wagon drivers he dreamed of children who would laugh at his numbers and would scream "Do it again!" He dreamed of his mother who would send him her handkerchief with an embroidered monogram.

When he was awakened by the deep voice of the hairy Stefania extolling her thick sweet porridge, it became clear to him that he was now completely alone. Fate had changed the sad clown into a riddle, into a tricky problem for the city to solve. This was even clearer now that he had lost the clothing of the bright splendor of the circus atmosphere and was laid open to strange curiosity, and he stood revealed in all his painful nakedness to the curiosity of strangers—human curiosity in all its mercilessness. From a bearable anonymity, someone emerged who was a sty in the eye, a person who radiated many mysterious meanings, or so everyone thought. Could it not be that he was a ghost, who had materialized, unbidden, at one of the spiritual sittings of Auntie Know-it-all? How did this person have the audacity to stay in the city just like that, without having been born there or having grown up there? Even the fact that he stayed away from the places where people met, the coffeehouse and the taverns, Trentcho's barbershop and the Rabbit's Blood, was something so unusual that he changed into the very imposing form of a presence that gave even more occasion for scratching one's head.

Provocatively, the man was dressed very poorly in his striped trousers, which were stuffed at the left knee, his sports jacket with the worn sleeves, the shirt that had been washed to death, and the fluffy collar under his neck, which did more harm than good to the man's constant attempt to hide his discomfort with his own existence. Later in the year one's eye fell on the long winter coat, which was more like a cape, and on the patent leather shoes with their spanking new metal clasps, which made the direction of his footsteps on the sidewalk of Main Street as identifiable as if he were clicking his rosary. So he announced his arrival long before he appeared, and he kept going even after he had long disappeared. Without chalk, his face was sadder and showed even less expression. His ever-present flute had taken on the look of the fall season so poetically in the glitter of its brass surface that one glance at it was enough to make the observer melancholy.

Although people urgently scrutinized him when he left the caravansery, they still had not given him a name. Perhaps he was hurrying after the circus, which was still quite close to the city. However, he did not make for the fortress, from which one could hear the groaning of the ungreased axes of the circus wheels under the weight of the tent and the fattest lady in the world. No, he went in the direction of the market, and passed the stalls without any sign of curiosity, stopping in front of the Rabbit's Blood. The inn was freshly swept out and sprinkled with water. A cool feeling rose from the mats on the floor. A few men were drinking beer and talking politics about the upcoming war. They immediately noticed the man. If he had come in, they certainly would have greeted him heartily, talked with him, and listened to him sympathetically. They would have given him any necessary advice and support but . . . he did not come in. He stood by himself, silent, in a lonely way shriveled up against the background of the riverside park. He looked dreamily down on to the water, as though his eyes still had not become accustomed to the brilliant early-morning light, or else he was seeking in the eternity of the river some comfort about the moment he had just lost. If he had at least jumped in, the men would have had a last chance to save him, but he had let this opportunity pass on, the opportunity to become one of theirs, a person whom they could understand and who was close to them. He decided against the attempt at suicide and by so doing chose to close in on himself.

In order to protect themselves somehow against this affront, they now gave him a name—the Whistler. He was a heavyset man of undetermined age, with the bald dome reminiscent of a genius or of an idiot, with eyes that seemed to have been bleached out over the years. His eyes seemed to be filled with a very special sorrow, an infectious sorrow of unknown origin that seemed to suggest that something significant, something fateful, had been entrusted to *him,* but which applied to *everyone.* It was difficult to withstand his pain-filled days. People were so unsettled that they made haste to throw him some alms, less for the purpose of gaining credit in their own eyes than simply to get away from his.

He had acquired no skills. So he looked for work as a porter at the harbor, but the sacks with the wheat and the untreated lime tore at his flabby body, and he quickly gave up the work. Grateful Kotcho offered him work in his perfume distillery, but his clumsiness and his heavy-handedness were so obvious that people considered his actions as his best clown number. After he had smashed some of the simmering vials with their mysterious aroma, it was clear that he could do only one thing—play a musical instrument, no matter whether it was a piano or an accordion, a violin, or an ocarina ... Still, his favorite instrument was and remained the autumnal flute, with which he unlocked sounds of such painful beauty and sublime harmony that the music worked its way into your thoughts and—this was what was most frightening—to a certain extent raised this extraordinary situation into a normal state.

Most frequently he was hired for funerals. For two plates of meatless beans the owner of the Rabbit's Blood, Mr. Vodetchka, let him entertain the local people in the tavern. His reputation—his talent—for driving sorrow into one's very pores spread so wide that even the crème de la crème of Vidin society invited him to the salon of the Royal restaurant, where amidst the crystal mirrors and silk carpets he could unlock melancholic sighs from the hearts of the banker Gocho Pantov and his rail-thin wife Auntie Know-it-all, as well as from the Hungarian Babash and his big-busted daughter Bochura. He was revoltingly fat and bloated, absorbed in himself—in other words, completely alone, in the middle of the glamor of the aristocratic restoration, surrounded by human dullness and insuperable incompetence, which balanced the socially powerful situation of these people. Here the Whistler hesitantly took up a melody as though he had composed it at the very moment of sounding the note. He expressed its essence, not in the form of bare notes, but as though he were drawing his breath from the heavy, wasteful folds of the curtains, and as a sign of his ability changed them back into the magic of sound.

"*Oh, mein Gott!*" sighed Auntie Know-it-all in her affected German, thus substantiating her nickname, which she had received on account of her knowledge of about two dozen German words. Since she could not assume that the others had as much education as she, she continued on in Bulgarian: "Such inspiring sadness! Just like once in Vienna, isn't that so, my dear . . ."

Despite these public appearances, the Whistler continued to be a nothing and a nobody. Whether at the burials or in the hurly-burly of the Rabbit's Blood tavern, yes, even in the venerable sumptuousness of the Royal restaurant, people couldn't bear him any longer. They had enough of the misery that flowed from between his fingers. They interrupted his playing and kicked him out completely. His abilities forced them to drown their hearts in the sounds of heavenly beauty, in the expanses of perfection. Something in them appeared to feel apprehension that perfection lay only in sorrow and death—and they didn't want to know about that. They reached for their glasses in which the raw fire of the wine sparkled to be able to believe for at least one moment more that they were happy. More and more the bitter reproach of the sounds of his flute lost its special arousal, and people began to hate such sounds. In a devious way the sounds got mixed up in their words and seduced them against their will out of the provincial slumber of this small town scene, with its fortress (actually a symbol of being awake), with its old women, who even early in the morning were crocheting their blankets, with the hustle and bustle of the Friday weekly market, with the harbor, which expectantly held its breath, with the perpetually hungry children and the funereal silence of the cemetery, with the cravings of the mosquito, and with the fear of malaria and war. Yes, the Whistler crowned these with beauty, but that did not comfort his audience. He was and remained an outsider; he remained forever that sad clown with the chalked, expressionless face, a notorious Pied Piper who, instead of cheering people up, did everything that brought them into contact with immortal art—only now his circus was the entire city, and his tent was the pale cupola of the skies. This skill of the flute player brought them into dangerous close relationships with the river—and who needed this comic beauty here in their dusty and humdrum daily routine, which brought people nothing but pain and—to make things even worse—clearly had an interest in making pain into a necessary part of existence.

With his talent, the flute player resembled every significant disappointment. Turned into himself, self-contained, rolled over in an orderly way by his own talent, which could not be compared at all with anything rational and useful, he was simply the man without destiny, without sense or purpose, so completely superfluous that things could not go on without him. Exactly as the Grateful Kotcho had prophesied—the Whistler had awakened that merciless romantic spirit in them that they feared and were ashamed of. A plate of white beans always stood ready for him in the Rabbit's Blood, and the women, after they had finished their springtime laundry at the Danube, always gave him something worn-out to wear. Auntie Know-it-all presented him with a dickey to wear around his neck; the banker Panto Valtchev honored him with a valuable Brazilian stamp from his luxurious album and a butterfly prepared in Vienna; Babash the Hungarian gave him spurs and a riding whip. Even Shdrigo the anarchist favored him, and tended to stay overnight with him in the woodshed and to share with him the fresh aroma of the mountains, but even he, who with his black shirt and matted beard resembled the devil incarnate, was afraid of the Whistler. For Shdrigo, freedom meant anger and destruction in his desire for revolution; he looked for the world to be covered with flames and purifying acts of violence, at the end of which liberation would be a desirable joy, enticing and unending. He imagined the world revolution as a highly seductive nymph, who made love with every proper man but never became pregnant. Shdrigo had read Friedrich Nietzsche, was himself the anti-Christ, and did not believe in the world to come. For him everything was right now. Hell and the devil were always the others, especially those who stood in the way of Shdrigo's earthly paradise. In contrast, the sounds of the flute awoke in the listeners not only sorrow, but also an undesirable feeling of one's own weakness and impotence. Hell, they heard in their hearts, burned within the breast of every person.

Even the accommodating and easy-going pastor Anissi, who was worried about the roof of the church that leaked rain, even he, the incorruptible master of the kingdom of the good, was not able to decide in moments of theological brooding whether the Whistler, with his constant and penetrating melancholy, was a useful and agreeable person in the sight of God, one who with his gifts could clean the souls of his flock, or whether he was possessed by a satanic power to hold out beauty as a permanent guilty conscience. Those people who expected that the war would begin in Serbia claimed that the Whistler's mother was a Serb, and his father Romanian. Those people who expected that the war would begin in Romania swore that his mother was a Romanian, and his father Serbian. When he had come to Bulgaria and had learned the language of the country nobody knew exactly. But that was exactly the point—this man, forgotten by the circus, was not simply a foreigner, but . . . he was different; he was basically and forever *different* from them. It was exactly this oppressive quality of otherness that upset the people in the Rabbit's Blood; it questioned the naturalness of their existence and led them to the uncertain thought that hell on earth does not lie in us or in others, but lies in the uncertainty *caused by* the others.

Without virtue, but also without vice, the Whistler had only one bizarre tendency. At the end of May, when the danger of flooding had passed and the rainfall had stopped at the time of the cherry blossoms, he went down to the now quiet flowing areas of the Danube and let himself be taken up by the stream. Wrapped up in the clear sky of the early summer, he played his flute. Precisely at five in the afternoon from the state fortress of Baba Vida one could hear his playing coming. The stream carried his tones along the steep banks over to the park on the edge of the river, where the songbirds became so distressed that they grew silent, and the old people, who were seeking out the sun there, became exceptionally tired. Over at the officers' casino, where the young lieutenants were burning to go to war, the music was heard as a reproach. In the whirl of voices in the Rabbit's Blood, they perceived the sound as the light whistling of a kettle. Then in the end the sounds blew past the trusting market stalls, only to pop up in the dark shadows of the Zagorka brewery, and finally, with their pure sadness, to reach the Roma quarter, where bacon rinds were being rendered over smoking wood fires to make soap and tin was being melted in small pots. Somewhere in the distance, as though disarmed by human apathy, the melody got quiet and disappeared into the damp air that reeked of sludge from the reedy swamps. There the sound was buried by the strong hand of the wind.

Since people were hardly to be seen in the place that his notes reached, this unusual ritual gave the impression that the river was singing. The punctuality with which the Whistler carried out his ritual even brought the bell ringer to schedule his five o'clock ringing according to it. At Panto Valtchev's bank, the employees stopped counting the money when the sounds came. Auntie Know-it-all slammed shut the heavy leather-bound edition of her encyclopedia from which she drew her knowledge of world history and of great men. The poorer people crept over to Trentcho's barbershop or to the Rabbit's Blood for a beer. At the Esmero Esperanto club the first test match was opened. At the barracks, the coronet blew evening call. And the city governor got into his carriage to demonstrate the glamor and inalterability of his authority in the form of his scrupulously polished epaulettes.

Year-in, year-out the citizens of Vidin got used to hearing this song of the river for four months, a song released by the timid powerlessness of a troubled soul without any destiny, only then once again to lose the habit of hearing. Over time even losing the habit turned into a habit.

How a person lying on his back in water succeeded in playing his flute without getting it wet remained a secret. People imagined his greasy, bloated body, his fat, soft fingers—a butterball, unaffected by either the cold or their contempt. Even the miracle worker Jonka, with her knowledge of the hallucinogenic effect of herbs, someone familiar with what was invisible and with the hidden meanings of things, was powerless in the face of the striking naïveté of this man's behavior. "Everything truly mysterious and inexplicable, even death, has sense, and is preordained," she said darkly.

If the people believed in the existence of the Whistler, it was not so much because they, bent over and discouraged, saw him in the flesh when he returned to the Rabbit's Blood. If they believed in the song of the river, it was not so much because this was the echo of a legend about a man stricken by fate—no, they believed in his existence because life itself had unexplained greatness. They had been entrusted with the task of changing it into a mystery, into striving that was often mysterious and flared up only weakly, but which could not be overcome by general indifference.

In 1914 the prophecy of Shdrigo the anarchist came true—the First World War began. It was on a tricky path, for people actually saw hell in others. The unthinkable, which the drunks in the Rabbit's Blood talked about hotly, after the assassination of the Austrian successor to the throne in Sarajevo, had turned into a reality that foretold disaster. Even Pastor Anissi confirmed it, "This year the flies have increased terribly . . . That looks like war!" But what tied a dreamy little town like Vidin to the fate of mankind except for this general human sorrow? What would Vidin give to world history other than a handful of brave men, of young recruits who were ready to die for the fatherland?

After the wheat had been brought into the barns, one evening the sky in the west turned a threatening red, punctuated by the formations of flocks of birds moving south. Cruelly and confusingly, even lethargically, the war spread with a sleepy serenity, just like any plague in the land. The Danube seemed to turn to stone. It fell silent in the face of this city without men in the discouraged expectation of an end that would bring no salvation. This empty space of days, months, and years, lit only by the eternal light in front of the image of the Virgin Mary, filled with misery and hunger, with the raucous speeches at the charity association and the fearful whispering of the women, who thought, if only they had not lost their honor, if only they had not lost their husbands as well . . . But what could a little town like Vidin offer to the world other than a few hundred mothers who had suffered disaster, half a regiment of children made into orphans, and a century of exhausted widows, who brought six bastards into the world, three of whom were frankly for sale and who filled the back room of the Rabbit's Blood with the odor of lavender soap? People in the city were carried to their graves every day, and the cemetery still radiated an air of quiet and of being deserted.

Only one repeating wonder remained from this general frozen sound— the song of the river. It was as if the north wind had come down from Koshava Mountain and was blowing onto the reeds. The song itself seemed to have become one with the environment, practically a phenomenon of nature, but one which did not break the consolation and forgetfulness of the night. Still, just as much as people accepted the encouraging good nature of his playing, they still retained an inexplicable anger toward the Whistler. Whether young or old, all were made to go. They even took Sleepy Kosta, a widower and only half a man. Shdrigo the anarchist had the law and a uniform slipped over his head; his black shirt was ripped off, his desire for the world revolution was shaved off of him together with his matted beard. Only the Whistler, whether intentionally or not, was skipped; he did not appear on any lists, as if even the war did not want to have anything to do with someone like him. "How does it happen," people asked themselves, "that the burden of the war has passed him by, a person who is childless, while fathers and sons are falling without pity on faraway battlefields?" Jonka the soothsayer knew one answer: "A person without his own home, with only a flute, is not taken into war. People must have a home from which their souls can break out for the long voyage to the other world." During the war the Whistler got even fatter, as if he was fed by feelings of guilt against outsiders. He no longer trusted himself to look them in the eyes, in the eyes of the others who had even robbed him of the right of becoming a victim.

When the Romanians decided to stir up fear and to bring the war closer to home, they hit upon the idea of anchoring a dove-colored steamship in the middle of the Danube screen and from there to bombard the city of Vidin with its single cannon. They called this the "bombardment." As a result of the shaking, the church bells wobbled for the remainder of the fall. People fled. The sun took on a metallic glow. Cellars filled with quiet, and children's eyes filled with innocence. Most people hid in the walls of the old Turkish fortress. The mortar drizzled down from the joints in the wall. Mothers' hair stood on end. In old people, hardening of the arteries disintegrated like a curtain of clouds and opened up their vision to memories of their youth. In those moments, everyone protected what was dearest to him ... Pastor Anissi hugged to himself an edition of the Bible which his grandfather had brought to him directly from the grave of the Lord; Dora the seamstress pressed the authentic Viennese sewing pattern to her lap; the banker Valtchev held tightly to the heavy albums with his valuable stamp collection, and his wife—her encyclopedia, source of all knowledge. The area governor, however, lacking his carriage, clattered around incessantly with his parade saber in order to drown out the humiliation of his powerlessness. Silk clothing and simple dresses crackled; seconds of time became eternities; and the crashing of the big guns started to sound as though the ground on the other side of the vineyards itself was groaning ...

Nonetheless, a few minutes after the "bombardment" had begun, the sound of the flute could be heard coming up softly and almost shamefully from the bank of the Danube. Slowly and mysteriously it filled the quiet with its sound, and its melody rose up over the city, over the war. As though intimidated, the Romanian firing fell silent. It would have been a sin to fire a shot at a naked man, clothed only in the gentle tones of his resistance. What would it have looked like to fire on a song? Could you even hit it? Driven by the stream, the melody crawled over the fortress, touched the faded green of the garden on the bank, lit up the flaring fire, went along the market street with its abandoned stalls, washed the windows of the unfriendly building of the Zagorka brewery, and finally dissolved in the swamps around the city. It was an agonizing but still delightful sigh, dampened by the rain, sunk in thought, with the fog spread over the Danube, a sigh that was clear and resonant in the last hot days of Indian summer. That's the way it appeared, as though neither the government in Sofia nor the great powers could stop the war for even a moment—it was only the dreams brought on by the flute that could do that.

With people huddled together, the sweat rolling off their clenched lips, finally thankful for the temporary salvation, the people's hate for the man with the flute now became incessant and final. What right did he, that bastard, that world wanderer, have to save the city? Without any qualms of conscience he had proclaimed beauty against the war! And—what was even worse—he had exposed everyone to ridicule, since he himself, naively or fearlessly—whatever the reason—had placed himself in danger in the gray shadows of the day by placing himself under the protection of his music. What was so bad in that? "As long as everyone is scared," Jonka proclaimed later, "human fear is invisible; but only so long as everyone ..."

After a week filled with fire and destruction, the denizens of Vidin succeeded in setting up two guns behind the old fortress walls, and the

Romanian temporary warship disappeared. The church bells sounded long and loud, as they did on Easter, and for a short time it was quite lively at the cemetery—until the funereal silence of the war returned.

On a still October afternoon, Pastor Anissi sat at the open window of his bedroom, cursing the flies and the premonitions of bad things that he had seen in his sleep and that he had woven into his holiday theological reasoning. The moment had come in which his worldly wisdom and strictly maintained fast days had led him to his greatest desire, a revelation of a new proof for the existence of God. Barefoot and quite delayed, the Indian summer romped about in the city. It was so hot that the yellowing leaves began to blaze up on their branches. Pastor Anissi yawned heartily and sank once again into his thoughts . . . But something prevented his concentration. Something quite familiar was lacking in his mind, and it worried him. For him, it was as if the belfry, the churchyard with its box-tree aroma, the swampy lands, why even the entire city, had changed. He looked over at the wall clock. It was five minutes past five, then ten minutes past five, but nothing other than an unbearable silence seemed to pour out over the park on the riverbank.

"A soul has given itself to God," he turned to his wife. "Tomorrow there will be a burial, but this time I won't be singing my last respects to any soldier."

The pastor's wife looked out into the droning stillness and immediately understood him.

The river, however, sluggishly rolling eternally along with the color of unrefined oil, suddenly abandoned, suddenly dead and alienated, had turned its back on the city. That was it, that was the true proof of the existence of God.

Translated by Lawrence Schofer

DAVID ALBAHARI was born in 1948 in Peć (Kosovo, then Yugoslavia). He studied English language and literature in Belgrade, and since 1994 has lived in Canada. Particularly well known for his short stories, he has also translated Vladimir Nabokov, John Updike, and Sam Shepard into Serbo-Croatian. Books of his available in English include *Götz and Meyer* (2006) and *Leeches* (2011), both translated by Ellen Elias-Bursać.

VLADIMIR ARSENIJEVIĆ was born in 1965 in Pula (Croatia, then Yugoslavia). A master cook and travel guide, he worked as a taxi driver in London from 1985 to 1989. His *In the Hold,* which had been awarded the NIN Prize for the best novel in Serbian in 1994 when it was originally published as *U potpalublju,* appeared in English in 1996.

BORA ĆOSIĆ was born in 1932 in Zagreb (Croatia, then Yugoslavia). He studied philosophy in Belgrade and left Serbia in 1992, traveling to Rovinj and later to Berlin. He has won numerous awards for his writing. In English, his book *My Family's Role in the World Revolution and Other Prose* was published by Northwestern University Press in its Writings from an Unbound Europe series in 1997.

BEQË CUFAJ was born in 1970 in Decan (Kosovo, then Yugoslavia). He studied philology in Pristina, and now works as a journalist and writer near Stuttgart. He has published several books of poetry and short stories in Kosovo and has been translated into German; he is the author of *Der Glanz der Fremde* (*The Splendor of the Unknown,* 2005) and *Projekt@Party* (2012).

DIMITRÉ DINEV was born in 1968 in Plovdiv (Bulgaria). He fled to Austria in 1990 and studied philosophy and Russian literature in Vienna. Since 1991, he has been writing prose and theater pieces in German, including the short-story collection *Ein Licht über dem Kopf* (*A Light Above the Head,* 2007) and *Barmherzigkeit: Unruhe bewahren* (*Mery: Disturb the Peace,* (2010).

SLAVENKA DRAKULIĆ was born in 1949 in Rijeka (Croatia, then Yugoslavia). She studied comparative literature and sociology at the University of Zagreb. Now living in Vienna, Stockholm, and Sovinjak (Istria), she is a journalist and the author of numerous novels and works of nonfiction, including *As If I Am Not There* (UK, 1999), republished in the United States as *S.: A Novel about the Balkans* (2001); *They Would Never Hurt a Fly: War Criminals on Trial in The Hague* (2005); and *A Guided Tour Through the Museum of Communism: Fables from a Mouse, a Parrot, a Bear, a Cat, a Mole, a Pig, a Dog, and a Raven* (2011).

ALEKSANDAR HEMON was born in 1964 in Sarajevo (Bosnia and Herzegovina, then Yugoslavia). He has been living in Chicago since 1992 and writing in English since 1995. His internationally acclaimed fiction includes *The Question of Bruno: Stories* (2000); *Nowhere Man* (2002); *The Lazarus Project: A Novel* (2008), which was a finalist for the National Book Award; and *Love and Obstacles: Stories* (2009). He edits *Best European Fiction*, most recently the 2013 edition.

DRAGO JANČAR was born in 1948 in Maribor (Slovenia, then Yugoslavia) and lives in Ljubljana. He has written numerous novels, short stories, essays, and theater pieces, and been honored with the most important Slovenian literary prizes. *Northern Lights* (2001) and *The Prophecy and Other Stories* (2009) are available in English from Northwestern University Press in its Writings from an Unbound Europe series. His most recent novel, *The Galley Slave*, was published in 2011.

MILJENKO JERGOVIĆ was born in 1966 in Sarajevo (Bosnia and Herzegovina, then Yugoslavia). He reported for the Zagreb newspaper *Nedeljina Dalmacija* from a besieged Sarajevo, and now lives in Zagreb and Sarajevo. He is the author of *Sarajevo Marlboro* (2004), *Ruta Tannenbaum: A Novel* (Northwestern University Press, Writings from an Unbound Europe, 2011), and *Mama Leone* (2012).

ISMAIL KADARE was born in 1936 in Gjirokastra (Albania). He studied literature in Tirana and Moscow, and now lives in Paris and Tirana. At first primarily a poet, his extensive epic oeuvre has been translated into many languages and includes *Chronicle in Stone: A Novel* (1987) and *The Accident: A Novel* (2010). Kadare has received numerous awards, including the Man Booker International Prize in 2005.

FATOS KONGOLI was born in 1944 in Elbasan (Albania). He studied mathematics in Tirana and Beijing. Kongoli lives in Tirana, where he works as the cultural editor of various publishing houses and magazines. He is the author of the novel *The Loser* (2008).

MARUŠA KRESE (1947–2012) was born in Ljubljana (Slovenia, then Yugoslavia). She studied literature and art history in Ljubljana, doing residencies in London and the United States, then worked in Berlin as an author and journalist. Her books include *Alle meine Kriege* (*All My Wars*, 2006), *Gegenwelten: Rassismus, Kapitalismus und Soziale Ausgrenzung* with Robert Reithofer and Leo Kühberger von Leykam (*Opposing Worlds: Racism, Capitalism, and Social Exclusion*, 2007), and *Heute nicht* with Fabjan Hafner von Drava (*Not Today*, 2009).

CHARLES SIMIC was born in 1938 in Belgrade (Serbia, then Yugoslavia). He has been in the United States since 1953 and is a professor emeritus of English literature at the University of New Hampshire. Since the fifties, he has published poetry and received numerous awards, among them the Pulitzer Prize for poetry (1990). Some recent poetry and prose collections include *Weather Forecast for Utopia & Vicinity: Poems, 1967–1982* (2010), *Zbigniew Herbert: The Collected Prose, 1948–1998* (2010), *Oranges and Snow: Selected Poems of Milan Djordjević* (2010), *Master of Disguises* (2010), *The Horse Has Six Legs: An Anthology of Serbian Poetry* (expanded edition, 2010), and *Dime-Store Alchemy: The Art of Joseph Cornell* (2011).

BILJANA SRBLJANOVIĆ was born in 1970 in Stockholm, Sweden. She studied at the Drama School in Belgrade and lives in Belgrade and Paris. Internationally recognized for her 1999 *Belgrade Trilogy*, written while she was still a student, she is distinguished as a playwright and political publicist. Other plays include *Family Stories: Belgrade* (2000), *The Fall* (2000), and *Berbelo* (2008).

SAŠA STANIŠIĆ was born in 1978 in Visegrad (Bosnia and Herzegovina, then Yugoslavia). He has lived in Germany since 1992 and writes in German. His novel *How the Soldier Repairs the Gramophone*, translated by Anthea Bell, appeared in English in 2008.

LUAN STAROVA was born in 1942 in Pogradec (Albania). He grew up in Skopje, where he was a professor for Romance languages. He has worked as a diplomat at UNESCO and served as the first Macedonian ambassador in Paris. Since 1971, he has published novels, stories, and essays in Macedonian and Albanian, which have been translated into many languages.

RICHARD SWARTZ, the editor of this anthology, was for decades a correspondent in southeastern Europe for the Stockholm daily *Svenska Dagbladet*. He is the author of numerous books, including *Room Service: Reports from Eastern Europe* (1998) and the novel *A House in Istria* (2007).

LÁSZLÓ VÉGEL, born in 1941 in Srbobran (Serbia, then Yugoslavia), is a member of the Hungarian minority in Vojvodina. He lives in Novi Sad (Serbia), where he works as an editor and playwright. Since the end of the sixties, he has written novels, short stories, plays, and essays in Serbo-Croatian and Hungarian.

NENAD VELIČKOVIĆ was born in 1962 in Sarajevo (Bosnia and Herzegovina, then Yugoslavia), where he continues to live. A professor on the philosophy faculty at the University of Sarajevo, he has written numerous works for radio and theater, screenplays for children's films, short stories, and three novels, including *Lodgers* (Northwestern University Press, Writings from an Unbound Europe, 2005).

DRAGAN VELIKIĆ was born in 1953 in Belgrade (Serbia, then Yugoslavia) and has served as the editor at various newspapers, most recently as editor in chief at *Radio B92* in Belgrade. He lives in Belgrade and in Vienna, where he served as the Serbian ambassador until 2009. He has published short stories, novels, and essays, many of which were translated into German and received awards.

IRENA VRKLJAN was born in 1930 in Belgrade (Serbia, then Yugoslavia). She moved to Zagreb in 1940 and went to study at the Film School in Berlin in 1969. She now lives in Zagreb and Berlin. Her volumes of poetry, essays, short stories, screenplays, and literary translations have received numerous awards, including in 2006 the Vladimir-Nazor Prize, which is given annually by the Croatian Ministry of Culture. Vrkljan's "*The Silk, the Shears*" and "*Marina; or, About Biography*" was published by Northwestern University Press in 1999 in its Writings in an Unbound Europe series.

VLADIMIR ZAREV was born in 1947 in Sofia (Bulgaria) and studied Bulgarian literature. Since the early seventies, he has been an author and the editor of the magazine *Savremennik* (*The Contemporary*). He has been editor in chief since 1989. He is the author of numerous short stories, novels, and works of nonfiction.